BAD DOG!

*a memoir of
Love, Beauty,
and Redemption
in dark places*

BAD DOG!

*a memoir of
Love, Beauty,
and Redemption
in dark places*

LIN JENSEN

WISDOM PUBLICATIONS • BOSTON

Wisdom Publications, Inc.
199 Elm Street
Somerville MA 02144 USA
www.wisdompubs.org

Library of Congress Cataloging-in-Publication Data
Jensen, Lin.
  Bad dog! : a memoir of love, beauty, and redemption in dark places / Lin Jensen.—
1st ed.
    p. cm.
  ISBN 0-86171-486-5 (pbk. : alk. paper)
  1. Jensen, Lin. 2. Zen Buddhists—United States—Biography. 3. Spiritual biography—United States. I. Title.
  BQ966.E596A3 2005
  294.3'924'092—dc22

                              2005009868
First Edition
ISBN 0-86171-486-5
09   08   07   06   05
5   4   3   2   1

Earlier forms of some of the essays herein have appeared in the following books, mag-
azines, and journals:

"Bad Dog," "Maintenance," "Swallowing," "The Egg Barn," and "The Jury Room" in
Turning Wheel, The Journal of Socially Engaged Buddhism; "Bad Dog," "Maintenance,"
and "The Mind of the Mountain" in *The Journal of the Order of Buddhist Contempla-
tives;* "Gathering" in *Mountain Record: The Zen Practitioner's Journal;* "The Bidwell
Park Goats" in the *Butte Environmental Council Newsletter;* "Eclipse" in *The Journal of
the Pacific Zen Institute;* "Shaking Down," and "Vestments" in *The Quest;* "Shaking
Down" in *World: The Journal of the Unitarian Universalist Association;* "Window Birds,"
"Empty Fields," "The Mind of the Mountain," "Maintenance," and "Real Estate" in
Bowing To Receive the Mountain; "Bad Dog," "The Killing Shed," "The Catching
Crate," "The Egg Barn," "The Debeaking Machine," "Vestments," "Night Talk,"
"Limit," "The Mind of the Mountain," "I Speak for My Father," "Empty Fields,"
"Shaking Down," "Window Birds," "Real Estate," "Maintenance," "Bicycling,"
"Margie's Room," "Noise," "Gathering," "Things," "The Cry of a Fawn," in *Uncover-
ing the Wisdom of the Heartmind.* "Bad Dog," in *Not Turning Away.*

Cover design by Joel Holland
Interior design by Dede Cummings. Set in AGaramon 12/15.5 pt.

Wisdom Publications' books are printed on acid-free paper and meet the guidelines for
permanence and durability set by the Council of Library Resources.

Printed in Canada.

Dedication

To my father and mother,
Morris and Lucy Jensen,
my brother Rowland Jensen
and my sister Evelyn Elliot.
You alone are the ones who were there
to witness our beginnings as a family
and whose lives have shaped the world of my mind.

Contents

Acknowledgments

I wish to thank Soto Zen Master Eko, Abbot of Shasta Abbey, and Rinzai Zen Master John Tarrant of Pacific Zen Institute for the training and encouragement offered me in the practice of Zen, without which I might have lacked the courage and the clarity to bring to light the events covered in these pages. I thank Susan Moon, editor of *Turning Wheel,* for her support throughout the years, having published several of my works and given aid in editing and improving the quality of my writing. I thank poet Jane Lawrence who taught me much about tightening and strengthening my prose. In particular, I thank Josh Bartok of Wisdom Publications for his precise and inspired line-by-line editing and for his unwavering belief in the worth of this book. I also thank the many members of the Chico Zen Sangha who have given me a reason to write and who have been a constant inspiration and guide to what finally needs to be said. Last, I thank Karen Laslo, my loving wife and best friend, for her unflinching and honest critique of my work and for her unflagging support of all my literary efforts.

Dust and Feathers

AN INTRODUCTION

I'd been writing this book for several years before I thought to ask why I was writing at all. And further, why I was writing it in the particular way that I was. Did I expect others to read these words of mine and, if so, why would they want to?

There are two things you can expect in reading this book. The first is that it is essentially autobiographical—though telling my life's story is not my primary intention. I didn't set out to chronicle the events of my family and the community in which I was raised. What I set out to do was to share what I had learned in my life that might be worth knowing and passing on to others. And all I really know, after all, is what I have truly experienced and observed for myself. Everything other than that is mere conjecture. So: the pages of this book are written in the first person *I*, a narrative option best explained by Henry David Thoreau, who wrote *Walden* in the first person for the very reasons governing my own choice: "I should not talk so much about myself if there were anybody else whom I knew as well. Unfortunately, I am confined to this theme by the narrowness of my experience." The result in the case of this book is not the story of anyone's life told for its own sake, but rather a drawing out from that life those incidents that serve to illuminate wondrous redemption, the kind that the old Zen masters knew for themselves and offered to the world. The second thing you can expect in reading this book is that the events described may at times seem harsh and raw with details one might rather not know. Why do I ask the reader to accompany me through such dark passages? I do so because I've been there myself and I've learned that when the universe offers the gift of darkness and I refuse it, my refusal invariably forfeits the very light I seek. I wouldn't ask anyone to take this journey with me if it were merely the story of my journey alone—but it's not. Though the details of our lives vary, we share a common humanity. If I've written truly you will find nothing outside yourself in these pages. I hope my story teaches that if we will accept whatever pain or distress life gives us, then that pain summons its own healing. If pain is what you have, embrace it, honor it, and care for it with all your kindness. Truly, within grief is power that transforms darkness to light.

The events of my own life have brought me to be a Zen teacher. But soon after I began teaching I found, as my own teachers had before me, that I had little to teach. Zen has no absolute truths, as such, to pass on. Zen is not something to think about or believe in—and I'm not very good at believing things anyway. I prefer questions to answers. A question opens my mind in a way that an answer shuts it down. Realizing this, I've tried to live a life of inquiry rather than one of conclusion. Zen itself draws no conclusions and is too alive to be captured in thought. Having staked out no fixed territory of its own to defend, Zen is free to roam at will, encountering, with curiosity and surprise, the world as it actually is.

As a result, I've written a book that seldom takes sides, preferring to remain undecided and watch what develops. If you really pay attention, life itself teaches the suspension of judgment. In life itself, the fiercest anger often issues from the deepest love, courage is discovered in the greatest fear, an unsuspected tenderness is found in the cruelest hand, a sudden clarity is born of utter confusion, and the one light that never dims is wrested from the blackest darkness. *Bad Dog!* is written in the knowledge that opposites merge in ways that are often contrary to all expectation, and that our perception of things opposing each other may be little more than the consequence of a linguistic convention.

Roshi John Tarrant, one of my own teachers on the Zen way, tells of an evening when his friend's girlfriend was having a birthday party for her daughter. Balloons trailing pink ribbons, half-eaten bowls of ice cream going soft in the heat of the kitchen, messy gobs of chocolate cake, and lots of chattering, gooey little girl's faces. When parents had hauled the other children off, the daughter came to her mother complaining of a stomachache. "Honey, you ate too much cake and ice cream," her mother told her. But the boyfriend, flaked out on the sofa and having never raised a child of his own, told her, "Maybe you didn't eat enough."

I doubt the gastronomic accuracy of the boyfriend's diagnosis but I like the way it turns things upside-down. "Maybe you didn't eat enough" is so contrary that it teases the mind out of its conventional expectations. *Bad Dog!* is like this, encouraging a tolerance for contradiction that frees us from whatever argument we're having with circumstance. If I find myself in one of life's distressing events, I can lobby the universe for relief or I can get curious about what's being offered. While I may prefer sunshine to the clouds massing overhead, if I'm willing to let fall my preferences, I'm free to explore all sorts of rainy-day possibilities.

One of life's interesting contradictions is that the best intention is invariably wrong. When I've taken the time to notice, it wasn't hard to see that anything we humans think or do is bound to be mistaken one way or another. "Ten thousand beautiful mistakes," the Chinese Zen masters were fond of saying. An old

Christian story attributed to the Desert Fathers touches on the innocence of this human fallibility. The story goes that a monk asked Abba Sisoius, "What am I to do since I have fallen?" The Abba replied, "Get up." "I did get up, but I fell again," the monk told him. "Get up again," said the Abba. "I did, but I must admit that I fell once again. So what should I do?" "Never fall down without getting up," the Abba concluded.

Falling down is inevitable; it's what we humans do. When I acknowledge this it brings me to an unguarded kindness and sympathy. Falling makes us human and, if such a thing can happen, it makes us wise. Abba Sisoius is showing us that the trick of falling is just falling itself and that the only thing we need do is get back up so we're ready, when the time comes, to fall again. Some perilous falls are taken in the chapters that follow these introductory words, but they are falls that reveal the obvious truth that we can only get up in the place where we fell down. And even more pointedly, it is our falling that teaches us the way back up. "The coin lost in the river is found in the river," old Master Yunmen told us ages ago.

Bad Dog! is about specific things—the stories, events, and images of things I have known and observed for myself. No one's life is a generalization. Our lives are singular events that lie right before us in all their curious detail and beauty. I trust things a great deal more than I trust ideas about things. I've had my own teachers, Soto and Rinzai Zen masters, and none of them gave me their ideas. They taught me instead to look at the details of the story that life itself was writing, knowing that there alone would I find the teaching I sought.

The old Chinese teachers understood this, and taught by pointing directly to life itself. You could never get these old masters to explain anything. If you asked one of them to teach you about Zen, they might set you to cooking rice or they might reply as Master Gensha did long ago in China when a monk said to him: "I am a novice just arrived at this monastery. Please, master, tell me how I can enter into Zen?" Gensha said, "Can you hear the creek down beyond the gate?" The monk listened for a minute and said, "Yes, I can." "Enter Zen from there," was Master Gensha's answer, returning the student to the intimate journey of his own life.

My way of entering from where the water flows will be to tell you a story. "Tell me a story" is an ageless appetite of the mind so simple and understandable that its appeal requires no explanation. *Bad Dog!* relies on story rather than lesson to carry its message more to the intuition than to the intellect. It's not always an easy story to read just as life is not always easy to live. It's a true story as faithful to fact as memory will allow. It begins with the life of a troubled family where the constant threat of economic failure makes hard work the one salient fact of life, and where mutual safety and affection could at any moment be overwhelmed by sudden fear and violence.

The story begins on a Southern California turkey farm. Imagine a hundred thousand birds, acres of milling feet, the earth perpetually ground to a fine powder of dirt and dried manure that the wind carries up through the barns to the house. Everything in such a world is coated gray—the pickup parked in the driveway, the leaves of the sycamore trees, the lawn chairs, even the lawn itself. Dust piles up on windowsills and insinuates itself into the house, coating tabletops and dressers and lying like talcum on the surface of the piano. And drifting feathers too blow downwind where they snag on every fence line and hedgerow and clump of weeds, and even wedge against the dog asleep in the shade of the barn. The acrid smell of turkey manure, where it piles up beneath the roosts, seeps into your skin and hair. The incessant cackling racket of the turkeys grates like the distant whine of a chainsaw or the droning motor of a kitchen refrigerator that never seems to switch off. The ever-present flies go after your breath and the moisture of your eyes.

We were a family of five. My father, a Danish immigrant whose parents had died when he was just a child leaving him to fend for himself, arrived at Ellis Island in 1923, penniless, ill, and with virtually no command of English. My mother was born somewhere in Montana of a mother who abandoned her as an infant, leaving her to be raised by the Goslees, an elderly couple who viewed the adoption of the child as insurance that they would be cared for in their old age. In time, the Goslees moved to the city of Orange in Southern California, and my father, having found his way there as well, met my mother when she was but seventeen. They fell in love and, before my mother's eighteenth birthday, they married and proceeded to make a household for themselves and raise a family. Neither of them had ever lived in a functional household under the care and guidance of their own parents, and so they had no model for what they were setting out to do. Not only that but they began their lives together at the outset of the Great Depression of the thirties and were soon to know the added hardship of all poor and immigrant households. My brother, Rowland, was born within a year of my parent's marriage. I came two years later, and my sister, Evelyn, six years after that.

Whatever my parents had hoped for in the beginning, our five lives together turned out to be a daily enactment of inadvertent cruelty and sudden love that we never quite managed to reconcile. But we were a family whose hunger to love one another could not finally be refused. Understanding and tenderness would arise among us no matter how bad things got, and we found redemption in the very places we hurt most. Sometimes in the midst of the worst anger or accusation or threat, an unaccountable hush would suddenly settle over us. In the momentary reprieve of this unbidden quiet the whisper of our five separate breaths could be heard rising to the high ceiling of the old farm-house living room. Our chests rose and fell with each breath, and there was a wondrous tenderness in the moment that we all recognized and felt for each other.

From these early beginnings on the farm, the story of *Bad Dog!* expands into the succeeding years, bringing the insights born of one family's intimate struggles to bear upon the lives of people and communities elsewhere. The book unfolds in chapters of birth and marriage, school and work, friends and colleagues, coastline, valleys, mountains, cities and towns, love and anger, old age and death. Its seven decades spans the startling losses and gains America has witnessed since my birth in 1932 to my present age of seventy-three.

Don't be deterred by the sometimes troubled landscape visited in these pages. I have returned to these regions not for the sorrow or pity of it, but for the wonder of how love and beauty take root in even the most barren places. *Bad Dog!* occupies a world in which people with every reason to misunderstand each other, miraculously meet, and find their lives less lonely. Your consolation and mine is that no matter how difficult life can be, its sweetness is always with us.

Bad Dog!

I am eight years old, my brother, Rowland, ten. We follow Father up the steep wooden stairs to the second story bedroom. He doesn't say anything. Our steps echo in the hollow of the stairway enclosure. Father holds the lath stick by its end. It's stiff and splintery and it hangs from Father's hand almost to the floor. I swallow the words that would beg Father, once more, not to do this.

In the upstairs bedroom, Father shuts the door behind us. A ceiling light hangs from a cord. It shines on the bed, leaving the corners of the room in shadows. Father stands by the bed. He looks at us. Rowland and I stand backed up against the closed door. We don't move. Outside in the hall, Laddie, our farm dog, scratches at the door. Father looks sad and serious like he wishes he didn't have to do this. He points toward us with the lath stick, and I hear him ask, "Which of you goes first?"

Rowland goes to the bed. He wants to get it over with. It's worse to go last, but I can never make myself go first. Rowland unbuttons his jeans and pulls them down to his knees. He does this without being told. He knows he has to pull his jeans and underwear down and lie face down on the bed. He pulls his underwear down at the very last because he doesn't like to show himself. He waits for the first blow. I look away. My body shivers and I feel cold. I hear Laddie snuffling at the door, and then I hear the crack of the lath stick. Rowland doesn't cry. He holds his breath. He has told me that this is the way to do it.

I hear the lath again and then again. Still Rowland doesn't cry. Laddie whines at the door. I don't know why Father is whipping us. Rowland teased me and punched me behind the barn, and I called him bad names. Did Mother hear us? I had some bad thoughts. Did Mother know them? Mother was angry and then she was sick and lay on her bed and put a wet cloth over her eyes and told us that we would be whipped when Father got home. I got scared and tried to talk to her and make it okay again, but the cloth was over her eyes and she wouldn't talk to me.

Rowland's turn is over and he gets off the bed. I pull my shirt up and tuck the end of it under my chin to keep it from falling. I pull my pants and underwear down. My penis feels rubbery where I try to hide it under my hands, and Rowland watches me. I hold my breath. The first blow comes. It hurts more than I can stand. My hands stretch back to cover my bottom and I hear myself whimper, "Please, Father, please." "If you do that, you'll only make it worse," Father warns. Sometimes Father says it hurts him more than Rowland and me. I don't believe him. He doesn't say it tonight.

When it's over, Father goes out. Rowland is in the dark near the wall. I'm under the ceiling light. Rowland can see me wiping at my runny nose with my shirt, but he looks away. We have something wrong with us. We both have it. We do not like to look at one another. It makes us too sorry.

After a while I go out. Laddie is waiting. He's glad to see me and wags his tail and rubs himself against me. "Go away, Laddie," I say. Later, in the dark when I can't sleep, I slip from my bed and open the door onto the hall where Laddie waits. Clutching him to me, I tell him how sorry I am.

2.

I am eleven years old. Laddie has done something bad and Father has seen him do it and I don't know what is going to happen. Rowland says that Laddie killed a turkey. When Mr. Post's dog, Starkey, began killing our turkeys, Father told him about it. And when the dog didn't quit Father shot it. I saw him do it. Starkey was dragging a turkey from the roost when Father shot him. Starkey whined and went round and round in circles until he fell down. Blood was coming out of his nose and pretty soon he died.

In the barn, Father has a rope around Laddie's neck. When Laddie tries to pull away, Father jerks the rope. It chokes Laddie and makes him cough. Laddie's fur is tangled and dirty like he's been rolling on the ground. A dead turkey lies on the floor. It's torn and bloody and its feathers are wet. "Oh Laddie," I cry out, "what have you done?" I squat and put out my hand. Laddie wags his tail and comes toward me.

Father jerks him away with the rope. "Don't be good to him, Linley," Father says. "Now that he's tasted blood, it's not likely he'll quit."

"He doesn't know, Father." I am trying not to cry, but I can feel my face screw up and my voice goes high.

Father hands me the rope tied to Laddie's neck. "If he kills again, Linley, we can't keep him. If you want your dog, do now exactly as I say." I know what to do without Father telling me because Mr. Post tried this with Starkey, but it didn't work. It's what everybody does with a dog that starts killing. If we can't make Laddie stop, we can't keep him. But we can't give him away either. Nobody will take a dog that kills.

I tie Laddie by the rope to a post in the barn, and gather the bailing wire and wire cutters and roofing tar that Father told me to get. The dead turkey is covered with flies. Tiny yellow eggs are already stuck to the places where the blood has dried. I take a stick and dab tar on the turkey until its feathers are all plastered down and the torn places are filled and its eyes are stuck shut. This way, Laddie won't chew it off. I punch the baling wire through its body and wrap one end around each of its legs so that I can tie them around Laddie's neck. Father says the turkey has to stay there until it rots off because we have only one chance. I'm not supposed to be good to Laddie. He has to learn not to kill.

I take the rope off Laddie. He's glad to have the rope off and wags his tail and tries to lick my face. "Bad dog!" I tell him, "bad dog!" The turkey hangs from his neck and the tar sticks to his fur. "Bad dog!" I say again.

After three days Mother won't let Laddie near the house anymore. We are told to keep the yard gates shut. "It's intolerable," she tells Father. "I can smell him even here in the house."

I watch father. He doesn't look up and he doesn't say anything.

"It's not just the smell, you know," she says. "I can't bear the thought of it."

"That doesn't help any," is all Father says.

At the end of a week, Laddie quits coming for the food I carry out to him. I find him where he has crawled back into a space under the floor of the storage shed. I call to him but he won't come. I push the food under to him. I bring a basin of water and push it under too. I do this for two more weeks. Sometimes a little of the food is gone and some water but most of the time he doesn't eat anything.

Once during this time I see from a distance that Laddie has come out from under the shed. The turkey sags from his neck and drags on the ground when he walks. Even from far away I can see that the turkey is slimy and bloated. "Laddie!" I call. I run to him but, before I can get there, he crawls back under the storage shed.

I see him there in the dark. I try to crawl under the shed but it's too tight and I can't get to him.

And then one day he's out. I find him in the barnyard, the baling wire still wound around his neck where the turkey has rotted off. I remove the wire, but he doesn't wag his tail or try to lick me. I take him to the washroom and fill the washtub with warm water. I lift him into the tub and wash him with soap. I scrub him and rinse him and draw more water and wash him again. I dry him with a towel, and brush him, and I keep telling him that it's okay now, that it's all over. I let him out on the lawn by the house where the sun shines through the elm tree, and then I go back to clean up the washroom.

When I come for him, he is gone. I find him under the storage shed. It's months before he will follow me out to the turkey yards. He never kills again.

3.

I am sixty years old. Father is ninety-three and he is in the hospital with pneumonia. It is not at all certain that he will survive this illness. Rowland and I take turns watching him through the night. Now it is nearly two in the morning and Rowland has gone to rest. Father is fitful. He suffers from diarrhea, and it wakens him frequently in such a state of urgency that I don't dare doze off myself. Father refuses to use a bedpan, and he is too weak to reach the toilet by himself. He needs me to get him there.

I watch him on the hospital bed where he labors in his sleep to breathe, his thin chest struggling with effort. Father is much softened with age and with grandchildren and great-grandchildren whose innocent loves have reached him beyond his fears. They have coaxed him out of his darkness.

A quarter past three. Father calls. "Linley, I need to go." He tries to sit up and get his feet to the floor even before I can reach him. I help him up. He has so little strength, yet he uses every bit he has to get himself to the bathroom. I support him as we walk around the foot of the bed and through the bathroom door before I realize we are too late. His hospital gown is pulled open in the back and feces runs down his legs and onto the linoleum where he tracks it with his bare feet.

He looks at me with the most urgent appeal. He is humiliated by what he has done, and his eyes ask of me that it might never have happened. He would cry with the shame of it had he not forgotten how to do so. I back him up to the toilet and sit him down. A fluorescent ceiling light glares down on us. In the hallway beyond these walls I can hear the voices of the night nurses on their rounds. I shut the bathroom door, and when the latch clicks shut on the two of us the sound of it sends a shiver through me. Once again I wait for the crack of the lath. For a moment this old man, sitting soiled in his own filth, disgusts me. But in the cloistered silence of the room, his helplessness cries out to me and the sight of him blurs beyond sudden tears. Laddie whines somewhere in the dark. And from that darkness there rises in me an unutterable tenderness.

"It's okay, Father," I tell him. "It's okay." I find clean towels and a washcloth and soap. I run water in the basin until it is warm. I take off his soiled hospital gown and mop the floor under his feet with it and discard it in a plastic bag I find beneath the sink. I wash Father with soap and warm water. I wash him carefully, removing all the feces from around his anus and in the hair on his testicles and down the inside of his legs and between his toes. I wash him until all the rotten things are washed away.

The Duck Pen

My baby sister, Evelyn, six years younger than me, wasn't much more than a year old when Mother took to setting her out on a little patch of shaded grass under a tree in the backyard and putting me to watching over her. I loved my little sister so this was fine with me. At the time, Father was raising a few ducks along with his turkey operation, and it so happened that the duck pen was right there in the back yard as well. Evelyn always wanted to get into the duck pen, especially when there were newly hatched ducklings running about, downy little puffs with tiny sticks of legs and two dark spots for eyes looking at you from over the ridge of a flattened little pink bill.

Mother would no sooner have set Evelyn down and gone back into the house than Evelyn would be tugging at the fencing of the duck pen, trying to get in. She wasn't big enough to manage the gate, but I could and so I'd open it for her and let her in with the ducks. She'd plunk down on the mud and manure and let the little ducklings peck at her. Sometimes I'd help things out by tossing a handful of grain from the feeder bin in her direction, and the ducklings, little more than miniature eating machines at that age, would walk all over her to get at the feed. I'd been a duck pen–sitter myself once, so I understood exactly why she liked baby ducks on her lap.

The principle of duck pen–sitting is one of simple delight. It's entirely uncalculated, an innocent inclination to like what the moment offers, a kind of freshness that can surprise you in stale places. After all, we're each sitting in some sort of duck shit—yet the whole world is brightened with little peeps and peckings and downy little discoveries of a sort we'd probably never think to ask for. And it's not just that sitting in duck shit is tolerable because the ducklings are so cute, it's that duck shit is pretty amazing stuff in its own right.

Duck pen–sitting is a state of mind that you can't initiate by an exercise of will. It's rather something called up in you, often at times when you least expect it, a grace given without the asking. It's not something you happen to deserve. It comes unbidden and is virtually unavoidable regardless of your merit or lack. It can come upon you like a blaze of yellow daffodils breaking through rotting leaves on a dark February morning, or the noisy sucking of a nursing newborn calf, a girl tossing her hair forward over her head to dry in the sun, the call of sandhill cranes passing overhead in the midnight sky.

Once you've sat among the ducks in this way, you never forget what it's like. It will sustain you, redeeming the sourest of circumstances—like suddenly remembering in the throes of a divorce settlement how much you love your adversary, or like the unexpected and perfect beauty seen in a lover's anger, or like that precious instant of recognition in the eyes of a loved one whose mind has been taken from him by age or disease. There's a power of surprise and delight adrift in the universe that can settle on the most unlikely and difficult situation, transforming it in ways you'd never suspect.

Like all farm families, the Jensen family cultivated a large garden, particularly during the years of World War II when food was scarce. We didn't have the cash to buy much of what we ate and without the garden we would have gone hungry. Mother always put up vegetables for the off season, stacking the pantry shelves with hundreds of Kerr mason jars, each labeled according to its content. One of the things she always canned was stewed tomatoes. When they appeared on the table, I only had to look at them to know that I didn't like them. The plump little tomato halves looked so slimy floating in their own juices that I knew I'd throw up if I tried to swallow one of them.

You need to know that the refusal of good food was not readily tolerated at the Jensen table. We children were expected to eat what was given us and not waste anything. Whenever stewed tomatoes were included, I'd load my plate with carrots, beets, spinach, string beans, anything but tomatoes in an effort to show my good will and gratitude. In this way I had somehow managed to get by for years without ever tasting a single bite of stewed tomato. And yet whenever the tomatoes came out of the pantry, there was a certain tension in the air regarding my refusal of them. Once or twice Mother had spooned some tomatoes onto my plate, and when it was remarked that I hadn't eaten them I'd plead my case with such an urgency that I'd be let off without a showdown. Still, no one likes to hear an ungrateful boy say that the food on his plate makes him want to gag, and the evening came when I'd run out of time. Father himself grabbed the serving bowl and spooned not one but two tomato halves onto my plate and told me to quit my foolishness and eat what I was given. I knew I was up against it and that I'd have to eat the dreaded things, but I was absolutely sure I'd vomit if I did. I simply couldn't bring myself to put the stuff in my mouth. But Father had no such misgivings and he came around the table and grabbed me by the neck and proceeded to stuff stewed tomatoes down my throat. I struggled, trying to keep my lips sealed against the invasion, but Father was having none of it and he forced the spoon between my clenched teeth and shoved stewed tomato into my mouth.

I didn't vomit. I didn't even gag. I *liked* them! I sat there with tears of defiance streaming down my face, and was startled to realize that the tomatoes *tasted good*. This is the sort of sneak attack that delight seems to specialize in. I'd been ambushed by a pleasure I couldn't anticipate or defend myself against. Father was looking as close to apologetic as he was ever likely to get, but I was already moving beyond the outrage of his treatment of me to the undeniable fact that I was about to ask for a second helping of stewed tomatoes.

I think you see now that the gate to the duck pen can open for you at any time. A Zen acquaintance of mine, who for years had been a member of the zendo where I teach, once came to a teacher/student interview for the express purpose of telling me what she really thought of me: "I think you're a phony," she said, "and only pretending to be a Zen teacher." I would expect myself to be scrambling to put up the barricades, especially with this coming from someone I would never have guessed felt that way. Even now I can imagine all sorts of defenses I might have offered on behalf of my teaching competence. But at the time I wasn't doing any of those things. Instead I was checking the situation out. And when I finally spoke, I had to say, "You know, I think that myself sometimes." My accuser would never know that in some unaccountable way she'd opened a gate onto the past, and with a whole brood of ducklings suddenly tracking mud all over the interview room I was able to find some agreement with her characterization. To this day, I don't know any response of mine to a criticism that's given me more pleasure than that unguarded admittance.

The old Chinese Zen masters were wary of categorical thinking and of the way it serves to control our response to the world. A world order viewed in this analytical way is merely an order of one's own devising. The trouble with categorical thinking is that it leads you to believe that you're seeing what you've seen before. But sometimes the sheer wonder of the moment breaks through these classifications of ours. The names of things vanish and, though the daily arrival of the sun is an accustomed fact, we are astounded to see a great glowing ball of light rise from the eastern horizon.

The old Zen master Lingyun must have felt this way when, on his walk, he rounded a mountain and saw peach blossoms on the other side of the ravine. Nothing would be more common than peach blossoms in the Chinese spring countryside where Lingyun walked. He would have known at a glance that they were peach blossoms, but at that moment he saw them for the first time and was awakened to a world no name can capture and where nothing ever happens twice. Another old master was sweeping the walkway when the motion of his broom threw a pebble against a bamboo stalk. *Tock!* For the instant, there was nothing in the universe but that singular sound. A Zen poet once sang, "How wondrously strange and how miraculous this! I draw water, I carry wood." In other words: I'm alive!

Zen master Yunmen was brought to life in this way when his teacher slammed the door on his leg and broke the bone in two. Elder Ting, surprised by a sudden slap in the face, stood motionless for a moment, not knowing what to do. When a monk standing by said, "Elder Ting, why do you not bow?" Ting bowed and suddenly the whole world opened up and took him in. The delight of simply being alive doesn't depend on whether something is pleasant. It can come with the sudden brilliance of peach blossoms or a slap in the face.

It no longer surprises me that some sort of simple joy will shine out from places where you'd not expect to find it. It appears in its own unlikely time, like chancing upon a faded snapshot of your own face grinning back at you from under a stack of old bank statements in a desk drawer.

The inclination toward delight is redemptive, awakening a wonder in us that doesn't worry itself about the mud and manure of circumstances. Duck pen–sitting is a perfect model for its workings. When Mother would find Evelyn in the duck pen, she would grab her up out of there as though she had no understanding of what was going on at all. Yet she must have known that Evelyn was there all along, since the kitchen window where Mother was often working looked right out on the back yard. But she had her duty as a mother and she would say, "Oh Linley! I told you to watch over your sister. Can't I trust you to do anything I ask?" But of course I was watching over my sister, and it seems a curious omission that for all the times she had to clean Evelyn up and launder her soiled clothes Mother never punished me or specifically ordered me to keep Evelyn out of the duck pen.

The Killing Shed

I huddle by the tub of scalding water. Steam rises from
its surface and a little warmth can be gotten from the gas jet
underneath. Through the open door at the rear of the shed, I
can see into the holding pen where forty or fifty turkeys stand
jammed together in the rain. Their wings, heavy with rainwater,
drag in the mud as they mill about and push themselves against the
fence looking for a way out. In the shed, seven of them hang dying
in a row suspended from the ceiling by cords cinched to their legs.
Their feathers are smeared with mud and manure and their necks
are stretched toward the floor by lead weights hooked into their
nostrils. Their bodies alternately relax and contract in sudden
spasms. Blood drains from their bills into buckets beneath them.

I wear heavy yellow rain gear and rubber boots, splattered now
with blood. In my hand, I hold a boning knife. It too is sticky
with blood. Where some of the blood has soaked into a cuff
beneath my rain jacket, I can feel a little of its residual warmth.
The turkeys now hang dead, the last of their convulsions over,
their necks limp, their weighted heads gradually swaying to a
stop, their eyes vacant above the bloody rims of the buckets.

At the sink, where the slaughtered turkeys will soon be gutted
and dressed for sale, I wash the blood from my hands and from

the boning knife. I lay the knife on a workbench alongside a cleaver and meat shears. I drag a ladder out from the wall to the center of the shed. The raingear presses cold and stiff against my body as I climb toward the ceiling to take the turkeys down.

I was nine years old at the time and I don't recall who in the family gave the shed its peculiarly stark name. It was probably my father, a Danish immigrant, whose choice of English possessed a literalness that could sometimes expose the heart of a matter. The killing shed was part of a plan to get us out of the poverty we were left in by the Great Depression. Father had gone into farming, which was what he had done in Denmark and the only thing he knew to do. He'd chosen to raise turkeys because it was something he could get into with almost no money for a start.

By the time of the killing shed, the farm had done pretty well. The idea was that we could make more money if we retailed holiday birds directly from the farm. An old garage and attached shed were adapted for this purpose. The garage became the salesroom and the attached lean-to the killing shed. Like everything else we did on the farm, this plan took the entire family to make it work. Evelyn was too young at the time, but my mother and Rowland and I were all put to the task. One of my jobs was to help out in the killing shed. Father had anchored seven eyebolts in a row across the ceiling of the shed. From these hung lengths of cord. On the floor below each of these seven stations was a bucket and a lead weight with a stiff piece of bent wire attached to it so that the weight could be hooked into the nostril of the turkey. The idea was to keep the turkey's head from thrashing about so that the blood drained into the bucket.

It was raining the day Father taught me to kill the turkeys. The two of us went out to the turkey yards in our rain gear and herded a bunch of them up to the killing shed and shut them into the holding pen Father had built there. Father grabbed a turkey by the legs and carried it into the shed. I did the same but, since I wasn't very big for my age, I had to more or less drag mine in. Father hung his turkey up and went back for another. I hauled my turkey up the ladder we had put there for my use, but I couldn't get the cord wrapped around the turkey's legs because it kept flopping its wings and I hadn't the strength to hold it in place long enough to get it tied. When Father saw this he said, "Okay, son, I'll put them up. You take them down afterwards." I liked that because it made our jobs equal. Father must have known how important I felt doing something as grown up and serious as killing the turkeys.

When all seven of the turkeys were hung, Father took the boning knife from the work bench. He grasped the head of one of the turkeys and stretched its neck down hard. He forced its bill open with his thumb and finger. Father told me to watch carefully, that the way to kill the turkey was to punch the point of the knife up through the roof of its mouth into its brain and then to slice the veins in its throat to start the blood flowing. Suddenly I saw the magnitude of what was going to happen. "Does it hurt?" I asked. "It's all over in a minute," he answered. I watched Father slide the knife into the turkey's mouth. I saw his wrist cock upward. The turkey exploded, its wings contracting violently. Its head jerked about in father's hand, blood gushing from its throat. Father hooked the lead weight into its nostrils. The turkey's bill opened and closed. Its neck repeatedly contracted upward causing the weight to sway about. Blood splashed into the bucket below. "Now you try it," Father said.

It was hard for me to force the turkey's bill open. "You have to squeeze harder," Father said. I knew this but, as illogical as it might seem, I didn't want to squeeze down harder because I didn't want to hurt the bird. My hand shook and the knife was unsteady. I held my breath. I stabbed and sliced up into the throat. The turkey recoiled upward, its head slipping from my grasp, its whole body arching upward, blood spraying against the ceiling and on the walls and raining down on Father and me, our hair and faces splattered with it. Father got the turkey back under control and held it down until I could get hold of it again. "You have to hold tight," he said. "Is it dead?" I asked him. "Yes, it's dead, Linley," he replied.

When I had killed a second turkey, Father said, "I think you've got it now. Finish the rest and when they stop bleeding, take them down and put them on the workbench. I'll be back to show you what to do next." With that, he went out the shed door into the rain. The four remaining turkeys hung from the ceiling, waiting to be killed.

In time I got the hang of it and the work in the killing shed went smoothly. Father taught me how to scald the turkeys and pluck the feathers clean. He taught me how to gut a bird properly and showed me what the giblets were and how to wrap them in wax paper and tuck them back into the clean body cavity of the finished bird. Father said that what I was doing was called "dressing" the turkey, which was a new use of the word for me but one I liked because it made what I was doing somehow more official.

When a turkey was all done, I'd carry it into the salesroom and Mother would check it for any pinfeathers I might have missed and put it on ice. Sometimes a customer would be in the salesroom and Mother would tell them they could thank me for how beautifully the turkeys were dressed out. As the holidays got closer, there was a steady stream of cars turning in off Seventeenth Street and coming up the dirt drive to get their turkeys. It seemed to me that everyone in Orange County wanted a Jensen turkey. At Schneider's Market in Garden Grove, there was a big sign that read JENSEN'S TURKEYS SOLD HERE: PLACE YOUR ORDER NOW. All in all, I felt very important doing what I was doing.

Looking back on that time now, I realize that for all the sense of purpose that I felt there in the killing shed, I was never indifferent to the regret that accompanies killing, no matter how unavoidable or necessary the killing might be. And the killing shed wasn't the only place that killing went on: there were diseased or injured birds to be disposed of as well. And most farms like ours raised pigs, cows, sheep, rabbits and chickens, all of which must eventually be put to death if the farm is to survive and the family to be able to feed itself and others. Sometimes killing was a matter of putting a creature out of its misery. But I discovered that even when killing is done to prevent suffering, you can never really kill with impunity. Some degree of regret, some sorrow, invariably accompanies the taking of a life. This is a truth that farm boys, and most farm girls too, discern early in their lives. Within our family, it was a truth we held in common without any of us ever specifically saying so.

Farm people are intimate with the facts of human survival, and both the cost and the gift of this knowledge is a certain inevitable sadness. Yet it is a sadness that doesn't ask that things be different from the way they are. And it's not a sadness that can be avoided by simply avoiding meat, for any farmer knows that the growing of field crops displaces and dooms to extinction thousands of little lives whose home the plow has taken from them—moles, mice, gophers, snakes, rabbits, meadowlarks, the hawks whose shadows no longer pass over the land, all gone. It is a consequence of being human that we find in ourselves the heart of genuine sadness that resides in the beauty and wonder of our human circumstance and that saves us from being merely brutes and that alone redeems the sacrifice of other lives.

But there are other killings of course that should never have happened, and an incident that occurred the summer after I was first put to work in the killing shed taught me more about this matter than a boy so young ought to learn. A few turkeys always managed to get out of their pens and one of my jobs was to put them back. To do this, I had to catch them first and, if the turkey was especially large, it was sometimes nearly impossible for me to chase it down and get hold of it. This was the case one hot August afternoon when I tried to catch a large hen that had gotten out. I repeatedly drove her into a fence corner but, just when I thought I had her, she would break away and slip past me. I had a summer cold and was short of breath. My nose ran and my head ached. Finally, I threw myself on her, grabbing for both her legs —but I got only one. She scratched at me with her loose claw, tearing into the flesh of the one hand I held her by but I wouldn't let go. I tried to pin her against the fence but she scratched her way up the wire, her wings thrashing so that one wing stung me across the eye. But I got hold of the wing and, still gripping the one leg I had managed to control, I raised her above my head and slammed her against the ground with all my might.

I still had hold of her when she struck. I felt the impact. I felt something break. She gasped with the shock of it. For a second neither of us moved. Then I felt her stir beneath my hands, struggling to get to her feet. I let go of her, and feathers came loose in my hands. She tried to rise but repeatedly toppled back into the dust.

She was horribly injured. I would have to kill her. It was suddenly urgent that I do so. I'd been taught to kill injured and diseased birds in the field by wringing their necks. I caught her by the feet and the base of her head and stretched her neck as hard as I could, but her size was beyond my strength and her neck wouldn't snap. I twisted and pulled on her neck until the outer skin ruptured beneath my hands and peeled itself, inside out, up over her eyes like a hood, leaving the flesh and tendons of her neck exposed. Still she was not dead.

A sudden sense of Father nearby. Had he seen? Could I get his help? I spotted him working in a field some distance away. I called to him. He didn't hear me. I thought of calling again. I thought of trying once more to wring the turkey's neck, but I couldn't bear to touch her again. I ran from her, leaving her stumbling about in the dirt, blinded by her own inverted skin.

I ran to the shelter of some cottonwood trees that lined the banks of the Santa Ana River beyond the farm. I sat in the fallen leaves and pulled my knees up tight to my chest and rocked myself. I bit my lip to keep from crying out. But I was hardly there a minute before I knew I had to go back. I needed help. I went looking for Father, an urgency rising in me to confess what I'd done.

The turkey was gone, only a few loose feathers left scattered on the dirt. Father was no longer in the field where I'd last seen him. When I located him cleaning manure trays in the brooder house, he spoke first. "I found an injured bird," I heard him say, "down by the breeder pens. I've put it in a coop behind the feed barn. I want you to see that it's kept in feed and water."

I tended the turkey until it died. It stood in the corner of the coop. I never saw it move. The exposed flesh of its head and neck gradually blackened and crusted over. It never ate or drank. At the end of a week, I found it stiff on the bedding of straw I had spread there. It looked to me as if it had lain down to die.

The pit that Father had dug to dispose of the bodies of dead birds lay at the far end of the farm as far away from the house as possible. I knew without asking what was expected of me and what had to be done to finish what I'd set in motion seven days before. At the pit, I took a deep breath and held it while I lifted the lid and dropped the turkey in. But then I did something I had rarely, if ever, done before. I looked down into the pit to see if I could see where the bird had fallen. Before my eyes could adjust to the darkness, I had to take a breath, which sickened me horribly. But, in the instant before I clamped the lid down and ran for air, I saw her there.

I had killed uselessly and in anger. I saw there in the darkness of the pit how such killings ended and knew what it felt like to have done such a thing. It was a killing that couldn't easily be absorbed into my life in any way that would allow me to find peace with it. No rationalization or excuse would do to set aside the simple fact of having done something very wrong. My father, knowing perhaps what was at stake in it for me, had set me to a task that, like some ancient ritual of atonement, allowed for no escape and prevented me, in my pain and anguish, from hardening my heart beyond regret. From that day forward, I would remember to carry clean water and feed to the sorrow that ever abides in the killing of things.

Vestments

side from those attached to my car, I own two mirrors. One hangs by the bathroom sink, a mirror just large enough to give me the image of my face and hair. The other is a full-length mirror stored in the back of a bedroom closet. I have recently hauled this mirror out and propped it against the bedroom wall where I can look at myself in new clothes I have bought.

In the past I can recall nothing beyond an almost studied indifference to anything other than the utility of what I wore. My clothes had to be practical, durable, and cheap. Once purchased, they had to be faithfully cared for and made to last as long as possible. I would no more think of discarding a usable garment for its lack of stylishness than I would think of throwing away a hammer that still had some work left in it—a virtue acquired from days of need.

As a child, I watched my father go off in the dark of the morning wearing the stiff gray work shirt and pants issued him by the gas company and carrying a lunch pail with his name scratched on it. I watched his return in the evening, where he often worked until bedtime trying to make the farm pay off.

In those days, my father and mother and my brother and I, even my baby sister Evelyn, seemed to live out our precarious lives in deadly earnest. My father was proud and scorned those who had to settle for jobs with the National Public Works Project. "Make-work," he called it. But when the gas company laid off his entire crew, my father too had to accept help from the project. He no longer had work clothes issued to him and he sometimes had to go to work in old Sunday clothes that had become too frayed to wear on that day.

I suspect my parents initially put my brother and me into jeans because jeans were durable and could be bought a size too large and still last long enough to be grown into before they wore out. Along with a few simple shirts and a jacket, these jeans constituted our school clothes. When they became too frayed for school we wore them for work. Each of us, my parents included, had one outfit that we wore only for church or other dress-up occasions. Otherwise, our good clothes hung in the closet safe from wear or harm. The necessities that drove my family to these frugal measures ended long ago, but the habit persists. I have seldom regarded my own clothing as a source of pleasure or beauty. I have carried austerity into all my doings, a certain strain of renunciation that seemed to come quite naturally to me. I believe I was drawn to Zen partly because of the unadorned practices I associated with Buddhist monks.

But recently, with practically every item of clothing I'd allowed myself pretty well worn out, I went out shopping. The first thing I found was a pair of tightly woven sandwashed khaki cotton pants. In the dressing room, I unbuttoned my jeans and slid them off and hung them aside on a peg. I pulled on the new pants. They felt and looked unfamiliar: the fabric lay smoother against my skin than the jeans, the cut was roomier so that the garment felt almost airy in its lightness. But they were comfortable, and in some indefinable way, the image reflecting from the dressing-room mirror pleased me. There were cuffs, and there were pleats that spread when I pushed my hands into the pockets. I took the pants home, and that was the beginning.

Since then I have bought three more pairs of pants, some T-shirts in soft colors with a pocket on the front, a cotton seersucker shirt in a pattern of thin alternating stripes of green and bone, a short-sleeved cotton shirt of tan, and a dozen pairs of socks in tones of earthen green and light brown. I like wearing these things, and I have recently found myself recalling with pleasure the remarkably beautiful robes the Buddhist monks wear for special ceremonial occasions.

Sometimes when I see my new clothes hanging in the bedroom closet, some unexplained tenderness, some melancholy, some softly rising joy comes to me. This puzzled me until on one such occasion I recalled the time of my father's new suits.

By 1945 the farm was finally paying enough that my father no longer had to work a second job. In fact, earnings from the farm had reached a little beyond absolute need. For the first time since immigrating in 1923, he had a small surplus at his discretion. He spent some of the money to have two suits custom tailored for him. The social circumstances of this tailoring was an issue of some delicacy to my father for reasons that I must explain.

My father had a deformity on his back in the form of a hump that bulged out on one side in the area of his shoulder blade. This defect was not severe but certainly noticeable enough to draw a child's attention and elicit questions. But my mother intercepted any such curiosities while I was still very young. She expressly forbade us children to ever speak of it to my father. She gave only vague intimations of early injury or sickness in explanation of the source of the deformity. Then we were instructed to put it out of mind and out of speech. Being thus enjoined to silence on the matter, this unspoken dialogue between my father and me became for a time our most persistent conversation, the language of an obvious and awkward avoidance audible in all we said.

I was always intensely aware of any circumstances pertaining to what I had come to designate as "Father's Back." If he took pain medication for his back, I knew of it. If he undertook any physical therapy or received chiropractic intervention or took heat treatments, I knew of it. In the same manner I somehow learned that my father's new suits were to be custom fitted to accommodate the hump on his back. For the first time in his life he would have a jacket that hung properly. Though only twelve at the time, I understood the significance of this. His tailor, I learned, was an acquaintance who had also immigrated to this country and with whom my father felt comfortable. I understood the point of this as well. It must have seemed to me as if everyone I knew was conspiring to guard this most public of secrets.

The formal declaration of these undertakings came one night at the supper table. Whenever Father had something important to announce such as the birth or marriage or death of one of our distant Danish relatives, he would stop eating, lay whatever utensils he happened to be using at the side of the plate, fold his hands in his lap, and look out on the rest of us in an attitude of expectation. Since he would do this in the midst of eating his meal, it would naturally draw our attention and signal to us that Father had something to tell us.

On this particular night, he proceeded to tell us something to the effect that the ranch had done very well that year and had cleared over twelve thousand dollars. We would be buying some things we needed but we couldn't buy whatever we wanted because, if we weren't careful, he could find himself "out carrying a lunch pail again." And then he added, "I am having George Wanger cut me two dress suits." This said, Father resumed his meal. And though none of us pursued this subject any further, I remember being pretty impressed with the event, as if I had been present at an important public function.

During the next several weeks, I was aware that my father went regularly to the tailor's shop for fittings. I couldn't prevent myself from trying to imagine how George Wanger could get the cloth to fit properly to Father's back. I imagined him stretching the material to form a sort of accommodating bulge or stitching in extra material where it was needed. I was driven to these speculations by the heartfelt wish that Father's suits would turn out right and by the heartfelt fear that they would not. I had come to think of my father's deformity as a sort of painful disease, bad enough that it mustn't be spoken of, and from which he could never be cured. I earnestly hoped that the suits would somehow help to make my father okay again, the way he must have been before whatever it was that had happened. My fantasies of tailoring were prayers for his healing.

The suits came home without my ever knowing of it—so I was surprised when my father gathered up my brother and me shortly after lunch one day and told us, "I have something to show you boys." He led us into our parent's bedroom, an act which in itself was unusual because it was somehow understood that we boys were to stay out of there. He pulled open the closet door and stood aside, inviting us without a word to look within.

And there were the suits. They were unlike any other articles of clothing that hung among my father's things. One was dark, a blended wool of rich browns; the other was light, a blended gray with closely spaced darker threads running through it. They were both double-breasted and had wide lapels. Father took each in turn from the closet and laid it on the bed so that we could better see the front with its pocket and the lining, which he exposed for us, and the startling inside pocket, a feature I had no idea existed. And then he put one of jackets on and I tried to make out what George Wanger had done to the back to make it fit so well but there was nothing obvious to be seen. And of course I couldn't ask because the subject was forbidden. Father also showed us the trousers that day with their pleats and cuffs. And then he held the suits up by their hangers, one in each hand,

and with the air of one who is disclosing a confidentiality of the most serious kind, he said, "These suits are made of the finest material money can buy." I had a habit in those days of whistling tunes a lot, particularly when I worked. All that afternoon while I went about my farm chores, I kept whistling, feeling that now things would be okay.

In the following year the ranch continued to prosper. Father began to do things he had never done before, and he did most of them in his new suits. He and my mother took lessons in ballroom dancing from Carla Wanger, the tailor's wife. When they had learned a new dance, they went to Vivian Lairds, a dine-and-dance club all the way over in Long Beach, thirty miles away, to try out what they had learned. They looked grand to me going out the door together, Father in one of his new suits (he was quite whimsical about which one he might on any occasion choose to wear) and Mother in a slinky mauve gown with a matching jacket she could discard when they took to the dance floor. Father seemed to love wearing his suits, and he would sometimes dress up just to go to a dance lesson or to do some banking or other such thing. I recall him on one occasion driving away in our old Hudson sedan wearing his gray suit with a handkerchief folded in the pocket, on his way to the dentist to have his teeth cleaned.

In those wonderful days of my father's new suits, I felt safer than I had ever before felt as a child. And the safest place of all was at Sunday service in Trinity Episcopal Church where my father had begun to serve as an usher. He greeted the other members as they arrived and showed them to their seats, helping some to remove their overcoats and hanging them in the cloakroom. Best of all, he distributed and collected the offering plates during the service. Sitting in a pew beside my brother and sister and mother, I felt that some mournful curse had at last been lifted from my father's back, that we were all rich, and that Father would never have to carry a lunch pail again.

And he never did. Yet in the course of a few years, my father quit his new church functions and withdrew once more into the guarded privacy of his past behaviors, devoting his energies almost exclusively to keeping the ranch solvent. "One really bad year could wipe me out and I could lose everything," he would sometimes say. His suits hung idle in the bedroom closet.

Nevertheless, standing before the mirror in my own new garments, the resurrected father in his marvelous new suit, his face as serious as if our collective salvation had been put in his hands, carries the offering plate up the aisle to the very altar itself. It is received by Reverend Hailwood, who lifts the plate up, up, upward, and we all rise and sing the doxology, and my father is still there, there where the whole congregation can acknowledge the importance of what he has just done, there at the very front of the church, clothed in the very best material money can buy.

Oh Father, is it not strange that after all the frugal self-discipline and denial, after all the secrecy and fear, we are drawn now toward one another as much by our minor self-indulgences and the small amenities we have allowed ourselves as ever we were by our shared sacrifices?

In a Zen monastery outside Mount Shasta, California, I watch a group of Soto monks gather in the temple. There are forty of them, all clothed in dark robes draped with ritual cloths of deepest purple and saffron. They approach the altar where they form themselves in four equal lines facing the figure of the Buddha. Their movements are measured and exact as they unfold their kneeling cloths, forty squares of embroidered white silk drawn off their shoulders and spread on the floor before them. The temple gong sounds. The monks drop to their knees and, in a movement as sudden and delicate as the beat of a moth's wings, arch forward to touch their foreheads to the floor, the purple and saffron of their vestments fluttering and settling over the squares of silk like brilliant insects drawn to white blossoms. It is an homage paid in beauty to the source of beauty before the altar of its being. It is the chrysalis unfolding to the light of its own awakening. It is the bright face of mutual recognition reflecting itself in the image of its own true nature.

The Catching Crate

The catching crate was a structure designed by necessity and arrived at by error. It took its eventual form from what was left after the mistakes were discarded. What the crate was intended for was to catch turkeys. Several times a year, each of the hundred thousand turkeys that were distributed over a 360-acre hillside of weeds and dust had to be caught for vaccination, breeder selection, or marketing. The catching crate figured so importantly in this need that it is hard to imagine how we could have managed without it.

All of us—my father, my brother and I, the farmhands, even my mother and little sister—called this simple structure "the catching crate." It was a name spoken in reverence and in aversion. To catch turkeys in the thing was to know that misery is relative: we were always thankful that our situation wasn't worse. Since "worse" would have been more or less intolerable, we looked upon the catching crate as a sort of saving presence, and our loathing of the task associated with it was tempered with a grudging yet heartfelt gratitude verging on the religious. This needs explaining.

Turkeys are hard to catch. Just to get them into some kind of enclosure and keep them there long enough to get your hands on them is an ambition fraught with serious difficulties. For one thing turkeys can fly—not well, but well enough to get them sufficiently airborne to clear an eight-foot fence. So you can't just herd a bunch of turkeys into a fence corner and expect to hold them there long enough to catch them. As soon as you grab for one, the others, frantic to escape, explode upward in a colliding tangle of thrashing wings. They pile up against the fence, claws scratching for a foothold, straining to get to the top, some scrabbling over the fence and dropping off on the back side, a few managing to get airborne and, in a directionless frenzy of flight, crashing into the fence or each other or into whoever is trying to catch them. The dark side of this absurdity is that the birds trapped on the bottom of the heap are being smothered to death, their bodies raked by the claws of those above them.

When you realize what is happening and start throwing turkeys off the top trying to save those underneath, you find yourself reaching down into a pile of limp turkey carcasses, their feathers wet with smeared manure and blood. When my father first went into the turkey business, we tried to catch turkeys this way. We ran a bunch of them into a corner and started grabbing. It was a method abandoned after first try.

A second difficulty in catching turkeys is that they're big. A full-grown tom can weigh as much as forty pounds, a hen thirty. Much of that weight is concentrated in the breast muscle, and it is this powerful muscle that drives the wings and legs. This accounts for the third major difficulty: turkeys are strong. So even if by chance and adjustment you eventually design a catching crate that is portable, strong, yet light enough to be moved, a crate that restricts the birds' flight, and prevents their piling up, you will still find that the three dozen birds you hope to contain in the crate will simply walk away with it unless the crate is staked to the ground.

Now aesthetics has always recognized simplicity of form as a fundamental virtue. This is not to say that we should admire any object that happens to lack complexity; such a thing might be merely dull. The simplicity I speak of has an inevitability about it that suggests that a form cannot be otherwise than exactly as it is. It is frequently a form required by utility. The lines of a canoe or sailing ship, for example, bear a clean and unadorned beauty necessitated by function. The catching crate was like this. It could be nothing other than what it was.

After all the modified fence corners, the cages of various designs, the darkened and lidded boxes, and the adjustable squeeze chutes which could never be made to accommodate more than a dozen turkeys, the structure that finally emerged was a simple three-sided containment that could hold up to thirty-six turkeys at a time. It consisted of two right-triangle side-pieces fronted by a gate that could be shut after the turkeys were driven inside. The back of the crate—and here is where the genius of its design is realized—was a panel angled inward at forty-five degrees, which prevented the birds from piling up on one another. The crate was built of slats, because we discovered that although turkeys balked at entering a solid structure, they walked unperturbed into one they could see through. They would try to push right on out the back, thus wedging themselves into the slant. With the gate closed, there was just enough room for a sin-gle man, kneeling on pads, to reach in and grab the turkeys by their legs. Shaped by necessity, the catching crate with its slats and baling wire reinforcement was a most unlikely candidate for a kind of spare utilitarian beauty that even the dullest of us who worked with it tacitly acknowledged.

The catching itself was a ritual requiring a fair amount of skill, poise, and self-containment—especially if you hoped to survive the ordeal with any of your dignity intact. For one thing, it had to be done kneeling. For another, it exacted of the catcher a dis-cipline of some severity in order to stay at the task for more than a few minutes. Catching turkeys required character. To catch a turkey, you must put on a pair of stout leather gloves, get down on your knees in the opening of the catching crate, pick out a pair of legs that belongs to a single turkey, and make a swift, hard, backhanded stab at them, hoping to pin the legs together in your grip so that you can yank the bird off its feet before it loosens one of its legs and claws itself free of you.

A frightened turkey shits. Fresh turkey shit is a smeary mess of yellows, greens, and whites that smells utterly vile and has the unfortunate consistency of soft pudding. When the catcher yanks the turkey's feet out from under it, those feet are invariably standing in a pile of this stuff, which flicks back on the catcher, again and again, until the catcher is plastered with it from where his knees contact the ground right up to his throat and, not infrequently, even into his face and hair. As the hours go on and load after load of turkeys is herded into it, conditions in the crate grow worse. The catcher's clothes stiffen with accumulating layers of drying turkey shit, and there in front of the whole crew he suffers the humiliation of spitting out filth and wiping shit from his eyes. No one ever offers help. No one ever laughs.

So naturally no one really wanted to do the catching, a fact that obligated every one of us to do our share. This is no small matter. The manner in which labor is distributed measures the heart of any work community, even if it's just a bunch of ragged farmhands trying to make a living or a family maintaining a household. To ignore this matter is to forfeit the one point of honor that gives work its integrity. Who cleans the toilets, washes the dishes, picks up after the party, takes out the garbage? To ask this question is to inquire into the heart of fairness, where justice either succeeds or doesn't. Of course, those of us on the turkey crew never spoke among ourselves about justice, but we were nonetheless bound by its dictates. What I want to suggest here, because I feel it so strongly myself, is that this is not a matter of principled behavior but one of love. It is a natural sympathy for others that moves us toward fairness, and it is this sympathetic capacity that brought each of us in turn to put on the kneeling pads and get down into the filth of the catching crate.

Yet there was a time when turkey-catchers lost faith—a dangerous time, a crisis that happened to coincide with my own childhood initiation into catching. It was also the time when Hector Berrens, driving home from the farm with the sun in his eyes, crashed into the rear end of a parked truck.

There were five hired hands on the farm who, along with my father and my brother Rowland and I, could make up a crew of nine. The hired hands had been taken on over the years as the turkey flock grew. Al Messeral had been the first, hired when I was just a baby. From my viewpoint, Al had been around as long as my parents had. Pete Haney came next, a refugee from Depression-era Oklahoma; then Bob Townsley, who had lost his sharecropping rights to a small plot of gravelly ground in southern Arkansas. Hector and his brother, Ernie, arrived only a year before the accident.

Hector had come asking for work when the eighty-acre lease he horse-farmed was sold and he was left with no way to care for his aging parents and for Ernie, who was retarded and couldn't make it on his own. Hector had never married. He had been unwaveringly obedient to his father's request to "stay home and take care of things." He had no pretensions, yet he carried himself with a degree of dignity that even a child such as I could sense. He came to my father's office, standing dark and stocky in the doorway, a powerful man, big-boned, with a thick neck and broad forehead. He took his hat from his head, stepped up to my father's desk, and asked for work. He offered Ernie, at half wages, saying that Ernie was a hard worker but that they would have to work together since no one else could understand him. Father, realizing he needed more help, took the two of them on.

The next morning Hector was there at dawn, wearing new work gloves and carrying a lunch pail. His face that morning bore a certain characteristic flatness of expression that suggested reserve, resignation perhaps, or maybe just dullness. Ernie trotted alongside him in little spurts and stalls like a squirrel that can't quite make up its mind whether to cross the road. He clutched his lunch pail in both hands as if he thought someone might take it from him, and his eyes, a little wild, darted from face to face. Hector had to calm him, show him where to stand, and separate him from his lunch pail so that their lunches could be put up in the lunchroom. It was later that same day that a danger, grave with consequence for us all, first arose.

We were in the midst of selecting breeder turkeys on that first day of Hector's and Ernie's employment, which meant that in the space of a few weeks every bird on the farm would have to be caught. As the day began, Al, Pete, and Bob took turns catching. Except for an occasional grab at a turkey or two, I had not yet taken my first turn in the catching crate. I was small and thin for my age. It was understood that catching was still beyond my strength and beyond that of Rowland as well. I never saw Father catch. He was the one who selected the breeders and it seemed obvious to me that he had more important work to do.

About mid-morning, Hector, seeing how things were done, strapped on the kneepads and took a turn. He made the usual mistakes of a beginner: he grabbed only one leg and the turkey clawed itself loose with the free one; he failed to guard against the bird that had turned itself in the crate, and all forty pounds of it launched from the back of his neck out the opening. He learned through error how to look away at the right moment, his eyeglasses with their scratched lenses taped onto the frame so splattered that he had to wash them off under a faucet in order to see what he was doing. But by the time Hector had finished his turn he was doing as well as anyone could expect.

As near as I can remember, it was a little before eleven when Al told Hector that he would take over for a while. I heard Hector say something to the effect that he would take a turn for Ernie, since we could all see that Ernie was not up to the task. How this could have happened I don't know but, after the mildest protest, Al let him do it. We all let him do it. We let Hector go back down on his knees and catch the turkeys Ernie couldn't catch. As a child, I simply remember feeling that something was terribly wrong. When we shut down for lunch that day, Hector was still in the catching crate.

After that the situation worsened. Hector, first insisting on catching for Ernie, later resisted being relieved from the task at all. He would be the first one in the catching crate in the morning, and it was hard to get him out of there. He took on this hardest and dirtiest of our labors as his natural lot, as though by right of some inherent virtue lacking in himself, the rest of us deserved better. He deferred to us in everything, anxious to sacrifice himself to us as he had to his father. In the beginning the others tried to take their turns, but when he declined, they were willing to let him have his way. By the second year of Hector's employment, no one even made a pretense anymore. Hector did all the catching.

We had lost our way. Even I knew this. We had forfeited the one ritual that, above all others, redeemed the misery of our work and bound us together in common regard. In the off season we would come upon the catching crate idle in some corner of a field, weeds sprouting up through the slats. None of us could look at it without knowing our loss.

Driving home from work one evening, Hector saw the truck at the last second, too late to avoid hitting it but not too late to jam on the brakes. Ernie was thrown under the dash, which probably saved his life. Hector, with his great power, had kept his grip on the steering wheel, the impact bending it over against the dash. He'd managed to stay in the car, but his head slammed into the liner above the windshield. In less than a week he was back at work, his head stitched and wrapped in bandages that made his hat perch off to one side, an angry swelling above one eye. His eyeglasses had somehow survived, though they were patched up even more than before. We were in the midst of breeder selection once again and everyone watched Hector put on the knee pads, drop to his knees in the catching crate, and begin catching. Father, sitting on his stool, watched him; Al and Pete and Bob watched him; Rowland and I watched him.

Before an hour had gone by, Al put on the knee pads and began catching, insisting to Hector that that was the way it was going to be. Seeing this, I resolved that when Al was done I would take a turn. When I asked Al for the pads, he at first looked questioningly at me, and then handed them over.

It didn't matter now how hard it was. Al had taken his turn and I was taking mine. Afterwards, Pete would take his, and then Bob, and maybe even Rowland. We'd found our way home again. There, under the slanting roof of the catching crate with its two triangular sides and a gate that snapped in place, I knelt at the site of our return.

The Sweetness of Making Beds

It's best to tuck the bedding in. That way the cold won't get to your feet. Smooth the wrinkles out and fluff the pillows until they're plump. A bed like that makes you want to crawl right back in even if you've just gotten up. But it's not like this when you awaken in a puddle of your own stale urine. The first thing you feel is the cold. The chill air of the upstairs bedroom penetrates the soaked bedding. You lie shivering in pajamas that are drenched from the small of your back down to your knees. Your skin rubs wet and raw against itself. The least movement is unbearable. The first gray of dawn leaks through the bedroom window. Outside the farm begins to stir. You stare into the dark ceiling, trying to will the daylight away.

But already the room is lightening and soon everyone in the house will be up. They will all know what you have done. It's your dirty secret. Soon it will be your brother's dirty secret as well, and later when the bedding is stripped and the mattress is airing in the backyard where your mother and father and little sister can all see the wet stain on it, it will be everyone's dirty secret. You shake your brother who lies asleep in the bed beside you. "Wake up, Rowland. Wake up." You hate sharing a bed. Both of you hate it. You can't remember a time when you didn't want a bed of your own. "Rowland, get up!"

Rowland stands beside the bed. He looks at you through eyes puffy with sleep. He knows without asking what's wrong. He's thankful it isn't him this time, because even though he's older than you he too still wets the bed. Neither of you can stop, and you don't know why.

You pull off your pajamas and wipe yourself with a corner of dry cloth. You put on pants and a shirt, and Rowland helps you roll up the soiled bedding which you will wash as your mother has instructed you to do because nobody else wants to wash something you've peed on. The bundle of bedding smells bad. You try to pick it up without touching the wet parts. Rowland takes his coat from the closet and puts it on over his pajamas. He wraps himself in the one blanket that's left unsoiled and curls up on the dry side of the bare mattress with his face toward the wall, trying to get a few more minutes of sleep. He hasn't said a word.

No one says a word. No one tells you why you still suck your thumb and don't even know you're doing it. No one tells you why your teeth stick out in front or why your father whips you so often. And though you wouldn't know to put it this way, you've staked your only hope for redemption on a dry bed. But four years later, having received confirmation in the faith, you will kneel at the altar of Episcopal Trinity Church in front of the entire congregation before the eyes of God himself and receive from the hands of Reverend Edward Hailwood your first sacrament of Holy Communion knowing that you still wet the bed.

That's the way it was at one time. But in that same year of my confirmation, I was somehow able to quit. I'm not sure why. It might have had something to do with the fact that the farm had begun to pay off and my parents could afford to have my teeth straightened. Also it was the year my father quit trying to beat my brother and me into compliance with a lath stick. It might have had a lot do with our having moved to another farmhouse where

Rowland and I, though still sharing a bedroom, had at last acquired separate beds. But I think my deliverance had most to do with my mother's illness.

In June of my thirteenth year Mother went to bed for the summer. She had undergone a surgery in May about which Rowland and I were given few details other than that it had something to do with what we called Mother's "sex organs." I think now she had a hysterectomy. She initially recovered from the surgery well enough but apparently a serious complication subsequently arose which made her gravely ill and put her back in bed from early June through the last of August. The onset of Mother's illness coincided with the closing of the school year, which always meant long days of summer labor for Rowland and me. The summer Mother got sick, Rowland, being the oldest, was sent as usual to the fields but I was sent to the house to help Mother.

Rowland was relieved that he wasn't the one to do the housework but to tell the truth I was secretly glad to do it. I was glad to be out from under my father's stern supervision and, while Mother was not above reporting me to him for the least offense, she was, nonetheless, easier to work for. The housework that summer was a haven for me.

There was a lot about housekeeping that I didn't know how to do, certainly not on the scale I was required to do it. I had to do the cleaning, washing, and cooking for all five of us, and I had to take care of Mother as well. Mother could barely manage to get herself to the toilet, and so had to supervise me from her bedroom. I would trail in and out of her bedroom to get instructions, sometimes carrying things like a pot of potatoes to see if I had cut the potatoes the right size and had added enough water to boil them.

Mother's housekeeping standards were exacting, and at first things were hectic for me. But in time I began to take a great satisfaction in seeing the family sit down to a supper that I alone had cooked for them, wearing fresh clothes I had washed and ironed with my own hands. I loved seeing Mother eat from the trays of food I carried to her. She was so weak at times that I was genuinely afraid she would die. I imagined my cooking might save her life. Keeping house that summer, brought me into a familiarity with the family that few children (certainly few boys) will ever know. I knew how much starch my father wanted in his dress shirts and exactly how he liked his collars and cuffs ironed. I knew how to iron my sister's sometimes frilly blouses and dresses without leaving any creases in them. I knew how everyone in the family liked their eggs cooked, those who couldn't tolerate them to be the least bit runny and those who wanted the yolk left soft.

On washdays, I would bring the finished wash to Mother's bedside to be inspected by her. She'd look to see if I had folded and creased her handkerchiefs as they should be. She taught me to sort Father's socks into pairs and stack them according to color and weight. Mother was naturally disposed to privacy and at first it was an embarrassment for her to watch me handling her underwear, folding her panties and bras into a drawer fragrant with the scent of a sachet. In time, however, we both became matter-of-fact about such matters, even to the point where Mother could instruct me in how to remove a stain from a nightgown she'd dirtied in her sleep. Mother could be a difficult and distant person even to her own children, but the two of us that summer entered into an intimacy understood only by those who truly depend on each other.

I became proficient at making beds that summer. I changed bedding on all the beds once a week and even more frequently on Mother's bed so that she wouldn't have to lie on stale sheets. Mother would sit on an upholstered chair at the side of the bed in her bathrobe and nightgown while I stripped the bed and remade it. She watched to see that the sheets had been ironed smooth and that the finished side of the hem showed when I folded the top sheet back over the blankets. She saw to it that I fluffed the pillows and that the embroidered pillowcases were lined up and matched to each other. When she was satisfied that the bed was properly made, I would bring her a basin of warm water and a washcloth and towel. I set these things on the nightstand beside her chair and laid a fresh nightgown out on the bed. Then I left her alone, shutting the door behind me. These procedures often left Mother exhausted, and when I returned a few minutes later, I sometimes found her asleep in her clean nightgown, snug between newly laundered sheets.

A couple of weeks before school started that fall, Rowland caught a cold. He couldn't sleep nights, repeatedly waking himself up with a hacking cough. I'd lie awake hearing Rowland spitting up phlegm into a handkerchief. And then one night somewhere between midnight and dawn, I awoke to the acrid odor of stale urine. Rowland was sitting up in the dark somewhere. I waited. I could hear him breathe. He didn't move.

At length I turned the lamp on. Rowland sat with his back to me on the far edge of his bed. He'd wrapped himself in one of his blankets. "Rowland?" I questioned. He didn't respond. For as long as I could remember, the understanding had been that you cleaned up your own mess. But for some reason unclear to me even now, I did something then that neither of us had ever done before. I went to the bathroom and got a warm wet washcloth and a towel and brought these to him and told him to take his wet things off and wipe himself down. When he didn't do anything, I took the blanket from him myself and pulled his pajama tops up over his head. I told him then to take the bottoms off, which he did. And then he wiped and dried himself and put on the clean pajamas I brought him. I pulled down the covers on my own bed and told him to get in. I thought he'd refuse. And then I thought he'd cry. But he got into my bed, and I turned the lamp off. In the darkened room, I gathered up his wet bedding and carried it past the bedroom where Mother and Father slept and out across the lawn to the laundry room.

I discovered that night that I was so intimate with the workings of the laundry room that I could wash a tub of laundry, tumble it dry, iron, and fold everything in the dark without once using the laundry room lights. I discovered as well that I could make a bed without the aid of sight, managing in the dark to turn Rowland's mattress and get his sheets and blankets back in place.

In the morning no one but Rowland and I knew what had happened. I had learned, once and for all, the sweetness of making a bed. I never wet my bed again. Before the year was over, Rowland too had quit.

The Debeaking Machine

*E*rnie was the only one who openly dissented. The rest of us insisted that the process was painless, and we did so, reciting this fiction, chapter and verse, with the anxious certainty of believers whose faith is called to question by fact.

Ernie's lone dissent could easily be discounted because he was only Hector's retarded brother. He couldn't read. He couldn't write. He couldn't even carry on a conversation that anyone other than Hector could understand. So what could Ernie possibly know about how much pain a turkey might or might not be feeling? Besides, Father said it didn't hurt, that it was no different than trimming a toenail, as long as you were careful not to cut "into the quick." I clung unwaveringly to Father's reassurance, because I didn't want to admit to yet another shame among the shameful acts I already felt myself involved in.

The debeaking machine was delivered to the farm by the company representative himself, and he demonstrated its use on the morning of the very day we debeaked our first flock of five thousand turkeys. The company brochure that Father had studied for some weeks prior to ordering the machine advised that it was best to debeak the turkeys while they were still quite young so as to minimize any shock the birds might feel from the procedure. "The older the turkey, the greater the stress," the pamphlet explained. It was an item of advice similar to that given to mothers to have their infant sons circumcised while they are "still young enough that it doesn't hurt," a theory flatly contradicted by the response of any baby whose foreskin is being cut away.

Nonetheless, our first "debeakers" were little more than a month old. They hadn't acquired their true feathers yet, and were still caged in the rows of coops they occupied before being put out on the range. On the morning of the demonstration, Al Messeral, who was the farm foreman, Bob Townsley, Hector Berrens and his brother Ernie, and I were all waiting at seven when the company representative drove up. Father came out from the house and the two of them got the machine out of the trunk of the representative's car. Al had already strung an extension cord from an electrical outlet in the barn out to the coops, so everything was set for the demonstration to take place.

The representative, who introduced himself as Terence Ferguson ("Just call me Fergy"), was dressed in a dark suit with a white shirt and tie. Even with a shop apron strapped on to protect his clothing, he looked impossibly out of place standing among the rest of us with the smell of manure and the hum of flies all about. He began his instruction by emphasizing what we already knew: that some form of debeaking was essential to prevent cannibalism. He stressed the word "essential" in such a way as to imply that it might be a debatable point.

But, of course, he was right. Even with a hundred acres of fenced range to accommodate the hundred thousand turkeys my father raised annually, that's still a thousand birds an acre, a density intolerable for turkeys whose nature it is to gather secretively in small family flocks. They are animals wholly unprepared to deal with the presence of such numbers of themselves concentrated into one place, and their response to the distress this raises in them is to eat each other. They pick and stab with their sharp beaks until blood is drawn, and then converge on the bloodied one, standing and pecking at it or taking a swipe at it in passing. The victim, still on its feet, wanders about the flock with bloody, gaping holes eaten into its body and half its head pecked away. Some seem unable to fall and die. By the time of the debeaking machine, I had seen one such bloodied horror sitting at roost with both its eyes eaten away, acting on one of its few surviving instincts, asleep side-by-side with the others, everything apparently normal, as though being eaten alive were the natural order of things.

We all of us who lived or worked on the farm suffered with the knowledge of this awful aberration. We didn't like to think that such a thing was the result of our own doing, though we knew it was. Even as a child, I felt the taint of this as of some shameful wrong we all somehow had a part in. Father, who often had to haul the mutilated carcasses of cannibalized turkeys to the pit to dispose of them, was I believe as pained by this as the rest of us, though lately he'd begun to reduce the whole matter to terms of economic loss, complaining that he couldn't afford to lose so many mature birds, that the cost of it would drive him out of business. But the very vigor of his protest revealed the presence of an uneasy remorse. We all had more than cause enough to want to believe in the efficacy and humaneness of the debeaking machine.

We stood around Terence Ferguson that morning, eyeing him, in his black suit and tie, with wariness and hope, while he pointed out to us, with a fair degree of proprietary pride, the various patented components of the debeaking machine, which turned out to be an almost preposterously simple mechanism for something as expensive as it was. The whole thing consisted of little more than a stationary metal "bite" rod, about the thickness of a pencil, with a movable, electrically heated, red-hot blade positioned above it. The idea was to split the turkey's bill over the bite rod with the upper half exposed on top so that the electrified blade could sear it off. A foot pedal operated the blade, which sprung back up on the force of a spring when the pedal was released. These working parts were mounted in the open end of a sort of hinged box set on three legs adjustable for height like those of a tripod.

By the time Ferguson had finished with these first fundamentals, Pete and Rowland had joined the six of us who were already there, father having called them in from their other work because he wanted everyone on the farm to be properly instructed in the use of the machine. Ferguson, who seemed to relish this increase in his audience, recounted a few particulars the others had missed and then, rubbing his hands together as if in anticipation of doing something quite extraordinary, said, "Well, then, let's get started, shall we?"

Hector grabbed a turkey out of the coop and handed it to Ferguson. It was a scruffy looking thing. A turkey that age has lost all the plump, downy appearance of a new hatchling and has become little more than a pair of twiggy legs supporting a sort of prickly-looking, half-naked body with a few wing feathers growing out of it and a knot of fuzz, like a boy's flat-top, sticking up on the crown of its head. If you look at its face straight on, a bird like this appears crazed. Ferguson took the turkey from Hector, letting it hang from the tips of his fingers on legs that looked about as sturdy as strips of dry spaghetti. He held it up to the debeaking machine, the ball of his foot cocked above the pedal in readiness to push down. The rest of us crowded in around him. Ferguson, absorbed in the particulars of his demonstration, explained how the prescribed procedure for a right handed operator was to "hold the bird's legs with your left hand while forcing its bill apart with the forefinger of your right hand" and so forth, but we weren't hearing much of what he said because we could all see the electrically-heated blade, glowing red in the open end of the debeaking machine.

Ferguson had trouble getting the demonstration turkey's bill pried open. I could see that this flustered him considerably. When he finally managed to get the job done and had the head of the bird shoved into the debeaker with its bill split over the bite bar, he paused to give final instructions on the "depth of cut" which he explained was crucial to the operation. "If you don't cut off enough," he explained, "it'll grow back before you market the bird and you still have to contend with cannibalism. It's like getting your money's worth out of a haircut. You need to whack off enough so that it will last a while." With that, he seemed ready to make the cut, and I actually saw his foot start to compress the pedal, but before he could continue, I heard myself asking with more urgency than I had intended, "Does it hurt?"

"Does it hurt to cut your toenail?" he responded. He sounded annoyed. "Just don't cut into the quick." At the time, I didn't know what "the quick" was, but before I could follow up on this, Ferguson pressed down on the pedal, and we could all see for ourselves that debeaking a turkey was nothing like cutting a toenail. And I suppose it was exactly then, when we saw how awful it really was, that we became such religious adherents of Ferguson's toenail theory, silencing thereafter any suggestion to the contrary with our own glib reassurances. I was expecting to see just the tip of the beak cut away, but Ferguson made the cut so deep that the bird was left with nothing more for an upper beak than a charred stump barely long enough to accommodate its nostrils. Though probably swift enough, the electrified blade seemed to burn its way through with an intolerable slowness. You could hear it sizzle. A kind of oily smoke came curling up about Ferguson, making him look all the more remarkable in his suit and tie. When he pulled the turkey's head out of the debeaking machine to check the cut, a bead of blood was still oozing from it. So he shoved it back in and sort of smeared the stump back and forth against the hot blade for a second, explaining that it was important to "seal the cut" adequately. I don't know what it looked like to Ferguson, but to the rest of us the face of that mutilated little demonstration bird looked something like a cigarette butt that had burned itself out. He handed it to Hector, and Hector dumped it back in the coop where it stood teetering for a moment before its legs folded under it and it came to rest on the wire in a sort of shocked daze.

Ferguson demonstrated a few more times, and then each of us had to take a turn. We all tried to get away with a cut shallower than was prescribed, but Ferguson was having no truck with such squeamishness. And neither was Father, who was pinning his hopes on the machine to save him from some unsupportable losses. Al went first, and then Hector, Bob, Jim, Rowland, Father, and me, in that order. Ernie refused his turn, and Hector said that it was OK, he didn't have to do it. By the second go-around, we had all of us learned to keep our fingers as far from the hot blade as possible and to lean away from the rising smoke because the smell was so bad. Before the hour was out, Ferguson, satisfied with our progress, had stripped off his shop apron and was gone, Father was back in the farm office, the others had returned to their earlier work, and the four of us who made up the day's crew were left with five thousand turkeys to debeak by nightfall.

At noon, Ernie wouldn't eat his lunch. He sat beside Hector with his lunch pail on his lap, but he wouldn't open it. At length, Hector opened it for him and showed him that the sandwiches were the same as his own and that they were good and he should eat some. "Cold ham, Ernie. You like cold ham." But Ernie seemed not to hear him at all, the opened lunch pail resting across his knees with his ham sandwich still wrapped in wax paper, an apple and a thermos of coffee untouched.

He'd been like this all morning. We'd divided up the work so that Hector and I took turns catching and debeaking, Al vaccinated for a disease called blackhead, and Ernie returned the turkeys to the coop. Hector, who took the first turn catching, leaned into the coop and brought out a turkey which I debeaked. The plan was that Ernie would take the turkey from me, pass it by Al to be vaccinated, and release it back into the coop. But when I pulled the debeaked turkey off the blade and tried to hand it to him, Ernie wouldn't take it from me. I held it out to him, but he shook his head and backed away, leaving the bird dangling from my fingers. Hector eventually got him to take the turkey and things went smoothly for a while, but then Ernie would balk again. This went on throughout the morning, and once he even walked away from the job and Hector had to bring him back with Ernie repeating over and over, "It's no good, Hector. It's no good. No good. No good." And of course it was no good. We all of us knew it was no good, which is precisely why we had to concur when Al parroted Ferguson and said, "It doesn't hurt them, Ernie; it's just like cutting your toenails." But Ernie wasn't capable of so obvious a lie to himself. His innocence exposed us and made our own dishonesty nearly intolerable.

The morning after that first day of debeaking, I woke early. The farm was silent, the turkeys still at roost, the bedroom windows without light. I thought of the rows of coops lined up in the dark beyond the barn. They would be wet now with fog drawn off the sea, the corrugated metal roofs beaded with drops of water, the wire floors cold to the touch. I wondered how a baby turkey could eat with a third of its bill gone. Rowland was still asleep. I wanted to wake him, but instead I pulled on my clothes and went out.

The turkeys were just beginning to stir when I got to the coops. I had never seen a flock awaken to anything quite like the conditions of that morning. Some looked as if they'd not gone to roost at all but had spent the night on their feet, their eyes a lusterless vacancy, their heads hanging down. Others tried to eat, stabbing repeatedly at the mash and pellets in the feed trays, uncomprehending as to why they weren't getting more food.

Though Hector and I had cauterized the wounds until we feared the heat itself would kill the birds, a few that morning still dripped blood from the stumps of their amputated beaks. The water in the crocks was tinted red where they'd gone to drink. In every coop a few birds lay dead.

I gathered up the dead ones, counting them as I went, fifty-six in all, a loss that father later that morning would compare favorably to the losses and the suffering he expected to avoid from cannibalism. I heaped up the feed trays in the hope that the birds might get more food in their mouths. I emptied the bloodied crocks and put in fresh water. And when I couldn't think of anything more to do, I went and stood by the little pile of dead turkeys I gathered from the coops. They smelled like burnt garbage. Their silenced lives rose in my ears like the voice of deepest conscience, asking that I not turn away: "It's no good, Hector. It's no good, Al. It's no good, Linley." But I did turn away. We all of us turned away—except Ernie, who wasn't clever enough to outwit himself.

In time we got the hang of the thing and our debeaking was less messy. Ernie quit refusing his lunch and all of us were a little more comfortable with what we were doing, though it was never something you wanted to be doing to a bird even if you believed, as we did, that it was something that had to be done. We quit lying to ourselves, forced to acknowledge that no matter how necessary the task, it was, in just the exact sense that Ernie must have felt, "No good." It was, in fact, a considerable cruelty to do what we were doing, and to pretend otherwise dishonored ourselves and every bird we'd ever debeaked. It took the courage of this eventual honesty to set us right with the world again.

I think the range of "no good" is broader and more comprehensive than our typical deceptions allow us to recognize. I'd like to think I'm now living harmlessly, but I'm not. I don't think the universe is put together in such a way that I can. No matter how hard I try, I'm not going to succeed in isolating myself in some kind of purity denied all the rest of creation. I don't complain about that. I celebrate life and don't argue much with its circumstances. I accept as best I can whatever the universe offers me.

That first year of the debeaking machine, as in all the years before and after, the five of us Jensens gathered round our Thanksgiving table knowing, as all farm families know, exactly how our food got there. Without this knowledge, we wouldn't deserve to eat a bite. Of course that means that the faces of happy anticipation seated at that table were touched with a shadow of the old regret that one can never dispel. So we didn't try to dispel it. What we did instead was to reach deep into ourselves for the gratitude that alone redeems the sacrifice of other lives. That done, five hungry plates were sent up to the head of the table where Father carved white or dark or some of both if you liked; and heaps of mashed potatoes, giblet gravy, cornbread stuffing, sweet yams, and tart cranberry sauce were passed round in an ageless ritual celebrating the earth's great harvest.

The Egg Barn

The egg barn was little more than a shed really, about the size of a garage. It stood on the outermost perimeter of a 360-acre farm located in a remote area of the Irvine Hills in Southern California. In addition to the egg barn, the farm also had a feed barn, stalls for two work horses, a small house and yard, a well, and thousands of feet of poultry fencing strung on metal T-posts to form enclosures for a hundred thousand turkeys.

None of these other structures could be seen from the egg barn, which stood down a long hill on the edge of a wash. The wash itself was a narrow crease of moist earth where a few willows survived. In the early mornings or late evenings when the turkeys were restless, one could hear them from the egg barn, their cackling faint in the distance, the smell of them on the wind. But all one could see of the rest of the farm were tire tracks disappearing in the weeds up slope.

As a boy, I worked long hours in the egg barn. I lost my childhood to such work. As far back as I can remember I had to rush home from school to do chores; but the summer Rowland was ten and I was eight, Father put us to work full time. My mother supported Father in this new regimen, seeing to it that Rowland and I were on the job by seven and that we didn't overstay the lunch hour. Both Father and Mother were so stern and formal about the arrangement that I took it as a punishment for something I'd done wrong. From the hot summer fields where I chopped weeds or rolled up poultry fencing, I could see the laundry drying in the shade near the house, and I yearned for the cool return to a refuge from which I felt exiled.

The whole of that summer's labor passed in tight little increments like the staccato advance of the second hand round the face of a clock. It was the longest ninety days of my young life, yet it was not time enough to make right again whatever it was that had gone wrong. Rowland set his face hard against whatever feelings he may have had. He went through his days without disclosure of any sort. At night we lay in the upstairs bed we shared, staring into the dark, each knowing the other did the same, and we never spoke. I had already been cut off from my schoolmates who did not go home to chores. Now I was being cut off from my family, even from my brother. But worse, an intransigent and divisive doubt had now begun to cut me off from myself.

As the breeding operation grew, Father set me to gathering eggs from the nests and hauling them to the egg barn, where I cleaned, sorted, and stored them ready for the incubators. It was work a boy could do better than an adult because the nest houses were cramped, and one had to crawl into them on hands and knees. Inside, the hens settled into hollows they'd scratched in the deep beds of rice hulls that cushioned their eggs. The bodies of the hens were hot. I smelled their acrid breath where they panted in the tight enclosure. I pushed my body in among them, dragging a wire basket along to hold the eggs. Some of the hens scrambled out of my way but others slapped at me with their stubby, nest-worn wing feathers and hissed and stabbed at me with their bills. I crawled the length of the nest, forcing the hens aside to get at their eggs, raking my hands through the rice hulls to bring up any that were buried. The sheer intimacy of this violence sometimes left me disheartened, kneeling among my antagonists, clutching hot eggs in my hands.

Back at the egg barn I loaded the baskets of eggs onto a table. Through the open door, I could see the wash where the willows stood out green against the fields of bleached weeds. I took each egg in hand, one at a time, and if even the faintest manure stain was found on it or a smear of blood from a hen's egg tract, I scoured it clean with sandpaper. Father had warned me that the slightest impurity that found its way into the incubator could sicken a whole hatch of chicks. When I was sure the eggs were clean, I put them into the incubators where, after a few weeks, I took them out again to be candled, putting a light to the eggs in a darkened room so that the inside of the eggs were illuminated and I could see the developing embryos. In the living eggs, I could make out the form of a tiny chick taking shape around its own beating heart. In others, I saw only the shadow of a lifeless yolk rotting in the warmth of the incubator. In the egg barn with the window shades drawn and incubators humming in darkness against the wall, I put the candling light to each egg, discarding the failures in a garbage pail that waited beside my stool.

I worked alone those days, and while I had no yearning for company, the solitude wore away at me. I stood by the table in the egg barn and sanded eggs until my hands and forearms, and even my hair and face, and the table itself was coated with chalky dust. I breathed eggshell and manure and traces of turkey blood. I felt increasingly vague, as indeterminate as the accumulating days and weeks I spent working there. Hour after hour I moved among the crates of eggs like a prisoner in solitary confinement who, when sentenced to the presence of his own person, finds himself locked up with a stranger. Under the unrelieved scrutiny of my own attention, I turned myself round and round in my mind like some unformed embryo that had failed to incubate and had so irretrievably lost the source of its own becoming that it was utterly unfamiliar to itself. Outside, the wind blew across the fields of dust and feathers and withered weeds. Sand scraped against the barn's corrugated metal sides.

Once in a while, Al or Hector or one of the other farmhands would come down to the egg barn to put in a spare hour helping me. They too were becoming like strangers to me. They might pull their hats off where the sweatband left a hot crease across their foreheads. They might wipe the grit and sweat from themselves with a handkerchief or a rag. They might complain about the heat or about the farm truck whose battery was failing. They might tease me about the Stillford girl who lived on a neighboring farm and whom they liked to imagine I had a crush on, but none of this penetrated the odd detachment that grew on me during the long hours I spent alone. I could find nothing of myself clarified in their company. I bore no necessary relationship to them nor to anyone else for that matter, not even my father whose visits to the egg barn were rare and formalized into employer/employee encounters, a stiffness that he must have felt necessary to my becoming a man but that only magnified the absence I felt in his presence there.

And then, one hot summer afternoon, six years after Father had first set me to work, he came to the egg barn to count the eggs we had in stock. As he left he did something unusual. He put his hand on my shoulder, gave a little squeeze, and said, "How's the young working man doing?" He stood there as if he were actually waiting for an answer, and he didn't take his hand away. I put my own hand over his and held it fast to my shoulder. And then I saw, in just the merest flicker of his eyes, that my father could not help me to know who I was because he himself did not know. I was as much a stranger to him as to myself. We were both made momentarily awkward by the unspoken disclosure of this fact in one another's faces. Father turned away first and went out the door, saying something about egg production being slightly improved over the previous month.

I heard him start the engine of his car and then I heard the sound of it recede into the distance. I went outside in time to see him disappear over the rise that separated the egg barn from the rest of the farm.

In the egg barn, I took up my work again. Down in the wash the willows shimmered in waves of heat. Then I was going toward the wash, down through the brittle stalks of weeds, the foxtails pricking me where they stuck to my socks. Under the willows, the sand was smooth and cool. I lay myself there, face down. It was not enough. I took my shirt off. Still, it was not enough. I pulled off my shoes and socks and stripped away the last of my clothing and pressed the whole of my naked body onto the ground. I dug a little concave in the moist sand, and I lowered my eyes and mouth into this space. And there, where the willows had found water, I breathed into the earth.

My name is Linley. I am lying on the ground, under the willows, in the wash beyond the egg barn, on my father's farm.

When I knew these things for certain, I dressed and went back to my work. In the silence of the barn the sound of my work seemed amplified. The drag of an egg crate on the worktable, the thin scratch of sandpaper, the scrape of a footstep, or the whisper of my breath; each was clarified and insistent. And every sound served to call me back to myself until the whole barn resounded with my name. Was it Father who called from where he sat at the farm office desk, his eyes blinking behind his glasses, his fingers pressing a sharpened pencil onto the columns of an egg ledger? Was it Rowland calling where he scooped grain into the turkey feeders, his back bending again and again to the task, his face wet with sweat? Did Mother call from the car where she turned onto the county road toward Schneider's grocery? Were Al and Hector calling from the fields? Had they set aside their tools and turned their faces toward the hill that hid me from their view, and called my name?

There in the egg barn I looked out on the wash where the sand still held the impression of my body. Weren't we all pressed to earth here in this field of one voice, calling our only name?

Venetian Blinds

We were getting Venetian blinds in those days. I don't know how it was elsewhere but in our end of the county a curtained window was swiftly becoming something of an historical curiosity. Ours was a farm district and our houses were mostly two-story structures with double-hung windows that were invariably curtained. For as long as I could remember housewives curtained their windows with ready-mades from Sears and Woolworth's or sewed them from cloth bought at Wilton's Department Store in Santa Ana. But now these new blinds were the rage; and up and down Smeltzer Lane perfectly good curtains were being stripped from farmhouse windows and stacked into the backs of closets. It was as if curtains were suddenly subject to some massive recall. In their stead window after window was upgraded with the Venetian blinds none of us could seem to resist.

I was just entering high school when this particular wave of modernization took hold. The year was 1946 and the prospect of installing Venetian blinds seemed to grip the imaginations of most householders with a persuasion that verged on patriotism. With the war effort behind them, everyone was ready to buy something. It was a matter of national pride to purchase, the moral equivalent of rationing during the war.

Hanging Venetian blinds wasn't all there was to it. Farley and Edith Head, who farmed the land next to ours, didn't stop with surface cosmetics like blinds. They yanked a whole set of multi-paned, double-hung windows right out of their dining room wall and replaced them with aluminum sliders. Edith, who had coveted these sliders ever since she'd seen them featured in a country fashions magazine, convinced Farley that they were the latest thing. "You just slide them open, Farley," she argued. "And they don't stick shut in wet weather. They're all glass. You don't have a bunch of dividers you have to look through in order to see out."

Neighbors traveling Smeltzer Lane had no sooner gotten used to seeing these sliders staring vacantly from the dining room of Farley and Edith's house, than the two of them tore half a wall out of their living room (which also fronted on Smeltzer) and installed a "picture window" big enough to frame an elephant. The picture window featured heavy drapes that opened and shut by hauling on a system of cords run through pulleys. On nights when the drapes were open and the living room lights on, you could see Farley and Edith from a mile down the road, moving in mute animation like actors on a set, the oversized window framing them like a proscenium arch. Confronted with an upgrading of this magnitude, travelers on Smeltzer Lane could see that any commensurate expression of patriotism had become a great deal more costly.

The Palmers, up the street from Farley and Edith, responded by cutting an eight-foot wide sliding glass door into their back bedroom wall. They didn't need a door there but now that they had one it had to serve some purpose, so they projected a redwood deck out over what had once been their salad garden. The Finleys, who lived across the field from them, pretty much duplicated these improvements with the exception that their bedroom slider was hung with green drapes while the Palmers' drapes were maroon. With their bedrooms facing each other's across less than five acres of pasture, both parties had to keep their drapes closed most of the time to avoid seeing one another in their underwear.

Mother, in one of her earlier enthusiasms, bought a modular sofa for the living room. Modular sofas, or sectionals as they were sometimes called, were regarded as the newest concept in household furnishings. Mother bought five upholstered sections with matching end tables finished in the new blonde furniture style that nobody around Smeltzer Lane could seem to get enough of. When we got our new modular laid out in the living room, it occupied an entire wall. The matching blonde coffee table was dwarfed to the size of a footstool when set in front of the thing.

How grand we all thought it was, Mother, Father, my brother, sister, and I all strung out along its great length, we kids giddy with excitement, popping up and down, trying out different locations. The sofa was so disproportionately large to the size of the room that Mother had to back into the hallway to get all of it into a snapshot. It's been fifty years since I've seen that photograph but I recall that my sister Evelyn's toy collie, Ring, who had been shoved off the sofa at least a dozen times by then, had gotten himself back up in time to be included in the picture. All of us, even Father, were grinning into the camera as if we'd just won a state lottery.

After a month or so, none of us wanted to sit on the sofa anymore. It was relegated to the use of visitors who had no prior experience of it and no alternative since those who knew were quick to occupy the few original chairs that had survived the general purge. The sofa's cushions were so soft that they more or less swallowed rather than supported you. In addition, the seat was so deep from the bend of the knee to the back that if you tried to keep your feet on the floor you ended up sort of lying down with the ceiling for a view. From the sofa, conversation with a visitor was difficult, a little like talking to someone who's bedridden. Elderly visitors often couldn't get out of the thing without help. Ring, who had become its primary occupant, loved the sofa.

It was a rare house in our county that survived improvement without forfeiting whatever aesthetic integrity it once had. Our very lives were being retrofitted. We'd disengaged from the talents of our own hands, allowing ourselves to be provided for. We'd purchased novelty in disregard of the sentiments of our hearts. We'd abandoned common sense, the extent of which we'd only just begun to measure in the disconcerting discovery that Venetian blinds weren't as convenient as we'd imagined they'd be. On farms, where blowing dust is a daily fact of life, Venetian blinds had to be dusted continually slat by slat—unto the hundreds of them if you'd hung them on every window of the house as we had. It was much easier to wash and iron curtains once or twice a year.

It took the wisdom of a child to bring at least a few of us back to our senses. Al Messeral, the foreman on our farm, lived about a mile away on a small acreage with his wife, Enid, his son, Jerry, and his eleven-year-old daughter, Ann. The Messeral house had only two bedrooms, one of which Ann had always shared with her older brother. But both children had begun to complain of the arrangement. It was decided that they were getting too old to share a room any longer. The plan was for Jerry to occupy a room in a shed that had once been converted to a bedroom for a farmhand. But from the very start, Ann wanted to be the one to make the move. Jerry was just as happy to stay where he was, and Ann lobbied so hard for the shed that they finally let her have her way.

The shed room was a mess. It took weeks to clean it up but from the moment Ann was given the go ahead she tackled the task with an energy and purpose surprising for one so young. She scrubbed the room down from ceiling to floor. She scraped off the old paint and freed up the double-hung windows, which had been painted shut for years. She repainted the ceiling and walls an antique white, and trimmed out the windowsills and the door in a soft green. In doing all this, she never refused help but she didn't encourage it either, seeming to prefer doing it herself. It was clearly Ann's room.

She refused Venetian blinds. Ann wanted curtains, and she wanted to sew her own. It was this turn of events more than any other aspect of the bedroom renovation that drew the others in. The prospect of an eleven-year-old who knew next to nothing about sewing undertaking to sew three sets of curtains was a circumstance irresistible to the women. All their talents were brought out of storage—Mother, Mabel Reeder, Thelma Buntin, Edith Head, Enid herself, and Enid's sister, Marjorie all becoming involved in the cause. Their first thought was that they could save the cost of cloth by cutting it from some of the curtains they'd all stored away. Surely they'd find what they were looking for with so much to choose from. They proposed this to Ann and she liked the idea.

Eventually, they'd dragged out just about every usable piece of cloth any of them owned but they hadn't found what they were looking for. Somehow a tacit consensus had formed among them that Ann's curtains had to be exactly right. The search ended when Thelma Buntin hauled out sixteen yards of new cotton calico she'd been holding back hoping to make something out of it for herself. It was a cross pattern of bright greens and yellows. Ann's eyes lit up. They all saw at once that it was perfect.

Mabel Reeder had the best sewing machine, a nearly new Singer Deluxe with all the latest attachments. So Mabel's Singer was hauled over to the Messerals, and the women gathered themselves into the little room that still smelled of fresh paint, and Ann's apprenticeship began.

Over the next few weeks, the women wore a path to Ann's door. They watched over her work as if it were their own. Ann was the most gratifying student imaginable. She cut and gathered and pinned and stitched and sewed as if there were nothing else she would rather do. The women could hardly keep their own hands off the project. With their coaching, Ann was probably turning out the most professionally finished curtains ever sewn by an eleven-year-old in Orange County, California.

Too soon, the curtains were finished. Mabel took her sewing machine back home. The women, lacking any ostensible reason to do otherwise, dispersed once more into the lives each had chosen for herself. They found excuses to drop in on the Messerals from time to time, where three sets of green and yellow calico curtains stirred their hearts and measured for them the extent of their loss.

Lucy

I think it's good, at least once in our lives, to call our parents by their names, not "Mom" and "Dad" but "Janice and Steven," or whatever their names happen to be. It's not absolutely necessary to do this in their presence; some of us were brought up on customs that would make it easier to cut out our tongues than to address our parents by their given names. But if we really want to know our parents as themselves, it helps to set aside the terms of parental relationship and speak their names outright, preferably to their faces.

My own parents' names are Morris and Lucy. As you may have gathered, my father was a rather formal person. The thought of my sitting down to play a game of chess with him and saying something like "It's your move, Morris" seems utterly implausible. Father lived to be ninety-four and that gave me sixty-two years in which to try out his name on him. I never did. Even the thought of it sticks in my throat.

The fact is that Father required Rowland and me to call he and Mother not "Mom," not "Dad," certainly not "Morris" or "Lucy," which he expressly forbade, but "Father" and "Mother" exclusively. We were in possession of these instructions before either of us had begun school. That my father had a role other than that of being my father and an existence beyond that of my seeing him as my father never truly dawned on me. It's a shame I had to wait until a chill December day in 1993 at Orange County's Fairhaven Cemetery to see the fact of it carved out for me on his gravestone: "MORRIS JENSEN 1899–1993."

It was different with my mother. Certain circumstances of her life brought me while still a child to question who this person I called Mother really was. Mother was still a nursing infant when a minister of the Episcopal Church of Missoula, Montana, delivered her to George and Amelia Goslee, two elderly members of the congregation who arranged to adopt the child. He carried her to the Goslees in a basket, receiving her from the hands of the birth-mother herself. He must have known the identity of the birth-mother, must have met her eyes or brushed against her as he took the basket. But my mother, innocent of all understanding, would know nothing but the naked loss and spent the better part of a lifetime trying to fit a name to the hands that surrendered her that day.

Mother can't remember a time when she didn't know she'd been adopted. Her foster parents disclosed this from the beginning. It was they who named her Lucy Beatrice, a name she bore along with the Goslee family name from the year of her birth in 1910 until her marriage in 1928 when she exchanged Goslee for Jensen. Her name always seemed provisional to her, a substitution until her actual name could be reclaimed. It was an alienation exacerbated by her foster parent's practice of reminding her that they had given her a home when she had "none of her own." Thus the name Lucy Beatrice Goslee was itself seen by my mother as the consequence of having no name of her own.

I was not yet in high school when Mother and I began to talk of these things. At that time, Mother undertook a systematic search for the identity of her birth-mother. Because I was genuinely sympathetic and interested, Mother made me her confidant. I saw how much it mattered to her to have her own family name back. We sat in the library corner of the old farmhouse and Mother explained her strategies to me. It was a long process with letters sent to various agencies of government, hospitals, churches, and individuals. Mother kept me apprised of the status of her inquiries and sometimes she was especially hopeful. I was hopeful with her, believing with all my heart that the next item of correspondence would tell us who she was.

During the three years that Mother and I shared this quest, we naturally focused on the fact of her name. As a result, the name "Lucy" became intimately familiar to me. I often spoke the name in Mother's presence, not as I recall in directly addressing her as "Lucy" but as if in reference to a third person known to us both. I began to discern in my Mother's person the presence of a stranger whose existence lay beyond the reach of my affection for her as my parent.

In the end all our efforts led to nothing. The last of the letters came back undelivered. Mother had no more strategies. We sat in the library corner, the letter lying face up on the table, the words ADDRESSEE UNKNOWN. RETURN TO SENDER. stamped across the envelope. I was about to tell her how sorry I was, but Mother spoke first. She said, "You know, my mother was probably English." I, who had been in the hunt with her from the start, knew there was no basis for this. "A lot of English immigrants settled in Helena," she went on. "Maybe my mother was from Helena." In the absence of facts, Mother was reduced to inventing them. I was witnessing the birth of a myth whose purpose it was to sustain hope where no hope was warranted. Over the next few years I watched her gradually elaborate on this beginning.

In the summer of 1948, between my sophomore and junior years of high school, Mother and Father packed their bags into the trunk of our old Hudson sedan and left for Montana. Mother explained that she and Father planned to visit Missoula and that they hoped as well to locate her birthplace in Helena. Apparently she'd come to believe her own story and expected the trip to confirm it. She was so matter-of-fact about the whole thing that I wondered if she knew something I didn't.

Mother came back from Missoula chattering like a travel brochure. What a good time they'd had! The mountains were beautiful. They had a nice room in the Missoula Hotel overlooking the river. She and Father located the Episcopal Church and the Goslee's house where she'd spent the first seven years of her life. But not a word about the birth mother. I hadn't the courage at the time to question her further, even if only to ask why they'd returned a week earlier than planned. To hear her tell of it the trip had been nothing but a vacation.

It took years of little hints and scraps of information for me to put together what happened in Missoula that summer. Mother and Father arrived in Missoula with the intention of going on to Helena within a few days. Mother had convinced herself she'd find records of her birth-mother there. It took them four days to reach Montana from Southern California. As Missoula grew nearer, Mother became more agitated, reciting endless details to Father of childhood sites she hoped to revisit. "I rollerskated," she told him. "My foster father taught me when I was only three. He made me do it right. He taught me to fold my hands behind my back and not let them flap about at the sides." She slid forward in the car seat to show Father how a skater's hands should be held. "I skated down the sidewalk from our house to the park. I wore dresses to skate in." She went on and on about such things. But once the door of their room on the fifth floor of the Missoula Hotel shut behind them, Mother fell silent.

She opened her suitcase on the foot of the bed and one by one laid out all her articles of clothing. Among other things, she'd packed a summer print dress with clusters of bright yellow daisies against a backdrop of stem and leaf. She hung it in the closet along with a pale lavender evening gown with thin shoulder straps and matching jacket to be removed when she and Father danced in the hotel ballroom. She'd brought a sun hat of yellow straw with a pale green ribbon attached. She hung it with her dresses on a hook in the closet. She set out her cosmetics, comb, brush, and a jewelry box, arranging them on the dark mahogany of the dressing table. Only when there was nothing more she could unpack, did she go to the window and look out on the town she'd left thirty-one years before.

The memory of the little girl named Lucy Beatrice Goslee simply could not grasp what she saw there. The town sprawled all the way to the river. Shops, sidewalks, gas stations, traffic lights baked in the heat where cool fields of sweet hay had once grown among pine wood lots. She strained to locate the bell tower of the Episcopal Church. She thought maybe she saw it but if so it no longer stood on the leafy residential street she recalled from childhood but was hemmed in among three and four story commercial structures with hardly a tree or a lawn anywhere in the vicinity. She felt suddenly tired. "It's been a long day's drive, Morris," she said. "Why don't we just rest up a little. We could have a quiet supper and go to bed early. Tomorrow we can go out looking."

In the morning, she was ill with headache and nausea. She hadn't slept. She thought perhaps the spinach quiche she'd eaten for supper had disagreed with her. She had toast and tea brought to the room. Afterward she went back to bed, a damp washcloth spread over her eyes. She'd be all right, she said, if she could just lie down for awhile.

Seeing she had fallen asleep, Father went out for a walk. He intended to walk to the river but before he was halfway there, he turned back. Suddenly, he didn't want Mother to awaken alone in a town where he feared so much disappointment lay in wait for her. He wasn't gone forty minutes, but when he got back he found her sitting in an armchair in the hotel lobby. She wore her dress with the yellow daisies. She had on leather flats and her yellow straw hat. When Father came into the lobby, she put a smile on her face.

They found the church unoccupied, its congregation having at long last abandoned it, the doors locked tight behind their departure. It looked shabby in all its ornate adornments, a decrepit relic of the past that might fall of its own neglect were it not squeezed in place by newer structures that buttressed it on both sides. A sheet-metal shop stood where the pastor's residence had once been, the clank and whine of machinery replacing the quiet conversations of the rooms where worshippers once came for counsel and where her foster father met once a month with members of the vestry.

Later they stood in front of the Goslee house, Mother reciting the street address aloud to herself, utterly dismayed that the house had been remodeled to such an extent that she couldn't convince herself she'd ever lived in it. "Three-Fourteen West Orange Street, Morris. This has to be it." Then nothing would do but that she had to have skates. She wanted to rollerskate to the park. "Don't you want to knock on the door, Lucy? Maybe the residents will let you look inside if you tell them who you are." "Who am I, Morris?" was her response.

They got rollerskates and shoes and hauled them back to 314 West Orange Street where Mother sat on the curb and strapped them on, Father trying to dissuade her all the time. He wasn't sure she'd skated even once in all the thirty-one years since she'd left Missoula. But nothing could stop her, and soon she was rolling down the sidewalk toward the remembered park. Father hurried along behind her as she pulled away in the distance. She looked positively gay in her splashes of yellow daisies with her hair streaming out beneath the brim of her straw hat. She was Lucy Beatrice Goslee, the only second-grader in Missoula Elementary that knew to properly skate with her hands behind her back.

Then Father realized that they were beyond where the park should be. He called out to Mother but she was nearly two blocks ahead of him. And then suddenly she was nowhere in sight. Father walked faster. He came upon her yellow straw hat lying on the sidewalk. He recovered it and hurried on.

He found her where she would never have gone voluntarily, sitting on a patch of dirt in someone's front yard. Her dress was spread out around her so that she looked as if she were sitting in a daisy patch. Her bare legs stuck out from under the hem, a few wheels on the skates still spinning. She'd veered off the sidewalk and more or less just sat down rather than fallen. "Are you okay, Lucy?" He squatted down beside her. "I rescued your hat." She looked at him then. "You know," she said, "my mother may never have lived in Helena." In the morning she asked to go home.

Mother left for Missoula bearing the name Lucy and returned home with the same. She thought that if she could only find her real name, the one her mother might have given her, she would know once and for all who she truly was. I, who had a name given me by a mother, knew this wasn't so. Had Mother found what she set out to find she would have realized this as well.

We truly know ourselves and each other only in this exact moment, and in this moment we are not who we once were nor what we happen to have been called, nor can we be summed up by any role or relationship. Real intimacy reaches beyond all our familiar designations. Until I'd gone beyond Mother to Lucy, I had no means to reach the person she was. In the end, I have had to go beyond Lucy as well, beyond all Lucy's personal history, in order to meet the stranger who bears her name.

Harness

S he was always a potential runaway. You needed to keep that in mind. If you didn't she could bolt and be gone before you could do anything to stop her. Smokey was a big horse. She could hit a full gallop in the space of a few yards, the bit in her teeth, her neck stretched taut, nostrils flared, powerful legs pumping her forward without direction or intent. Once started, nothing but her own exhaustion ever stopped her.

At times I could smell a runaway coming, feel the heat of it in the palms of my hands as though they were held over a flame. I would take up the reins, drawing in the slack ever so lightly, and tell her, "Whoa now, Smokey. Easy now. Whoa, girl," and whatever urgency was in her would subside—and for the moment there'd be no runaway.

She was a horse that should never have been put into harness. I think we all knew that from the start, even Father who bought her for that express purpose. She was a beautifully muscled smoke-colored Morgan mare, and when she was led into the corral at Ranney's Stables she was the very image of contained power. Ranney himself put her through her paces. Father and I watched. I never saw the signal that started her, but suddenly the big mare shot forward. She raced down the fence line, driving herself into the opposing corner at nearly full speed, skidding to a stop just before impact. She whirled about and trotted back toward us with her tail up and her head high. She made Ranney look as if he were just along for the ride. One could not imagine her pulling a cart.

But the mare was irresistible. To see her was to want her for your own. Father must have lost sight of his purpose. "Well what do you think?" Ranney asked Father. Father said, "She looks good." "She's a lot of horse to handle," Ranney said. He was looking at me. "I wouldn't plan to put that boy on her just yet. He could use a few more pounds before he's up to riding a mare like this." "I'm not buying her for saddle, I plan to harness her to a feed cart," Father said. There was a long pause in which Ranney looked at Father and then at the ground and then at the horse and at Father again. At length he took Father to the stable office to write up a bill of sale.

I followed the stable hand into the barn to watch him rub down the big mare. Her gray coat shone phosphorescent in the dim light of the stall. Her muscles rippled under his touch where he ran the currycomb over her flanks. I thought of her racing along the fence line of the corral, and I wanted more than anything to ride her. "Her name's Smokey," the stable-hand told me.

Within a month Father had gotten Smokey to tolerate harness. He was in fact a superior horseman, having learned from his own father who was one of the best on the Danish island of Funen. But neither Father's skill nor anyone else's was ever to cure Smokey of the propensity to run away. Despite this, she was soon indispensable. Rows of feeders were strung out across the turkey range and it was Smokey's job to pull the feed cart along these rows so we could scoop grain into the feeders. She was so naturally inquisitive, so alert to everything, that she often anticipated what was needed and did it before it was asked of her. One rarely had to touch the reins.

Father forbade Rowland and me to ride Smokey. It wasn't so much that Father feared for our safety. In fact we were both expected to work the horse, a circumstance at least as dangerous as riding her would be. Father's concern was that it would compromise her toleration of the harness. I rarely questioned my father's orders, but I wanted to ride Smokey so bad that I appealed to him to let me do it. Father just as rarely explained orders but this time he said, "She remembers the saddle, Linley. I want her to forget."

A set of harness is an instrument of economics, a system of cinches, buckles, and straps designed to subvert the will of an animal to human purposes. When you harness a horse, you harness a life. Smokey somehow never looked harnessed. She was worked from the time my father bought her to the time of her death. But some reserve in her remained untouched by circumstance. She was a horse undiminished by harness. This was so even when she was hitched to a feed cart, a thousand pounds of grain towed along in her wake. She had a will that refused to be subdued, a spirit that survived any restraint imposed on her. Her resistance was grounded not so much in any detectable stubbornness but in an irrepressible exuberance over which she herself seemed to have little control. Put into harness she was like one of those rare prisoners who survive freely within the confines of a cell.

A priest of a Zen order in which I once trained confronted me with a choice between obedience to the order or disaffiliation. His ultimatum settled on me like a set of harness. I could feel my neck thrust through the leather collar, the hames secured to it, the bit forced between my teeth, the weight of the load dragging on the traces. The priest sat across the room from me in his brown robes and purple *kesa,* his arms folded defiantly across his chest. He himself looked harnessed. He had institutionalized himself. He had forgotten how willful the founders of his own order had been, requiring of me that I conform to the footsteps of those who had themselves insisted on finding their own way.

Fifty years ago, an Army Field First Sergeant at a basic training camp in California slammed his fist into my face for stepping out of ranks to aid a soldier who had fainted and fallen onto the pavement in front of me. "Who told you to break rank!" the sergeant screamed at me. The sergeant's face was a blurred smear inches in front of my own, his hot breath laced with spittle. Blood leaked from my mouth. My whole body shook, trying to will the restraint that would keep me out of jail. I had a choice between compliance and court-martial. I thought I couldn't bear the injustice of it, that I would suffer any consequence rather than tolerate such insult. But still I held myself at attention, reaching for a grace first taught me by a smoke-colored mare when I was still a boy.

It was four years after she had first been put to harness, that I rode Smokey. Everyone was gone at the time, and I'd been left behind to finish the feeding. I was about to release Smokey into the pasture when instead I swung myself onto her back. With just a halter and lead, no saddle or bridle, I had little means of controlling her. She chose the direction, and within a few yards punched herself into a full gallop, almost losing me had I not grabbed a fistful of her mane and managed to hang on. She was headed toward the Santa Ana River, but to get there she had to cross Harbor Boulevard. I was suddenly afraid we'd be struck by a car. She was coming up on the boulevard fast. I tugged on the halter lead, desperate to prevent a disaster. She eased back a little. I let the lead out and she picked up speed. I pulled it in again and she slowed. Smokey wasn't running away! She was just running— and she was including me. Though Father had wanted her to, she hadn't forgotten what it was to run free of the harness and carry a rider on her back.

I slowed Smokey to a trot, crossed the boulevard, and headed her toward the river. She broke into a run again and I let her go, knowing that Father might return at any time and find out what I'd done. But for the moment I was determined to go on and didn't care what it might cost me. On the river trail, the bamboo and cottonwoods swept by in a blur. Smokey was running hard, her neck stretched forward, nostrils flared drawing great sucking draughts of air, as she settled into a rhythm that carried us farther and farther from the barn where the harness hung awaiting the next day's work.

Within the structure of every conformity, every confinement and restraint, dwells the heart of the runaway. It is a being spare, swift, original. It speaks words of its own telling, sings songs of its heart's consent, runs unhindered in fields of its choosing. It is the unimpaired body and voice of an irrepressible freedom. And it refuses to be forgotten.

Ditha

That first night together, Ditha sat cross-legged on the bed and showed me the twin scars that lay in the little hollows between her hip bones and pelvic bone. "They did this," she said, meaning the Nazis. "I'd have a nice body, if they hadn't done this." She seemed to think of herself as some kind of damaged goods and that she owed me an apology for not being better than she was. She was searching me with her dark frightened eyes for some sign of distaste or disapproval. When I reached out to touch the scars with my fingertips, she winced and twisted away. And then she was crying, and I held her, the two of us rocking back and forth where we sat naked on the tumbled bedding. Then, just as suddenly, she pushed me away and grinning through her tears, said "You're lucky to go to bed with someone as good-looking as me." Later, eating sandwiches together at the kitchen table, I asked, "Are you okay now?" "Yes," she answered, and then added on, "I can't have babies."

The year was 1954 and I'd been drafted into the Army and sent to Germany to serve in the occupation forces. I met Ditha through a German friend of hers who contracted with the Army to manage the mess hall at Friedberg Kaserne where I was stationed. As time went on, I learned something of Ditha's past. She remembered being left one day at her aunt's apartment in

Frankfurt because, as it was explained to her, her mother and father had "business" somewhere that day. But they never came back to pick her up, and that's the last she knew of them. Later the Nazi's came and took her aunt away and Ditha became a ward of the state, housed in an orphanage. In time the whole orphanage was organized into a factory for assembling field uniforms, and the child Ditha spent her days at a sewing machine, stitching together pants and shirts. She remembers being hungry most of the time.

At the time I knew her, Ditha worked at a travel agency in Frankfurt. Besides German, she was fluent in English and spoke Italian and French well enough to conduct business in those languages. She was taking a class in conversational Spanish, not because her work required it but because she wanted to move to southern Spain where it was warm. She'd lived her entire life in Germany, but she told me, "It's too cold for me here. I never get warm enough." She kept her apartment uncomfortably warm for anyone but her. If we were going out somewhere, she'd grab a coat to take along on the mildest days.

Before the sound had registered on me, Ditha clasped her hands over her ears. And then I heard the drumming and the squeak of horns faint in the distance, and I pictured the bedraggled little remnant of what was alleged to have once been the Führer's honor band goose-stepping their way up the Kaiserstrasse in all their soiled dignity. It was one of the anomalies of post-war Germany that I found the most difficult to account for, the difficulty being not in the sustained patriotism of the band itself but in the tolerance and response that others accorded to the little group. People would pause on the sidewalk to watch the band pass, some coming out of shops and restaurants to join the spectators. They would hiss and jeer and wag their heads in disapproval, and yet at times they would cheer the band on. But the most surprising reaction, one that was invariably witnessed up and down the street, was given by those who, with an arm thrust suddenly forward, shouted "Zieg hiel!" As often as I'd witnessed this, I always took the gesture to be one of defiant mockery, perhaps even self-mockery, an effort to make the whole cruel history into a bad joke.

The band always marched on Sunday mornings, and this Sunday morning, when Ditha and I had gone out for breakfast, she sat across from me in the restaurant booth looking as if she might crawl under the table. The music got louder as the band approached, and Ditha pressed the sleeve ends of her jacket into her ears. People were gathering on the sidewalk outside the restaurant, and then Ditha was suddenly out of the booth standing among them. Through the restaurant window, I saw her arm suddenly thrust forward. She came back into the restaurant with furious tears in her eyes.

The summer we were together, Ditha would catch the train from Frankfurt to Friedberg Kaserne and we'd walk the four-mile river trail to the park in Bad Nauheim where the summer lawn was let grow as high as pasture grass. Sanford and Calvin, two of my buddies from the orderly room staff, would join us, and Ditha's mess hall friend would make a picnic lunch for the four of us to share. In the park a string orchestra played on Sunday afternoons and we'd spread the army blankets Calvin brought and eat our lunch, drink Piesporter Moselle, and listen to the music.

The park was thick with robins, the trees hung with nests of squeaking chicks begging to be fed, the parents searching the moist lawn for worms. It wasn't that uncommon for a chick to fall from the nest or even be expelled by the parents if they had too many mouths to feed, but when Ditha found a fallen chick she was beside herself with the urgency to do something to rescue it.

There really wasn't anything you could do. Ditha herself probably knew how hopeless her efforts were. Still she went hunting for worms and when she couldn't find any she tried to get the chick to swallow little bits of picnic cheese—which it didn't recognize as food and wouldn't take. When she'd failed to feed it, she sat with the chick cupped in the palm of her hand, stroking it with a finger now and then. "I can't leave it for the cats," she said.

It was Calvin that suggested we take it to the park maintenance shed. "Maybe one of the workers there will know what to do," he said, catching my eye to let me know he understood how pointless the suggestion was. If Ditha understood this as well she didn't let on, and so the four of us went in search of the maintenance shed where, in fact, we found two workers in coveralls taking a break and sharing coffee from a thermos. Ditha held out the robin for them to see, speaking to them in German too rapidly for me to follow. The two workers listened patiently and, it seemed to me, sympathetically. When Ditha finally fell silent, the older of the two workers said something to her. Ditha handed him the robin, and when he cuddled it up against his cheek she turned and walked away. "What did he say?" Calvin asked her. "He said not to worry that he would take good care of it." "That's good," Calvin told her, throwing an arm about her shoulders and squeezing her up tight.

That evening when I saw Ditha off at the Friedberg train station, she said, "The baby robin's going to die. I hope they won't let it suffer." She started to board the train and then turned and held onto me for a long moment. In a world where young things fall from their nests, Ditha knew as well as anyone the difficult odds of survival.

The sight of her waving to me from the window as the train pulled out of Friedberg that evening was the last I ever saw of Ditha. A few days later I was reassigned—without notice and without a chance to let Ditha know what was happening—to an intelligence and reconnaissance platoon for two month's field training. But by then, I'd begun to realize that the one essential purpose I served in Ditha's life was to prevent her from being alone, a condition she couldn't bear for even the shortest duration. So I asked Calvin if he'd go to Frankfurt and look in on her once in a while. He did, and in my absence they took up with one another. But one day when he called her apartment to tell her he was coming, he got no answer. But he went anyway, and the landlady told him Ditha had left with no forwarding address. When I got back from the field, I called Ditha's travel agency, and they told me she'd gone on an indefinite leave of absence, saying that she'd let them know if she was coming back.

Ditha's been on my mind lately. Now that I've had children of my own, I sometimes think of the little girl in the Wiesbaden State Orphanage with no one left to look over her and who, when hospitalized for a tonsillectomy, awakened to discover two sore and reddened scars on her "tummy," and who as a grown woman would one day refuse to leave a baby robin for the park cats to get. I'd like to think that Ditha's somewhere in Spain now and that she's finally warm enough and not alone.

The High Cost of Justice

When I was in my early twenties, I suffered such a painful falling out with my parents that the estrangement lasted for nearly three years. During that time the three of us spoke not one word to each other. I was accused of an act of which I was innocent. My mother, swayed by circumstances that suggested otherwise, remained convinced of my guilt.

I'd returned from my two years military duty in Germany with the intention of making the family farm my life's work. I'd temporarily moved into the bedroom that Rowland and I once shared, planning to move into a place of my own as soon as I and Shirley Rice, to whom I was engaged, were married. Though the date was set for June tenth and we were already into the month of May, it was clear that Father was not pleased with the prospect of having a grown son living back home, however temporarily. But Father's uneasiness seemed to me to go deeper than his discomfort with having me under the same roof, and I began to wonder if Father questioned whether the farm could expand enough to support another family. I think perhaps he saw that there was no place for me in the business and couldn't bring himself to tell me so. Land had appreciated so dramatically in Orange County that farms all around us were selling at unimaginably high prices, and soon the forty acres on Harbor Boulevard, which housed the farm hatchery and brooding coops, would be surrounded by freeways, subdivisions, and shopping malls. Perhaps Mother and Father were themselves considering selling the farm and retiring to the city of Orange where their lives together had begun and where a few old friends lived and Trinity Episcopal Church stood.

Rowland had become the foreman of the farm by then and the one who handed out paychecks, so I asked him for an advance of a couple hundred dollars until I could get things in order. I had rent to arrange on a house and car expenses that I couldn't quite manage. Rowland's solution was for me to report additional hours on my timecard to be paid back later with equivalent hours of unpaid overtime, which seemed convoluted to me but which he seemed to think would "keep the books straight." Mother was writing the payroll at the time, and maybe Rowland thought she'd object to the cash advance and so was trying to accommodate me by doing it this way. But when Mother saw my pay card, she knew I hadn't worked that many hours and believed I was trying to claim money I hadn't earned. "Stealing" was the word she chose.

I have no doubt that my mother was disappointed and pained by her discovery of what she thought I'd done. I'm certain there was no malice or triumph in her accusation. But I wasn't stealing, and I told her so. I looked for Rowland to clarify the matter, but he was suddenly vague about the whole thing, simply pointing out that I could pay it back with overtime. I realized that he was not going to help me. Maybe he had overstepped his authority in agreeing to the arrangement and was reluctant to admit his part in it. Did he even remember what we'd agreed to? When I confronted him with this, he merely repeated that there was no harm done since I could pay the money back with overtime.

My mother's certainty regarding my guilt brought my father, and even my sister, to the same opinion as well. When I saw how it was, all I could think of was to get away. I left the farm within the hour of my being accused and never worked there again.

I found a job on a remote desert poultry farm twenty miles east of Palmdale in the Mojave Desert, and a few days after Shirley and I were married we moved there to begin our lives together. But within a year and half the farm I was working at went bankrupt and I ended up pumping gas at a Chevron station on the outskirts of town. It was there on an August afternoon—in 120-degree heat that had so softened the asphalt on the station's driveway that the soles of my shoes stuck to it—that Mother broke the long silence.

I was at the driver's side door, waiting for the window to be rolled down, before I realized who it was that had pulled up to the pump. Father was at the wheel. He glanced up at my face, startled to see me there. He was obviously unsettled and unsure what he should do. Mother said, "Well, hello there!" Her voice reached me, false with feigned casualness, from the far seat. I don't remember whether I hesitated, took a breath, swallowed, or what. All I remember is hearing myself ask, "Would you like regular or high octane?" Father answered, "High octane would be fine." I filled the tank, checked the oil and water, cleaned the windshield, took their money, and walked away.

I could barely breathe. I fled toward the rear of the station so as to avoid the others in the lube room. The rear of the station was treeless, the station wall baking in the heat. In the inch or two of shade afforded by a dumpster stacked with discarded tires, I stopped to catch my breath. And then Mother was there, her face flushed dangerously red with the heat, which she had never tolerated well. She came up to me where I stood backed against the dumpster. She said, "Linley, this has gone far enough." She tried to sound firm yet calm like a scolding mother who needs to correct the error of her child. But as she spoke the words, her false teeth (as dentures were more honestly called in those days) slipped loose, causing a little clicking sound. Mother, who had always been terribly sensitive about this, brought her hand up to cover her mouth. She had no hat and so she squinted against the sun that poured down on us and reflected off the station wall. Sweat formed in the creases of her neck. Behind the screen of her hand, I could see her mouth work as she tried to press her teeth back in place with her tongue. Finally, all her dignity undone, whatever small pride she had been able to retain compromised, she had to stick her fingers in her mouth to adjust her teeth. When she spoke again, her voice carried the grief of her three years' sorrow: "Son, it's time we ended this."

Of course it was time. But I saw in her, in the tilt of her head perhaps, or something in her eyes, that her opinion of my guilt was unaltered. What she offered was a mother's forgiveness; she was willing to let the trespass go unadmitted and unanswered so that she could have her child once more. Her love required this, making its appeal from the pain of its own loss. I saw this, but the error of the accusation, the everlasting injustice of it, made her offer of forgiveness as deadly to me as a drink of poison. In the end, I could say nothing. She tried to hold my eyes, her own imploring me to let the hardness go, but when she saw that I couldn't or wouldn't, her chin quivered and she blinked and turned away.

When she was gone, my eyes stung with a sudden rush of hot tears, I vomited all my bitterness into the station toilet. Kneeling on the floor of the stall, afraid that I would be found there, I touched within my mother's dark pain and my own a love for her more fierce and unchecked than any I had known.

Years later, sitting in meditation at Shasta Abbey Zen Monastery and long after I'd put aside my injured pride and reconciled with my parents, I would come to better understand this thing we call love. We were in the midst of a meditation retreat, and its theme and purpose was to raise the heart of Avalokiteshvara, the embodiment of compassion in the Buddhist tradition. He is an archetypal figure that represents the capacity for love that resides in each of us, and is described as having a thousand arms and eyes, one eye embedded in the palm of each hand, so that the organ of perception is also the organ of action. With his thousand eyes he can see all suffering wherever it occurs, and simultaneously with his thousand hands, he can reach out and aid each sufferer. The idea of the retreat was to call upon Avalokiteshvara, and I was doing my best, sitting in the meditation hall, hour after hour, with my knees and back aching, asking him to appear.

I don't know anything about magic and don't put much credence in "signs" or "visions" of a religious sort. But I do know about imagination and its artful power to bring up the very thing that's needed when the time comes. And what came to me at the retreat was not the expected image of Avalokiteshvara surrounded by a glittering halo of arms and eyes, but the plain, recognizable face of my father, who, though dead six years at the time, was as undeniably present as the pain in my legs. He didn't have myriad hands and eyes. He had but two of each. One of his hands gripped me by the shoulder and the other touched my check in a gesture gentler than any I'd ever known of him. His two eyes were simply the eyes of a father's love, inclusive and without reserve, and he said to me, "Oh Linley, you always wanted everything to be fair." And then, just before he vanished, he winked at me in acknowledgment of what was understood between us.

There's not much room for judgments of right and wrong, blame and praise, justice and injustice in matters of love. Love's not an orderly, unblemished affair. Father had come to see if I'd figured this out. I had, but his visit brought me once again to consider the waste of those three-years' alienation my family and I had suffered because I'd insisted that things be fair.

Later, on the evening of my father's appearance, I told the abbot what had happened and asked him if that was Avalokiteshvara who had finally shown up. He assured me it was.

Lunch

When *Shirley and I married,* my family didn't attend because they weren't invited. The three dozen or so folding chairs set out on the lawn under the trees outside the Anaheim Wedding Chapel were occupied by members of the Rice family and by the Willifords on Shirley's mother's side. I think at the time I felt self-righteous about my family's exclusion, my sense of being wronged by them was that strong.

The chapel garden was a relic, a quaint keepsake, of a time that was rapidly disappearing from our lives. Beyond the patch of shaded lawn and encircling hedges, the conversion of Orange County from farmland to city was already underway. Shirley and I had to raise our voices to be heard above the annoying hum of nearby freeway traffic and the clatter and grind of building construction. Our marriage vows were colored by a sort of defiance of all that we felt to be unfair or hostile to our lives, swearing to love each other to the end no matter what. With my long-held plans of joining the family farm gone awry and with the countryside in which I'd grown up being rapidly converted to asphalt and concrete, I poured all my hopes into the promises the two of us made to each other standing side by side that day on our isolated and threatened patch of grass in Anaheim, California.

We drove north to Santa Barbara for our honeymoon, but cut our stay there short because we were both worried about money. The Keithley farm, where I'd found work as a field foreman, was located twenty miles outside Palmdale, so three days after our wedding, Shirley and I were descending the long grade from Tehachapi pass into the scorching summer heat of the Mohave Desert.

It was afternoon and 118 degrees when we got to the farm. The Keithley house was a remarkable old adobe structure big enough to have been a resort of some kind. But now it stood in the midst of a tangle of poultry fencing where flocks of turkeys stood panting in the scant shade of what appeared to be a failed attempt at an almond orchard. Lining the driveway from the county road to the house was a column of ancient date palms that projected skyward, surviving somehow the oppressive heat and apparent lack of irrigation.

We were met in the yard by a pair of shorthaired terriers, barking and wagging the stumps of their cropped tails. Mr. Keithley was well over six feet tall, big-boned with a deep chest and broad shoulders. He came out of the house in cowboy boots and hat, looking more like a cattleman than any turkey farmer I'd ever known. Mrs. Keithley, who was as small as her husband was large, followed behind him, remembering as she greeted us that she was wearing an apron, which she stripped off in apparent embarrassment and held behind her. Shirley and I had driven straight from the coast and when we stepped out of the car and the full force of the heat hit us, it was all either of us could do to appear rational in our first meeting with the Keithleys.

B.A. Keithley was to be called "B.A." he informed us. "As soon as you and the missus get settled, we'll talk." He was glad I'd come early because there was a lot that needed doing. It had been agreed that I was to get $500 a month and a house for my work. "Mrs. Keithley will show you what's available," B.A. told us, and then disappeared into the house. We had a choice of two houses.

The first of the two was a recently installed prefab in a row of six other prefabs that sat out in a sage flat adjacent to the farm. The second, a couple miles further down the road, was a weathered and sagging one-bedroom farmhouse that sat under a canopy of cottonwood trees with a rusty water-cooled air conditioner jammed into a living room window. Shirley wanted the second because it was shaded and because it sat next to an irrigated alfalfa field, one of the few green fields, as it turned out, to be found in the whole district.

Mrs. Keithley left us there and we moved in. The house was only partially furnished: a maroon sofa faded to a sort of pinkish gray and one standing lamp in the living room; a table, and a couple folding chairs in the kitchen. In a small shed adjacent to the house, we found a nearly new washing machine that drained out through a flex hose onto the ground behind the shed. A clothesline was strung between the trunks of two cottonwoods. There wasn't much storage in the house but then we didn't need much. Everything we owned was in the trunk and back seat of the car. The kitchen turned out to be pretty well stocked with an odd assortment of old pots and pans, dishes, cups, and at least a dozen glasses, no two of which matched. We spent the rest of the afternoon sweeping and dusting and hauling our stuff into the house while the air conditioner labored away in the window trying to cool the house down.

Toward evening we drove the twenty miles back to the Palmdale Safeway for groceries. Shirley found a blue calico tablecloth and an ironing board cover in the housewares section. On the way out of town we stopped at Maggie's High Desert Café for hamburgers, where we treated ourselves to slices of Maggie's homemade blackberry pie, grinning at each other between mouthfuls, celebrating the start of our two lives together.

In the morning, I was over at the Keithley farm at the very first light of dawn. I wanted the time to see for myself what was needed, and as I suspected there was a lot. At noon I drove back to the "cottonwood house," as Shirley and I would come to call it, for lunch. The blue calico tablecloth from the Safeway had been ironed and spread over the kitchen table. On the table was a small vase Shirley had found somewhere among the kitchen things with a few sprigs of blossoming alfalfa arranged in it. Shirley had set two places with cloth napkins that she'd apparently packed and brought with her. There were small triangular-wedged deviled-egg sandwiches and a platter in the center of the table neatly laid out with carrot and cucumber sticks, celery, broccoli flowers, and green onions surrounding a little bowl of sour cream dip mixed with chives and sprinkled with parsley. There was iced tea to drink and slices of lemon.

It looked as if Shirley had called out to have lunch catered—but she hadn't. She'd done it herself. The lunch was an event for her. And the care she'd taken in doing it was a measure of the time she had on her hands. I looked out the window across the burning fields of desert scrub without a single neighbor in sight. What would she do this afternoon? And tomorrow? And the day after that? Here in this house with no car and no one to talk to. Shirley was finishing her junior year in college when she said to me, "Well, if we're going to get married, let's do it." So we'd set the date and Shirley quit college at the end of the year. It looked that first day on the desert as if Shirley had determined to throw herself wholeheartedly into being a housewife—but this was only the thirteenth of June and how, I wondered, would it be for her in September with the fall semester beginning and her classmates returning to the dorm? How could I have agreed to have her set the affairs of her life aside for mine?

Yet the woman who'd said, "If were going to get married, let's do it" was a lot more resourceful than my fears had allowed for, and Shirley made the most of her situation. She bought a used sewing machine and cloth to make curtains for the house. She found out from the alfalfa farmer how to open an irrigation hydrant, so she could flood our yard and we could sit outside on hot nights and eat supper at a picnic table with our feet resting in eight inches of cool water. On winter nights, when icy winds blew down off the southern Sierra, she dug her college texts out of a storage box and we sat wrapped together under a blanket on the sofa and read *The Thurber Carnival,* and Steinbeck, and even Goethe's *Faust.*

When Shirley found herself pregnant, she drove me to work and kept the car so that she could attend prenatal classes at Antelope Valley Hospital. And when our son, Dru, was born in our second year on the desert, and Shirley's parents bought her a baby buggy that was virtually useless considering our rural situation, she drove to the park in Palmdale, loaded Dru into the buggy and pushed him around on the sidewalk there. But, in the very energy and inventiveness of these pursuits, I was witnessing the force that would one day pull our marriage apart.

The next twenty-two years of our lives together took Shirley and me first from the desert to San Jose where I worked my way through San Jose State College and where our daughter, Krista, was born; then through four years of study ending in my graduation from State College, followed in succession by a year's fellowship to Stanford and a Master's degree in Literature and Language; then from Stanford to a teaching job at Monterey Peninsula College, and finally to the house I built for us on evenings and weekends in the Carmel Highlands.

And so we moved into our brand new house in the woods above the sea, where we lived in circumstances vastly different from the isolation of our first years on the desert. Behind us as well were the five lean years I spent as a student earning very little money to pay for anything. I felt that we had at last settled into our lives. Now, I hoped, everything would be all right. But in truth I already had misgivings, for I felt in Shirley—as I had at the beginning of our marriage—a sort of principled determination to do what she thought a wife and mother should, as if she'd struck some sort of a deal back at the Anaheim Wedding Chapel and was sticking with it now only out of obligation.

Nonetheless, through the years, by degrees nearly indiscernible at first, she withdrew her life from mine. Thoughts and experiences once shared weren't anymore, and there were more and more nights lying awake in bed, at pains to avoid touching. Shirley had come to the point where she was merely biding time until she could do whatever it was that present circumstances seemed to deny her.

So when Shirley was offered a partnership in a fine fabrics store in Carmel, I hoped this new interest of her's would ease whatever it was that stood between us and bring our lives back together. But instead things went the other way. Shirley seldom spoke of what was deepest in her heart, but had she been able to tell me what was happening to her then, I think she might have told me that though she'd loved me and given me children and kept my house for twenty-four years, would I please now let her go and please not suffer so that she'd have to feel guilty. Though she never said these things, I think I knew all along this was how she felt. But still I tried to hold on to her because I couldn't imagine a life without her. That Shirley and I were on the brink of a divorce seemed at the time the most regrettable failure and loss of my life.

Dru and Krista were both married by this time and on their own. And with Shirley working in town at the fabrics store I had taken to cooking supper for the two of us much of the time, though sometimes she showed up late, having had supper in town. One day when some classes of mine were cancelled at the college and I thought Shirley would come home for lunch, I stopped by the natural food store and hurried home to make lunch for her. I wish now I could recall what I fixed for her that day as well as I recall that first lunch she made for me on the desert twenty-four years earlier. A cold fog had rolled in off the ocean and so, thinking something hot would be good, I made a creamed soup of some kind and I think I had warm sourdough rolls with sweet butter. I made a yellow cake with crushed strawberries to put on top but forgot the whipping cream.

When Shirley came in, she must have seen the bowls set out for the soup and the rolls wrapped in cloth to keep warm. She must have felt the lingering affection that still rode between us in any room we both occupied. But she walked past the table and went to the refrigerator and took out the makings of a sandwich. "I have soup for lunch," I told her, though she could plainly see that for herself. She turned to me then and tears spilled into her eyes. "I don't want you cooking for me," she said. That was her goodbye.

In the months and years that followed our divorce, I watched Shirley flourish in her new independence, all her brightness and talent coming to the fore, so that I could no longer look upon our parting as something gone wrong. She soon had her own shop with all sorts of materials to beautify the rooms of lovely houses. Clients from as far away as Paris and London sent for her to consult on matters of interior decoration. She was bright and fresh and energetic. One day when we chanced to meet, she greeted me with an unguarded smile that said she was glad to see me again. We stood on the sidewalk talking as casually as simple acquaintances might, and I was struck with the wonder of how unforeseeable the consequences of our choices can be. What one fears seldom materializes. Here was Shirley laughing and chattering as if nothing would ever be withheld from her again. It was a bright autumn day for both of us that morning where we met with white clouds streaking over Monterey Bay and the cry of gulls on the wind.

Esther Shepherd

n two semesters of Masterpieces of the Western World, I never saw her lecture from the desk or the podium. She was simply not a stationary person. She strode back and forth sending a wake of charged air flowing over the front row students, reading passages from the pages of literature she'd been teaching since before the Depression. She'd burst into the room before the rest of us could get settled in our seats, reciting lines from Homer or Virgil or Dante with the door still swinging closed behind her. She had in her grasp a wealth of the finest words that had ever been written, and she wanted more than anything to hand this on to us before time ran out. The way she figured it, time would run out in exactly ninety-six hours—one hour every Monday, Wednesday, and Friday for two semesters. After that we'd be gone, moved on to survey courses in English and American literature. There was no time to waste. Yet Esther Shepherd never seemed hurried. What she seemed was engaged, completely absorbed in whatever she taught. With her, it wasn't a matter of getting us through the content of the course but *into* the content of the course. Literature wasn't something you studied; it was something you lived.

I don't know how I'd managed to refuse the literature that was offered me in my previous schooling. But I had. There was a moment of brief light in Garden Grove High School senior English when Eileen LaBarthe led the class line by line through Hamlet. But it was only a faint spark, and it failed to ignite anything. Later, when I was stationed in Germany with the Third Infantry Regiment, Calvin Floyd took me under his tutelage. He insisted that I go with him to the post library where he picked out authors for me as diverse as George Meredith, Thomas Hardy, John Donne, John Keats, William Wordsworth, Lord Byron, Virginia Wolfe, and William Faulkner. When he noted my growing interest in Donne's poetry, he told me to write a poem of my own. I did. When he praised it, I wrote more, sometimes making a tent of my blankets at night while I scribbled away with the aid of a flashlight so as not to awaken others in the barracks. And later yet, there were those cold winter nights on the high desert when Shirley and I read from the literary anthologies she'd saved from her own college days. But it was Esther Shepherd who first swept me across seas of time and change to the ancient Greek world of Homer, Euripides, Aeschylus, and Sophocles, where I found the strangely foreign and startling sources of my own mind.

The one abiding sentiment I felt during my student years at San Jose State College was one of gratitude. They were years of discovery for me when I could say as Keats said upon first reading Chapman's Homer that "Then I felt like some watcher of the skies / When a new planet swims into his ken." And it's not that I scorned in any way my roots on the turkey farm and the farm community in which I'd grown up. I was as much that person who'd knelt on his knees in the catching crate or scooped grain into feeders as I was anyone, but I was on a journey now from which there'd be no return. A new planet really had appeared in my sky from whose sphere of influence I'd not easily escape. I knew as I sat in that first semester's class with Esther Shepherd that I was already changed in ways that couldn't be undone, even if I were called back home to run the farm and spent the rest of my life raising turkeys.

It can be hard to know what to do with change that is so much within oneself and so consequential that your own name begins to sound unfamiliar. I was having such a good time as a student and yet it was a little unsettling not to know who it was that was having a good time. One day I overhead an exchange between the department head and Esther Shepherd that I wasn't meant to hear: Professor Shepherd was asked what sort of student I was. "He makes top grades," she said louder than intended because she herself was hard of hearing. "But he's better than that," she added. "He's a scholar and a gentleman." I blushed to overhear this appraisal of me, but afterward I thought about it with a kind of skeptical wonderment. A scholar and a gentleman, is that what I am?

To not be what I once was nor yet what I was to become was actually to be quite free. Almost anything felt possible. But, of course, I took it as a given that life required me to have some sure sense of who I was. Yet, in the meantime, not identifying myself as one thing or another left me free one week to be one of Chaucer's pilgrims telling his tale on the way to Canterbury and another week to be a stricken Trojan mother wailing over the body of a child left dead by the conquering Greeks and on yet another week a much saddened and sobered Wordsworth calling the spirit of Milton back to England. Being no one in particular I could be anyone.

I was in my junior year at San Jose State College when a classmate, Joseph Gallo, gave me a copy of a poem by Gerard Manley Hopkins. He said he loved Hopkins and wanted everyone else to love him too. It was two days later before I got around to unfolding the sheet of paper he'd handed me and read the poem. It was a brief lyric poem called "Kingfishers," and it began with images of kingfishers and dragonflies, stones, some sort of stringed instrument, and a bell, all of which seemed initially obscure to me. But in the heart of the poem I found these lines:

> Each mortal thing does one thing and the same:
> Deals out that being indoors each one dwells;
> Selves—goes itself; myself it speaks and spells,
> Crying, *What I do is me: for that I came.*

I saw in the instant and with great excitement how Hopkins had formed from the noun a previously unknown verb, giving to the world a new word: "selves." You can conjugate it: I selve, you selve, she selves, we are selving. That's it! I'm a verb not a noun. As useful as the convention might be, reality itself is too alive to be contained by names of person, place, or thing. The whole of this great earth and everything in it is inflected in this way, a movement that "goes itself." "What I do is me." In that line of Hopkins', I was touching the great mystery of a "self" in which the doing is all there is.

The year I studied Masterpieces of the Western World with Esther Shepherd was her last year teaching. She planned to retire at the end of spring semester and do some writing she'd postponed for the last forty years. Toward the end of spring semester, she'd moved us into a unit on English romantic poets. She was at her best one day, pacing back and forth reciting passages from the Lyrical Ballads, when she suddenly stopped in midstride as she sometimes would to make a point, bringing all her attention to bear upon the class. "The best I can offer you," she said, "is found in those unforgettable words of Percy Bysshe Shelley… uh…the words…uh—" and then nothing. I don't know whether she or some of us waiting in our seats for Shelley's words were first to realize that the unforgettable had been forgotten. Esther Shepherd seem transfixed for the moment, searching the air above our heads for the missing words, her lips trying to find the shape of syllables long familiar to her.

And then she was doubled over with the perfect absurdity of it all, laughing so hard at her predicament that she cried, dabbling at her eyes until she'd fumbled her eyeglasses onto the floor where she retrieved them and in a rare instance sat down at the desk to recover herself. At length she said, "That happens more often now, though not always so unforgettably. It's good that I'm retiring before I forget my own name or even who I am." With that, she was up and at it again, reciting from Byron's "Childe Harold's Pilgrimage."

The last time I visited the Campus of San Jose State College, the classroom where Esther Shepherd taught had been torn down to make way for new construction. Only the token tower itself was left to commemorate the site. I was a teacher myself by then and knew even less than before about who or what I was. But standing on the ground of that vanished classroom of years before, the question of identity didn't matter much. Whatever sort of entity I might imagine myself to be, Esther Shepherd was alive in it, her great heart and voice so commingled with my own that the two of us would ultimately prove to be inseparable.

Rocks

here were three of them on the hill above the road lying in the shade of an oak tree. The one Jack wanted was the largest of the three, a weathered granite boulder nearly twice the size of the other two. I doubted whether Jack and I could move anything that big. But Jack was the boss and he insisted it was no problem. Nothing I could say had ever deterred Jack from what he'd set out to do.

It was three o'clock on a hot August afternoon when Jack and I started digging the rock out from under the oak. At the time, I was working my way through college, and Jack, who had just gotten his general contractor's license, hired me to help him build a house in Blossom Hill Estates, a subdivision Jack's father owned. Jack was given to sudden inspirations. So when the buyers, Mark and Elaine Willoughby, dropped by the building site that morning to tell Jack they wanted an ornamental rock for their landscaping, Jack said he knew where to find just what they were looking for. Jack rented an equipment trailer and in less than four hours, we were headed back to Blossom Hill Estates with the Willoughbys' ornamental rock chained to the trailer bed, Jack exclaiming all the while what a beauty it was and how good it would look in the Willoughbys' yard. He was right. It was a beauty. At first I was as enthusiastic as Jack was. But then I began to doubt the whole thing.

We'd found the Willoughby's rock on a grassy hill under an oak tree whose limbs bent over it to form an enclosure. It felt private under there, the kind of place that makes you want to talk softly. Sunlight leaked down through the leaves onto the rock. Patches of lichen the color of burnt amber shone on its surface. The base of the rock was sunk deep in rotting mulch. Our boots stirred up the smell of it. Jack was explaining how we'd go about getting the rock loaded on the trailer, more or less thinking aloud, talking more for his own instruction than for mine. When he stopped talking, a hush as still as the rock itself settled on us.

Thousands, perhaps millions, of years before Jack and I came along, the rock dropped from the cliffs above and came to rest with its two sisters on the slope below. And the oak tree that shaded Jack and me and the rock we were straining to dig loose was there before either Jack or I were born. Now Jack and I were going after the rock with a pick and a couple of pry bars—but I knew that the rock belonged where we'd found it.

I wonder now why I never objected. Well, of course, I needed the job. How else would I ever make it through college? It wasn't the first time I'd compromised principle and done the very thing my heart told me not to do. And it turned out not to be the last either. Sometimes my life seems nothing but a history of such compromises. But it wasn't the Willoughby's or anybody else's rock to be had for the taking. It was its own rock, and if I hadn't come along and dug it out, it would have held its place on its hill for a lot longer than the years allotted me for compromising principles.

The Willoughbys loved their rock. Within a week, they planted a clump of birches beside it. They smoothed the ground around the rock and seeded a lawn. They installed sprinklers so that the rock would be splashed with water, hoping to keep the lichen alive. The rock was beautiful. But whenever I looked at it, I thought of a patch of raw earth beneath an ancient oak on a hillside in the Santa Cruz Mountains.

Too Much

"D-5" was stenciled over the door in fading black paint, the "5" looking a little smeared where the stencil must have worked loose during the spraying. The wall itself was an unrelieved battleship gray that had been acquired at cost from the nearby Naval Postgraduate School. The door was an obvious retrofit, a solid-core variety with a birch plywood finish showing through yellowing varnish. The only other detailing at the exterior end of the building was a single window cut into the wall and a set of "temporary" wooden steps rising to the door. In truth the whole arrangement was temporary and had been for over ten years when I took up residence in D-5.

Monterey Peninsula College first acquired the D building along with four other barracks buildings from Fort Ord at a time when the college population was expanding faster than the public was willing to pay for any new construction. Number five at one end of the barracks was assigned to me as an office to be shared with Elliot Roberts, who'd had it to himself until I came along.

The first notable thing about Elliot Roberts and me was how different we were from each other. Occupying halves of a single office only served to magnify those differences. I've always been at pains to keep things neat and in order, and when I first arrived, Room D-5 was to my eyes about as random as a room can get.

Nothing of Elliot's seemed to have a place of its own. The desk I was to occupy had only been delivered a couple of days before I got there, but Elliot's stuff had already spilled over onto it—books, a stack of student papers in the process of being graded, a couple of old lunch bags, and a pair of apparently discarded cotton socks.

Elliot greeted me from the midst of this debris, sitting behind a desk so cluttered he'd have to shove things around to get at the typewriter. He seemed glad to have company, shifting a banana he was eating from right to left in order to shake hands. Would I like a bite? No? Then finishing it off himself and lobbing the peel toward a waste basket where it landed dangling over the edge. *My* wastebasket as it turned out—his was already overflowing. "Here's coffee if you want some," he said, showing me where the can of drip grind was stuffed in among some English renaissance anthologies on a bookshelf. The coffeemaker was actually on his desk, though you could miss it if you didn't know where to look. I could bring a cup from home, he told me, but I could use his for now. "Let me get this out of your way," Elliot said, as he hauled his stuff off my desk and stacked it on one of the two visitor's chairs.

I set about moving in: putting my things away in the desk drawers, organizing a filing cabinet, negotiating for bookshelf space—"From here to the right is mine, and to the left is yours." When I got through with all this, the contrast was so stark as to disorient any unsuspecting visitor who'd never been to the office before. It was as if an inviolable line had been drawn down the middle of the room, like some natural barrier separating one distinct species from another. Elliot recalls how, on the day of my moving in, I sharpened exactly six pencils—half of a twelve pencil box, you see—and laid all six in the top drawer of my desk with the sharpened ends carefully lined up in the same direction.

Elliot also recalls an occasion when he needed a pencil and, not being able to find one of his own, borrowed one of mine—

and then inadvertently put it back with the point headed in the "wrong" direction. He tells me that when I opened the top drawer of my desk, I noticed the discrepancy and restored the pencil to its proper alignment. I don't doubt this. I have no recollection of doing it, but then I wouldn't. At the time, it was just the kind of asymmetry that I'd be likely to "correct" without ever realizing I was doing so. I mean, *three* pencils one way and *three* the other would probably pass without notice. But one and five? Never! It would take thirty years for Elliot and me to uncover our deep similarities. We were like a knock on the other's door or a ring on the telephone, one calling, the other answering, until the exchange of dissimilarities became the medium through which each of us found something of ourselves in the other. In 1997, Elliot and I would co-author a book, *Bowing to Receive the Mountain,* and Elliot would write these words of introduction:

> One of us: a son of a Danish immigrant; his childhood disciplined to the demands of a Southern California turkey farm. The other: a son of Jewish parents one generation away from Germany and Poland; his childhood attuned to the streets and back alleys of Brooklyn, New York.

> Thrown together in 1965—one in wingtip shoes and a three-piece tweed suit, pencils sharpened tip to sharpened tip, unmarked eraser to unmarked eraser; the other with long hair and shaggy beard, his desktop a shambles of papers, overdue books, lunch bags with day-old banana peels and apple cores—sharing an office at a small community college on the central coast of California. For twenty-four years, colleagues and neighbors. Different as day from night.

In the end, when we'd put Elliot's poetry and my prose together in a book, Elliot would conclude that "Placed together, essays and poems, for us, created new meanings, new awareness; a synergy." Perhaps the consequence of any abiding friendship is that one is transformed by it.

Whatever psychological support I might have gotten from wearing wing-tip shoes and a tweed suit, I was still a kid from a turkey farm, the first ever in my family to have graduated from college. The truth is I was uncertain of myself and more than a little frightened by what I'd undertaken. My very success was unnerving me. I latched onto Elliot with his street smarts, casual clutter, and assured manner as a much-needed mentor. I think I knew even then that whatever talent or gift I had to give as a teacher or just as a human being would dry up if I clung to my little conservatisms for the sake of safety.

Everything at the time conspired to shake me loose. Monterey Peninsula College is located just two dozen miles north of Big Sur, and this being the Sixties, Big Sur was a weekend and summer mecca for hundreds of Beats, hippies, and flower children hitchhiking their way down Highway 1. The hippie counterculture had even reached into the wealthy, conservative, gated and guarded community of Pebble Beach. The sons and daughters of staunch Republican Party donors could be seen in the college parking lot climbing out of the BMWs they'd been given for high school graduation and making their way to class wearing dirty T-shirts, scuffed sandals, and jeans with the knees and seat torn.

A lot of my students were convinced of the unquestioned efficacy of universal love and unhindered personal freedom in those early days of my teaching. They didn't bother to distinguish one from the other, so that universal love as they saw it was somehow characterized by a freedom notably intolerant of restraint or boundaries of any sort. I was teaching survey courses in English and American Literature, but both classes were clamoring for assignments in Kerouac, Ginsberg, Kesey, and Burroughs. Everybody was tuned into Dylan and the Grateful Dead. Timothy Leary was an idol of LSD advocates, and a student for whom I'd helped to secure Conscientious Objector status was forever extolling the spiritual virtues of acid and trying to turn me on to the hallucinogen.

Not only that, but most of my male colleagues were discarding their sports jackets, suits, and ties in favor of khakis or jeans with T-shirts or some other "psychedelic" shirt that didn't have to be tucked in. Still trussed up in my three-piece tweeds, I just didn't know what I was expected to wear anymore. Jeans were perfectly familiar to me. Aside from my teaching clothes, I'd worn Levi's and casual shirts my whole life, but at the state college where I'd previously taught, male professors were required to dress "professionally"—and that included a tie. My advisor at Stanford was a professed Maoist, but even with his impassioned revolutionary aims he never came to class minus a tie. I'm sure my quandary regarding clothing must appear to be lightweight stuff—and I'm not unaware of the absurdity of it—but as uncertain of my role as I was at the time, the question of what to wear did not feel so trivial.

Either by force or choice, my life had been characterized by discipline and order of a sort that defined for me certain boundaries of manner and decorum that seemed somehow advisable to maintain and respect. Or was I merely playing it safe?

Things came to a head in my English survey course when I began to get requests to sit on the floor. "What do we need chairs for?" "We sit on the floor in our psych class." I said, "You can sit on the floor if you want to." And they did. Not just a few but most of the class. But there was more. Two nursing women ("Earth Mothers") in nearly identical flowered skirts and peasant blouses had taken to bringing and nursing their infants in class. They also brought their dogs; in fact, dogs were a big counterculture thing on campus. The place was beginning to resemble a kennel. When I'd had to quell a brief classroom dogfight once, I inquired of a dean about the appropriateness of dogs in class, and his view was to just let the whole "hippie thing" work itself out without causing a fuss.

I need to tell you that I liked this wayward class of mine a lot. The students were bright and curious, and when they saw that I wasn't going to substitute Beat poets for the course content, they were willing to learn something about English classics. Besides, everyone including myself got along well with the two dogs and babies that were brought to class. We missed them on days when one of the mothers couldn't attend. It began to feel a little odd to be standing at a podium delivering lectures to students who were practically underfoot. Still, I wasn't sure if I could lecture effectively on *Paradise Lost* while sitting on the floor in tie and tweeds with a wet-nosed dog nuzzling me.

The first time I tried sitting on the floor, I came to school in jeans and a sport shirt, feeling as if at any moment I would be scolded and sent back home to dress properly. The students were discreet, not making a big deal of it when I put my briefcase on the floor and sat down with them. They must have known how spooked I was, but the lecture on Milton that day was more of a mutual conversation than we'd ever had before, the students joining in while one of the babies sucked hungrily and the dogs behaved.

So that was it. I kept on wearing jeans most of the time, and at eleven A.M. every Monday, Wednesday, and Friday, I taught while sitting on the floor. The word got out of course. As it turned out, aside from the psych teacher, I was the only one doing this. The attention this brought to me was troubling. A growing number of students thought of me as a "cool" professor, a faculty convert to the student counterculture. But I didn't feel particularly "cool" and doubted if I ever would no matter how many hours of floor-sitting I logged. The jeans I was wearing weren't any more reassuring than tweeds had been.

It's hard to account for the distress I suffered over these minor matters. After all, it was the teaching that was important, and the teaching was going well. My students were learning, and it was a joy to watch their minds opening to the great literature I'd only lately discovered for myself. After all, wasn't I doing exactly what I set out to do when I left farming to go to college? I told myself these things, but it was a long way from a turkey farm to the uncertainties of the Sixties when boundaries were being removed and familiar signposts disappearing. I felt like one who'd set out but hadn't arrived anywhere.

Of course I wasn't the only one having a hard time finding my way. I'd begun training in Gestalt therapy with a group that met under the guidance of George Brown from the Esalen Institute, and from time to time I'd lead therapy groups of my own. It was probably this activity of mine that encouraged one of the most conservative deans at the college to confess to me over lunch in the cafeteria one day how much he loved going to a nude beach on weekends. It was the last thing I would have expected to hear from him. He was absolutely ecstatic about the experience, imagining, I suppose, that anyone who ran therapy groups would be intimate with the joys of nudism. He was at pains to let me know that it wasn't just a "sex thing"; it was more spiritual than that. The women were "truly beautiful with their clothes off," he told me. I just bet they were, I thought. Of course it was all one could do to keep a straight face, but the dean was so genuinely enthusiastic that I was touched by the sincerity of this confidence. He was more alive than I'd ever seen him. If he'd found this much happiness so easily, I was glad for him. But it wasn't long after the disclosure that he quit meeting my eyes and rarely spoke to me at all. He'd gone too far and said too much, having ignored a boundary meant for his protection.

There were other colleagues as well that seemed too quick and willing with their revelations: Ryan listing off his seven marriages that ended in divorce, critiquing all seven wives; Marian, identifying herself to me as a lesbian at our first meeting, and then complaining to me that "young girls these days don't know anything about sex"; the psych teacher himself declaring to me that "you're never free until you admit you want to screw your mother." I suppose I should have felt more flattered and warmed than I did by the trust shown in sharing such intimacies. It wasn't that I was offended or even that I was put off by the sometimes odd perversity of these disclosures. But I did feel uneasy, as if I were conspiring with others to say things we'd all wish one day we had never said. I didn't want to be the source of another's regret. At times I longed for some rules, like those of dining etiquette imposed by my mother at the Jensen table: napkin on the lap, elbows out of sight, "Thank you," "Please," and "May I be excused"—simple procedures that kept chaos at bay. I wished for someone who could for once just say "No" to something—to anything at all!—with the same authority my father once wielded.

One day a student came to the office, explaining that she had a request of me that was very hard for her to make. She'd been thinking of it for months, but had only now found the courage to carry it through. She wanted to know if I'd make love to her. "It's okay if you don't want to." she quickly added. "But I had to ask. It seemed like the only honest thing to do." There was a second or two of silence while I wondered if she'd have made the same request of a teacher without a reputation for sitting on the floor three times a week. When I reminded her that she was my student and that I was committed to a marriage, she didn't seem particularly disappointed. I thought she left the office feeling pleased with the degree of her honesty.

When she'd left I closed up the office and went out, passing the student union where a colleague of mine was meeting with young Vietnam War protestors who, with his explicit encouragement, were planning to tear up their draft cards that day whatever the legal consequences. Across the way, students from the Black Student Union were gathered on the lawn by the flagpole, brandishing spears and waving signs disparaging the "Honkies" in protest of what they thought to be discriminatory college policies. It was just then that I happened to stop in at a restroom where a middle-aged Japanese gentleman in a gray suit was washing at a basin. He'd set his eyeglasses on the counter above the sink and was washing his hands and face, splashing water into his eyes to rinse the soap away. When he'd finished, he stood over the basin, blinking and dripping water and feeling for the paper towel dispenser which happened to be out of his reach. Wanting to help, I pumped the dispenser handle up and down four or five times and handed him the little stack of towels to dry off.

But he backed away from my outstretched hand, saying "No, oh no, no" and punctuating each refusal with a quick bow the way the Japanese sometimes do. And when I stood back and quit pressing the towels on him, he reached out and carefully tore away one of the five I'd offered. "Too much," he explained as he patted himself as dry as he could with one ten-by-ten-inch square of damp paper. Retrieving his glasses and still bobbing up and down with little bows, anxious to not offend me, he left the restroom, repeating once more before the door closed behind him, "Too much." Standing there, dangling an extravagance of wasted towels, I knew for a certainty that there was, in fact, such a thing as *too much*.

Back at D-5, I comforted myself by straightening things up a bit, clearing the desktop of items that belonged in drawers or files. Maybe D-5, like most things in those days, was merely temporary, but in the meantime I'd keep it in order anyway. I heard footsteps outside climbing the temporary stairs, and then there was Elliot, with a load of library books, opening the temporary door—dear, dear Elliot who would become my closest friend and who never confessed anything to me we weren't both ready to hear. And it wasn't wasted on me at that time that Elliot, while not wearing a tie, wasn't wearing jeans either. He was wearing slacks. The sharp division between Elliot's half and my half of D-5 was beginning to blur. He'd straighten everything up once in a while, seemingly just so he could get a fresh start at making a new mess. And I was becoming a little bored with so much neatness, though I had to smile when, from time to time, I'd catch myself checking to see if my pencils were still in good order.

Daughter Crying On the Mountain

*T*o *others* this might not seem like such a big deal. And I guess it isn't but to write of it is like swallowing something I don't like.

When my daughter, Krista, was thirteen, she and I began to take yearly backpack trips into the high Sierras. We'd climb above timberline where the whole range would lay itself out before us in a succession of peaks stretching north and south for miles. Up in the high meadows and cirques we'd find all sorts of lakes connected by small streams that splashed among the rocks and wandered through the fresh grasses and wildflowers of a delayed July spring. But for all the wonder and beauty of it, it was the chance to fish these waters that brought the two of us to these elevations. The first thing we'd do when we came upon water was to try it for trout—brook, brown, cutthroat, rainbow, golden. We did a lot of catch-and-release during the weeks we spent in the mountains.

Golden trout were the most elusive and the last of the trout species for us to locate, a fact that has something to do with what happened. I'd heard that Golden trout could be found at Sand-piper Lake below the west flank of Seven Gables Peak. So Krista and I left the trailhead at Florence Lake, and in a couple of days made the long climb over Selden Pass into the high country where the terrain leveled out and Seven Gables came into view. We headed cross-country and got to Sandpiper by mid-afternoon. The inlet to the lake looked especially promising and we both went for our fishing gear. It was then that we discovered that Krista had inadvertently left the bail open on her reel and that her line had fed itself out into a hopelessly tangled mess.

The minute I looked at it, I knew the odds of untangling it were nil. I'd tried such a thing before. The result was always the same: a knotted clump from which nothing will come free. None of this would be critical if I had brought replacement line. But I realized then that I hadn't. I'd forgotten. I knew Krista was waiting for me to pull out a spare spool of fishing line, and I had to tell her I didn't have any.

I got hold of the reel, which was still mounted on the pole with this big bird's nest sprung out of the face of it. At first I didn't do anything likely to succeed. What I did was find the loose end and give it a sharp little tug, a strategy almost certain to fail. But instead the snarl loosened a little and a foot or two of line unraveled. And then a little more and a little more until I had a couple yards of freed line. Suddenly there was a just shred of hope.

I got Krista to take hold of the freed end of the line so it wouldn't twist itself up again. "Just string it out as I loosen it," I told her, "and keep a light pressure on it, not too much but enough so that the line doesn't go slack." The line was nylon monofilament and if Krista put too much tension on the line the whole tangle would tighten up so that nothing more would come loose but with too much slack the line would bunch itself up again. Krista couldn't seem to get it right. I kept calling out to her things like "Ease up a little" or "Take up the slack, it's too loose." And then I was actually shouting. "Ease up will you! Can't you hear me!" That a situation such as this manages to take on the character of an emergency is one of the disconcerting qualities of the human mind.

We'd been at the task for over an hour, and fully half the spool of line was stretched out between Krista and me. I would never have thought it possible to untangle so much, but there was still one tight little clump of knots left to get by. I kept fussing and fussing with it but I wasn't getting anywhere. Not only that but a heavy mass of clouds was forming over Seven Gables and the wind was picking up. We would be in a thunderstorm within the half-hour, and the whole thing was my fault because I'd forgotten extra line—*If Krista would just pay attention to what she's doing!* "Don't yank on it! Can't you keep a steady pressure!" It was then that I heard the severity of my voice and actually looked at Krista for the first time since the whole episode began, standing out there among the boulders and stunted trees, holding the end of a fishing line with her dad yelling at her. I saw her shoulders shake, and I knew that she was crying.

Once again I open the door on something I never wanted to see. The year is 1954 and I am twenty-two years old, arriving home on a brief leave from the army before shipping overseas. I don't knock. I just walk in. The kitchen's empty. "Anybody here?" I call. No one answers but something is happening in the dining room. What is happening is that my father has backed my sixteen-year-old sister, Evelyn, into a corner and is slapping her repeatedly across the face. Evelyn's face is puffy and red and streaked with angry tears. She screams at Father through gritted teeth that he can slap her all he wants but she will not be shut up. My mother, in the living room beyond, covers her ears. She throws open the living room door and runs into the yard. "Lucy! Stop it!" Father commands. I want to shield my sister. I want to go to my mother's aid. But I am also strangely moved by some sympathy for my father as well. I feel the awful urgency in him. He is terrified that everything will go to pieces if he isn't there to prevent it. He is trying, once again, to beat some lasting order into his life. He is failing as a father and husband and can't seem to get control of things.

Krista is crying under the shadow of a darkening sky, and my fingers, fiddling with the knotted line, somehow discover the key to its unraveling. The last of the line is freed and the crisis has passed.

What actually happened? The bare details of the incident don't seem too bad: one time I forgot to bring some extra fishing line and got anxious and shouted at my daughter and made her cry. That's not much really in the scale of serious offenses. But into what future place will Evelyn carry the sting of a father's abuse? How will Father ever rub the shame of it from his hand? And in what vulnerable moment years hence will Krista recall a father's angry voice scolding her as clouds massed overhead?

Consequence is a fact of life; whatever we do, however slight, sets in motion a force we can never trace to its ultimate outcome. Regret comes to remind me of this truth.

Limit

*E*veryone *was catching fish* except my mother and me. There were nearly two dozen of us jammed onto a narrow strip of mud between the parking lot and the water's edge, and everybody was hauling in trout. My mother wasn't catching any because she refused to switch her bait from salmon eggs to worms, and I wasn't catching any because I had brought a fly-fishing rod and refused to fish with any bait at all.

Except for a few who fished from boats in the deeper water, every one of us was congregated on this single spot of shoreline, not twenty feet from where we had parked our cars. You could feel the heat from the engines of the new arrivals where they pulled in behind us, the dust they raised from the clay parking lot settling out on us like a dry fog. And then a newcomer would haul a plastic lawn chair and a fishing rod out of the trunk of the car, and addressing no one in particular and requiring no answer, ask, "Well, what're they hitting on today? The usual?" But he'd already be threading a worm on the hook and eyeing a patch of uncontested water for his cast. By the time he'd fold his lawn chair out and set down, he'd have his first catch.

The college was shut down for the summer, and I had driven south to Orange County to visit my parents. The two of them had recently taken up fishing and no sooner had I arrived than they had me packed into the back seat of their car headed out to Irvine Lake for some fishing.

Had I remembered to bring my fishing rod, they had asked before I was even inside. Their urgency it turned out was driven by the fact that Thursday, the day of my arrival, was also the day Fish and Game stocked the lake: if you wanted to catch fish, that's when you needed to get out there. That was also why we had to fish from a parking lot, because that's where Fish and Game dumped the fish into the lake.

Ten fish was the limit at Irvine. We hadn't been there much over an hour before Father was within a couple trout of limiting out. But he couldn't enjoy his good fortune because Mother was still without a single catch. Her stubborn insistence on using salmon eggs, because she loathed putting worms on the line, aggravated him. He wasn't pleased with me either. I couldn't motivate myself to fish at all under such circumstances. I spent the hour standing around with an idle fly rod in my hand refusing Father's offer of a bait rod he had brought just in case I needed it. It lay unused in the trunk of the car not more than twenty feet away. This left Father torn between the pleasures of demonstrating his own skills at getting fish and his distress that I wasn't getting any of my own. He wanted me to have a good time.

The truth is I felt superior to him and to all the others as well. As congenial as I tried to appear, I secretly scorned the lot of them, sitting on their plastic chairs, hauling in a limit of bewildered hatchery fish that knew nothing whatsoever about surviving in a lake and had never eaten a meal that wasn't thrown to them. I, after all, was a *fly* fisherman. I wouldn't degrade my sport with such easy takings. Still, I cheered Father whenever he hooked a fish. He saw through the falseness of the gesture. He knew I disapproved of what he was doing. The knowledge of it showed in his eyes.

Father kept his catch on a metal stringer secured by a short length of clothesline to a stake he'd pushed into the mud at the water's edge. From time to time, the stringer floated ashore and beached itself. Father would heave it back out into deeper water, trying to keep the trout cool in the heat of the afternoon. With nine fish on the stringer, he was down to one more catch.

Seeing that his very prosperity had run him headlong into a sort of poverty, he was saving this last catch so as to have something to look forward to for the rest of the day's outing. He fussed with mother over using some of her limit, since she hadn't used any of it herself and wasn't likely to as long as she kept to salmon eggs. But she didn't want to share. Still he kept after her; still she refused.

"You have your limit and I have mine, to use any way I wish," she explained to him quite logically. She sat on her beach chair, her fishing line hanging undisturbed where it entered the water. Father sat beside her, staring stiffly ahead, his arms folded across his chest. All around them, the others were dragging fish ashore. "But, Lucy, you're not using your limit at all. You haven't caught a fish." "Well then, it's my limit to not use at all, as you put it. I don't tell you what to do with your limit."

When I offered father my limit, he turned me down. "Well then, how about splitting it. Five each?" "I don't want to do that, Linley," was all he said. I thought about the bait rod in the trunk of the car. It was all set up with fresh hooks and weights. Father had bought new line for it in anticipation of my visit. I felt awful. "Look, I think I'll check out the shallows at the outlet. I might do some good down there with bass flies," I told him. He simply looked at me and gave no reply. "There might be some bass in the shade of the cottonwoods down there, I said, and walked out of the parking lot, knowing that I ought to take the bait rod out of the trunk and fish with him.

At the outlet, the lake narrowed into a long shallow pool where cottonwoods shaded the water. The bottom there was weedy, and patches of water lilies floated on the surface. Clumps of willow overhung the banks. It was, as I had said, a good place for bass. But I didn't at once set out to fish. The whole situation had put me out of the mood. The outlet was the only wooded portion of the shoreline. All the rest was exposed to full sun, with withered grass and a kind of gray, shrunken chaparral growing right down to the mud at water's edge. From the cool beneath the cottonwoods, I watched the group at the parking lot where they shimmered in heat waves that ran along the shore. I tried to make out my mother and father, but from such a distance their heat-distorted images were lost among the others. I felt—and this is the part that's hardest to account for—a sudden sympathetic tenderness for the whole wavery little group of them. Their cars, all lined up in the dust of the parking lot, looked sad and pitiful to me. It seemed for the moment as if everyone I had ever known was in transit somewhere, pausing briefly at the margins of some cooling place, hoping for the big catch and trying to extract an hour's respite from their worries and cares.

There, under the cottonwoods, a stillness rested on the water. From time to time a slight breeze wrinkled its surface. My skin and clothing smelled of the willows I had pushed through to get to the shore. Splashes of sun broke through the canopy overhead, illuminating pockets of water where waving stems of yellow and green bottom weeds stretched toward the surface. It reflected off the flutterings of butterfly wings, and sparkled the waxy leaves of the water lilies. And it showed something else I would otherwise have missed.

There, against the far bank, where a shaft of light penetrated the dark waters beneath the willows, a form moved among the weeds. I watched as it sank back into darkness. Then it reappeared. It was a largemouth bass and it looked simply huge. I had never seen the like of it anywhere in the county. Its presence confirmed what I had once been told: even though the lake had not been stocked for bass since before I was born, a few remnants of the original population still survived. I watched the shadow of the big fish as it moved in and out of the light. A gust of wind rippled the surface of the water. Dragonflies rested on the lily pads. Still I did not fish.

The sound of an engine shattered the quiet. A door slammed. I could see beyond the trees that a late-model pickup had stopped on some road I hadn't even known was there. Someone was coming down through the chaparral toward me. I saw that it was a man, tall and broad shouldered, and that he was walking not like one who is sizing up a situation, but like one who knows exactly where he is going and what he is going to do there. Chest waders were slung over his shoulder. A creel and net hung at his waist. He came in under the trees and pushed his way past the willows to an opening on the bank not forty feet from where I stood. Without a second's hesitation, he pulled on the waders and stepped into the water.

I could see then that he carried a long, single-pieced graphite fly rod with what looked like a bass lure tied to the leader. He waded out into the water far enough to clear some space for his cast. He threw the line back up over his head, fed it out forward, threw it back again, out, back a third time, and laid the lure right up the middle of the pool. He waited while the rings spread out a bit, then twitched the line. Twitched it again. Again. But even before he'd twitched it a second time, I saw the heavy shadow of the bass move out from the darkness of the willows.

The lure disappeared. The line straightened. The man in the waders set the hook hard, and with lots of pull against the fish, he followed after it down the length of the pool, dragging water-weeds behind him and churning up mud. When the bass was netted, he walked back down the pool to his point of entry and was gone as quickly as he came. I heard the pickup receding in the distance. I don't think he ever knew I was there.

It was the biggest bass I'd ever seen anyone catch, the track of its conquest marked in mud and floating weeds. But I couldn't discover in myself the excitement I ought to be feeling. Instead I felt disheartened, and was no longer sure of what I was doing there and why. There must have been a time, I thought, when the men and women who lived in the surrounding hills took the fish that swam in these waters because they needed to feed themselves and their families and not for the sake of getting a limit or for mere sport. I turned to go but just as I took my eyes from the water, something moved that shouldn't have. There, in the exact spot from which the bass had been raised, was the unmistakable shadow of a second fish. A great fish. A trophy like the first.

There was an instant of painful hesitation in which I almost walked away, but instead I tied a bass fly to my leader. I walked into the water in my pants and shoes and cast the fly as lightly as I could onto the leaves of the lilies where they floated against the bank. I waited until the shadow moved again into the light, and I twitched the fly into the water. The bass struck instantly but no sooner had I hooked it than I knew I didn't want to kill the fish. But with the puritanically light leader I had always insisted on using, the bass exhausted itself and floated up lifeless before I could bring it to net. I held it under water, trying to revive it, knowing as I did so that it was no use, that the fish was dead. Still, even in my regret, I marked the fact that the bass was not as big as the first.

Back at the parking lot everyone converged on me. None of them had ever seen a fish like it at the lake. They all agreed that it was "at least thirty inches if it's an inch." They hefted it to determine its weight, and estimates ranged from a modest twelve pounds to an extravagant twenty-five. It seemed important to them to get the weight right, and various figures were put forth and disputed. It was as if I'd uncovered the treasure we'd all been looking for, and seeing it in hand, they wanted to know the treasure's exact worth. To a person, they were all glad for me, yet they envied me as well. After all, if it couldn't be one of them, at least someone got the prize. Even my father's eyes showed his hunger to have been the one. "A fish like that is limit enough for a lifetime of fishing," someone said.

But I didn't want to believe that whatever it was we'd been seeking all these years was measurable in inches and pounds. I didn't want to show up anyone else's catch, didn't want anyone's admiration or envy, didn't want to limit out ever again. For I had seen that getting your limit, no matter how tastefully it was executed, meant ten dead fish for the sake of a few hours' recreation. It meant snatching a load of miserable hatchery fish from the confinement of a concrete tank and tossing them into Irvine Lake on a Thursday morning so that my mother and father could converge on them in the afternoon and put to a quick end their first and only release into open water. It meant preferring at whatever cost dead fish to live ones. It meant witnessing two normally sane and reasonably compassionate people squabble over who would get to do the killing. It meant remembering, for half a lifetime now, how the stain of mud spread in deadly stillness over a pool where only moments before the clear waters quickened with the gliding shadows of ancient bass.

I gave the bass away to an old couple who dropped their protest when I convinced them that it would otherwise go to waste. It turned out that Mother and Father had resolved their dispute. Father had baited worms for Mother and she had caught some fish and shared the rest of her limit. So now they had twenty trout on the stringer that they didn't want for themselves and would end up giving to obliging neighbors. We loaded the fish into a tub in the trunk of the car and all the while Mother lamented what a shame it was I couldn't take them back to Monterey with me.

As we drove away, with me once again in the back seat, my clothes still dripping lake water, I saw that the other Linley, the one who came to fish, still stood in the dust of the parking lot. I watched him until he was lost to sight. The last I saw of him he was looking down the shoreline to where the cottonwoods clustered around the outlet. For all his misgivings, sudden and unprecedented, he still coveted the larger of the two bass that had died there that afternoon. He wasn't at all sure what to do with such feelings.

"It's a shame there isn't some way you could take these back to Monterey with you, Linley," Mother repeated.

"Yes," I replied, "it's a shame."

Paths

The paths I have in mind are nothing like sidewalks. Nor are they like the curved walkways one finds in public gardens. They're not even like the Forest Service trails that twist their way into the high mountains. The paths I mean are not designed. They just happen.

In towns, such paths originate at the point where the walker abandons the sidewalk and strikes out on her own. You find them as shortcuts etched into lawns and tracked through the weeds of empty lots. No one intends to make these paths; it's just that one day someone cuts across. Then others follow. Paths like these are common in the country where they lead you from the house to the trashcan or compost bin or woodpile. They are worn into the sod between the back door and the garden plot. They connect the laundry room to the clothesline. They thread their way down through the fields to the creek. They often end at the family burial plot.

These paths are so interwoven with other living pursuits that they are an unwitting disclosure of a species' behavior. That's what makes them worth noticing. A well-worn path shows us where we've been going and how we've been getting there. They reflect character and value. It's heartening that in this age when all our travel is directed along predetermined routes of concrete and asphalt a true path is nonetheless certain to appear wherever the possibility for one exists.

There's a certain temperament however that resists paths, that resists anything random, anything governed by chance or mere opportunity. To such a temperament, a path lacks sufficient method and is an effrontery to a properly developed sense of order. My son, Dru, was in the seventh grade when I received a letter from the school counselor, Mr. Stipplewaite, informing me that Dru had been guilty of some unspecified infraction of the school rules. I was summoned to appear at a parent-teacher conference regarding the matter. It all sounded so ominous. I wondered what grave transgression on my son's part had necessitated such formal proceedings.

It turned out that Dru's crime consisted of having cut across the lawn. Not only that, but he was also uncooperative, having cut across more than once, thus showing a willful disregard for school policy. How many times had he been caught cutting across? I inquired. Twice. He'd been caught twice but the supposition was that he'd probably done it lots of times. I asked to see the scene of the crime. Mr. Stipplewaite was visibly annoyed by the request but drawing on his considerable skills in mediation he humored me by leading me to the spot.

The evidence was irrefutable. I was shown a quadrangle of lawn bordered by classrooms. Dead center across the lawn was a path worn through to the dirt. It commenced at the sidewalk where I stood with Mr. Stipplewaite and broke its way through a low cover of cypress bushes and tracked out onto the lawn and back again through some cypress bushes on the far side where it reconnected with the sidewalk. It was in every way consistent with the true nature of paths. But it was certainly not the work of a single culprit or even of a few. Dru couldn't have worn a path that deep all by himself if he'd spent every spare minute of his school day doing nothing but walking back and forth across the quadrangle. This particular path was a popular route.

Measures were being taken, however, to stem the flow of traffic, which in this case was like trying to stem the flow of human nature. The path had been barricaded with yellow tape strung on stakes, and the bare earth had been reseeded. New shoots of grass were already springing up, but right alongside the abandoned path a fresh track was already being laid down. I could see why. At the point where the two of us stood, the sidewalk took a ninety-degree turn to the right along the face of the building. If you were going to Rooms Four through Eight, the sidewalk served the purpose just fine. But if you were going to Rooms Nine through Twelve, the sidewalk made no sense at all. It so happened that Mr. Stipplewaite and I were conducting our parent-teacher conference in Room Ten, and when we got ready to go back it took all the adult restraint I could muster to keep from cutting across the lawn myself.

Mr. Stipplewaite seemed to have no such difficulty. I could see that he trusted sidewalks more than I do. Concrete is more or less permanent and it was clear to me that permanence was an article of faith with Mr. Stipplewaite. He liked things to stay put, and he feared that if you allow one thing to go astray all would go astray. It's dangerous to tolerate a disregard of rules.

But the kids keep cutting across the lawn. All efforts to prevent this behavior, all the taping-off and reseeding, all the threats and punishments have ultimately failed to produce a correction. Mr. Stipplewaite attributes this to laziness, or to a stubborn resistance to authority, a willful refusal to cooperate, whereas I see it as an innate and inescapable wisdom that arises quite innocently of any intent on the children's part. The shortest distance between two points is a straight line. Something deeper than mere surface logic responds to that simple truth. Children cut across lawns for the same reason any of us do: because they can't intelligently do otherwise. If in doing so they defy school authority, it's because they answer to an authority greater than that of the school. It isn't something they think about; it's simply something they do. As I assured Mr. Stipplewaite that I would, I asked Dru to try using the sidewalk. I think he made an effort but, if he's any son of mine, he's probably cutting across the lawn again.

True paths are a configuration of the present, answerable to the moment only. A genuine path is born when one trusts oneself enough to allow circumstance to show the way.

Hiking a trail in the Amargoso River Preserve southeast of Death Valley, I came to a place where the official trail swung to the right along the brushy banks of the river and where a kind of lateral canyon opened up to the left. The canyon looked inviting but the desert in that area is difficult for cross-country, so I thought I'd better stick to the trail. But then I saw something I hadn't noticed before. At the mouth of the canyon was a "trail duck,"—a little pile of stones balanced one on top of the other. I found the second trail duck a little further up canyon. And then a third. And then another, and another, all the way up to where the canyon opened out and I found myself on a high rise above the whole sweep of the Amargoso River Valley. Up there, a stiff wind rattled the desert brush. Ravens soared along the cliff faces. In the far distance, red rock plateaus were cast into alternate light and dark as thunderheads formed overhead. In the valley below, the river twisted among the smoke trees and cottonwoods. Someone was the first to come this way, an event that in the very nature of pathmaking was inevitable. Others marked the path piling stone on stone. I in turn had followed in their steps, casting yet another vote for the preservation of the way.

It is in this way as well that paths are laid down in the mind. No one creates them; they are found. Like the path at Amargoso or the one tracked into the lawn at my son's school, they exist long before anyone walks them. They appear as tracks in the landscape of the world's perennial philosophies. They lead us through thickets of confusion and doubt. They are discovered in the voice of poet and sage. They take the form of artistry and music. They unfold in the laughter of the comic. They are revealed in the joyful curiosity of children.

Each of our lives is a path. To know this requires intuition and trust. If we are true to the steps we take, the travel makes sense and the journey confirms itself.

Mother's Last Chess Game

ertainties fall away from me these days faster than I can accumulate them, so by simple mathematical consequence I am rapidly approaching a sum of no certainty at all. I used to be certain that it was best not to be angry, taking it for granted that anger didn't help. But lately I've remembered some occasions that raise doubts, one of which is the occasion of Mother's last chess game.

My father liked a game of chess in the evenings. Mother, on the other hand, had little talent and no inclination for the game whatsoever. But she would accommodate Father from time to time when he didn't have anyone else to play with. This arrangement might have gone on indefinitely except that Father wasn't content with an easy win; he wanted challenge. He considered each of his moves at great length and wanted Mother to do the same. He wanted her to be competitive, and this required of her intelligent play. My mother was quite intelligent, but her growing impatience with watching Father study his own moves for interminable periods of time wore on her as the game dragged on. In addition Father had the habit of humming to himself while he was plotting strategies. So sometimes when Mother's turn came she simply made the first move that occurred to her, hoping that she would lose quickly and the ordeal would be over.

But a dumb move on Mother's part spoiled the game for Father. "Lucy!" he would protest, "you don't want to do that." He would stare at the board and shake his head in disbelief and try to get her to take the offending move back.

Whenever I visited my parents, Father would try to press me into service. But I wasn't much help because I knew next to nothing about chess at the time. Father could hardly get much satisfaction out of reminding me of the names of the pieces and in what directions each was allowed to move. Despairing of getting much competition from me, Father would coax a game out of Mother. It was in this way that I was privileged to witness the last game of chess the two of them ever played.

It was after supper and Mother was playing the black. They'd been at it about an hour. I was seated on a sofa reading some poems of Wordsworth's from a volume of the lyrical ballads. Father was humming a lot. Mother was trying to screw her attention to the task of making intelligent moves. Father, typically relentless in his concentration, was sort of hovering over the game, never relaxing his attention, never sitting back in his chair or looking about the room or engaging in any unrelated conversation. Even when it was Mother's turn, he studied the board with an intensity that seemed intended to will her into making the best possible move. The atmosphere was positively suffocating. And then I heard the familiar, and this time, fatal incantation. "Lucy! You don't want to do that."

Perhaps fate had allowed Father a certain quota of this aggravating and oft repeated combination of words, but if so he must have finally exceeded the limit. Hearing him this one last time, Mother was released on the instant from all further obligations, practiced behaviors, restraints, or accommodations she'd ever imposed on herself for the sake of Father's chess games. Sitting there on the sofa, I looked up in time to see Mother slide her chair back from the chessboard about a half-foot as if to gain the perspective of a little more distance. I felt a change come over her as definite as a car shifting gears. Father didn't seem to notice. He was still locked into the game, trying I suppose to make the most out of the mess Mother had made. He was hunkered over the board and he was humming again. Mother had her eyes fixed on the top of his head, the spot where his hair was thinning out. Something was about to happen. I felt the imminence of some unprecedented action on my mother's part.

At length, Father apparently felt it too. He quit humming, and he looked up. And when he'd given her his full attention, Mother, in one brilliantly executed sweep of an arm, knocked all the chess pieces off onto the floor. "There, Morris!" she said, "How do like that for a move?" What I recall more than anything else was the *briskness* of the event. It was as if Mother had thrown open all the windows in the house, ventilating the stale air with a fresh night breeze. It was all so crisp and final.

Yet, Mother didn't storm out of the room or anything like that. Instead the two of them sat looking at each other across the vacant chessboard with faces of mutual defiance, mixed with what you'd have to say was the simple affection of wise old couples who've scattered the pieces of their lives more than once. At length, Father said, "I guess that's a checkmate." And then the two of them were down on their knees, laughing and retrieving chess pieces.

Since Mother's last chess game, I no longer conceive of anger in the absence of love. Anger seems more like love's protest than anything else, a way love has of voicing its complaint when slighted or ignored. Before the week was out, Mother had bought Father a computerized chessboard that he could "scold and hum over," as Mother put it, "until the cows come home."

Margie's Room

I f the door is closed, I don't go in without first knocking. She's taking classes at the local college, and she might be studying and not want to be disturbed. She might be looking out the window, watching a neighbor or a passing car or sparrows flying in and out of the pistachio tree. She might simply want to be alone. It's understood between us that it is her room to do with as she pleases.

When I first met Karen Laslo, I knew nothing at all about Margie. So I didn't know that Margie had never had a room like the one Karen now has. I only learned of Margie's existence when Karen and I decided to get married and sent for birth certificates. She told me at the time me that I would be surprised to learn that her actual first name wasn't Karen. Karen, she explained, was really her middle name. Her first name was Margie. "I switched to Karen when I was eleven years old," she said. "Why?" I asked. "Because I don't like Margie," she answered with an air of defiance I couldn't at the time account for. In the months before our marriage, Karen and I were living in an apartment in the seaside town of Pacific Grove. The apartment set above a garage and was barely four hundred square feet. But from the front windows we could see Monterey Bay between the intervening houses. And being a second story apartment we caught lots of sunlight. I liked it there.

Karen liked it too, but from the start, she showed the distress of feeling crowded. If you divide a twenty-foot-by-twenty-foot area into a kitchen, dining nook, living room, bedroom, closet, and bathroom, you have little space left for movement and none for privacy. At times Karen would grab for a jacket and head out the door, whatever the weather or hour. I could literally see her pulled back and forth between wanting me there and an equal need to have me out of there so that she could have some space of her own.

Nevertheless we agreed to keep the apartment. Housing in the area was expensive and the apartment was a third the cost of any other rental we'd priced. We planned to have a house of our own someday and needed to save whatever we could. Karen saw the sense of this, but still she searched the classifieds in hopes of finding another rental we could afford. Sometimes at her urging I went with her to look at places that were clearly beyond our means. Karen knew this, yet she examined the kitchen for cupboard space, noted what size table the dining area would accommodate, and measured the living room for furniture we didn't own. She inventoried each bedroom. This one would be ours, this for guests, this for a study. Heading back to our apartment after such outings, she was often subdued. After a little bit, she might say, "It was a pretty nice house, don't you think?"

When her birth certificate came, Karen barely glanced at it and then handed it over to me. "You can read it," she said and turned back to whatever it was she was doing in the kitchen. The certificate recorded the birth of Margie Karen Laslo to her parents, Francis and Eloise Laslo on February 20, 1947, in Nyack, New York. Who was this little Margie, I wondered, who had drawn her first breath thirty-seven years before in the maternity ward of Nyack General Hospital and whose record of birth I now held in my hands? What went wrong that she discarded her name and put herself out of sight?

In early June of 1984, six weeks before Karen and I were wed, I was to see for myself where Margie lived when she disappeared. On a patch of bare alkaline ground in a trailer park southeast of Death Valley, California, Eloise and Frank Laslo still lived in the same trailer they'd occupied since Karen was a baby. Throughout the whole of her childhood and adolescence, this trailer, wherever it was parked at the moment, was Karen's only home. I was the first outside the family to see it. None of Karen's friends had ever gone there. None had ever met her parents. Karen was apprehensive about our visit. She tried to prepare me and thus told me things she had hoped she would not have to tell.

She told me of a father who pried into everything personal, who ordered his wife and daughters and son to do his bidding, who bullied and struck out in rage when they failed to do so, and who sank into depressions from which he could not extricate himself. She told me she had never taken a friend home from school because she didn't want anyone to see how she lived. She told me of the nights she and her mother and sister and brother took refuge in a neighbor's spare bedroom or a motel room to wait out the times of humiliation and danger. She told me of the summer train journeys to the home of her maternal grandparents, William and Mary Kirby, her mother shipping the children to safety where they could be kids for a while and where Karen could pretend she'd never have to come back to the trailer again. When Karen and I passed over the Tehachapi grade into the desert that June, Karen had not seen her parents for ten years. We were traveling into the past.

We found the trailer in row E, space 15, of the Yolo County Park at Tecopa Hot Springs, a few miles from the crossroads settlement of Tecopa, California. The trailer had slumped down on its supports as though gravity itself threatened to pull it under, the tires having long ago rotted beyond use. Its sides were chalky white, like the alkali dust that spotted the ground of the trailer park. I had to squint to look at it in the afternoon light. The roof was covered with discarded tires painted silver to reflect the sun. With few windows, it looked more like a big metal box than a place where someone lived. In mid-June, the trailer stood alone in the shimmering heat, the others having left the park to escape the blistering summer temperatures.

Inside the trailer, all one could do was sit down. There simply wasn't space enough for people to move around. Everyone blocked everyone else's way. If one person needed to move, others had to move as well. Karen's mother, Eloise, sat the two of us at a small table shoved against a wall just inside the door. Once we were in place, she unloaded some boxes of cereal from the top of a stool and pulled the stool up to the table and sat down herself.

Frank Laslo sat where he had been sitting for years, in a frayed upholstered chair with the fabric worn through on the armrests. From there he could watch television. Half a lifetime before, when Karen was still a child, Frank Laslo, driving his milk truck in the rain in San Fernando Valley, saw through the splatters on his windshield the figure of a woman entering the street. He swerved to miss her and the truck, with no side doors and no seat belt, rolled over. After the surgery had gotten him back on his feet, Frank Laslo made the fatal decision to be an invalid. He might have found work he could do had he not been so angry at a world that he felt now owed him something for his misfortune. Instead he put his whole energy into getting what he felt was his due. He collected his monthly disability check and never worked for wages again. By the time I met him, his life was an endless round of TV game shows.

I could see that he was trying to be sociable for our visit but I felt how much of a strain it was for him. There was a dark brooding about him he couldn't hide. He sat in his chair and from time to time interjected some brief comment into the conversation, but he seldom took his eyes from the television screen. He spoke in quick short jabs like a boxer who had backed himself against the ropes and was trying to punch his way out. His comments were mostly complaints, which Karen pointedly ignored.

I felt a tension between them that had the capacity to explode. Karen's mother felt it too; the fear of it showed in her eyes. This was the daughter who had defied her father, who had hated his bullying and refused to be intimidated by it. I sat at the table with the three of them, the afternoon heat gradually overwhelming the trailer's inadequate cooling system, and I tried to imagine what it must have been like to live there. How had Frank and Eloise Laslo and their son and two daughters survived all those years within its confines?

By the end of the day, civilities had worn thin. Frank had had all he could handle. All of us had had all we could handle. We crowded into the trailer for a last cup of tea. Karen and I planned to leave the next day. Frank sat silent, watching the TV. Eloise was weary with her own apprehension. None of us had much left to say. I thought to myself that it was to this father and to this trailer that Margie had returned each day from school. It was here at the age of eleven that she had ceased to exist because she no longer wanted to be who she was. She told everybody that her name was Karen and not to call her Margie anymore.

One day not long ago, on her way out to meet a friend, Karen invited me to sit in her room. "It catches the morning sun," she said. "You can read your book there." I took her up on the offer. I closed the door as Karen sometimes does. I sat in her chair and pulled it up to the writing table where she studies for her classes. The room is not very big but there are two large windows that open onto the front lawn and a plot where gardenias and daphne grow. Even with the door closed I didn't feel confined. Besides a writing table and the castered swivel chair I sat on, the room is furnished with a graceful upholstered chair on elegant hardwood legs, a footstool, and a wonderful old floor lamp that Karen plans to restore. On the wall hangs a small picture of a country snow scene that long ago hung on the wall in the home of Mary Kirby, Karen's maternal grandmother. Alongside the snow scene hangs a framed copy of a 1929 calendar given out by Grandpa Kirby to customers of the West End Garage in Walker Valley, New York, ninety miles up river from Nyack where Margie was born.

Among her things on the writing table is a color photograph of Karen as a child. It is no larger than a snapshot and it's held in a gilt edged frame. With the exception of the faint green tint of her sweater, all the details have faded to a sort of pinkish-red hue. The girl in the photograph sits on a boulder in a stream. I can see a swift current of water bending around the boulder and rapids in the background. The little girl's jeans are rolled up to her knees; her legs dangle over the edge of the boulder. Her sweater is buttoned up the front and a collar shows at her throat. Her hair, parted in the middle, is pulled tightly back. Her hands are folded in her lap. She looks as if she likes having a rock of her own to sit on.

On the back of the photograph, Kodak stamped the date of the print: October 3, 1955. Karen was born in 1947. I realized then what I was seeing. This child, with features barely preserved in faded pink, was Margie. Sitting there where the click of the shutter captured her image on film that day, she would live three more years before she disappeared from view. I looked out the windows into the yard. I looked at the wall where a calendar hung displaying a January that was sixty-seven years out of date. I looked at the faded image of the little girl sitting at the stream's edge, her hands folded on her lap. I knew then that this was Margie's room. She had come home. Through all these years she had remembered that safety was possible. She had found within these walls a place secured against the dangerous waters running close by.

Peregrine Falcon Watch

The climb to Beckwourth Peak begins in the sage spotted grassland of Sierra Valley. I've made the climb so many times that it's as intimate to me as the path from my own back door to the garage. In the lower elevations, there is just the faintest track to follow winding through a forest of Jeffrey pines. And then I come out onto an exposed slope of rocky ground with patches of stiffened grass, and stunted junipers. From there I skirt past a little shelf of rock where a breeding Rock Wren bobs like some avian athlete doing morning knee-bends, all the while singing an amazing repertoire of wren melody. From there I work through a dense thicket of shrubbery that's impenetrable unless you know where to find the seam that lets you pass. Back in the open again, the climbing is steep, and the ground underfoot slips away, barren of any growth at all. And then finally, the cliff face itself comes into view. I work my way up a rocky spine that falls steeply away on either side until I come to a little patch of level ground where an isolated ponderosa pine has somehow taken hold and managed to survive. It is here, within a hundred yards of the cliff face, that I set up a spotting scope and begin my four-hour watch of the peregrine falcon eyrie.

Karen and I had been married five years when we retired to Sierra Valley, a remote mountain valley in northeastern California. It was the summer of 1989, and we'd spent the previous three summers building the little house that was to be our new home. We'd only been there a short time, when the Forest Service hired me to monitor the first-year's nest of a pair of newly-mated peregrine falcons. The species is endangered and this single nesting pair was the sole result of a peregrine reintroduction project underway in Sierra Valley. The peregrines, like Karen and me, were setting up household there for the first time. We were concerned that they succeed.

Karen and I had bought one of the few sites in the area that we could afford, and while the property wasn't ideal, it was, after all, ours to live on and do with as we pleased. We had a wonderful view of the surrounding mountains, and a night sky as vivid in my memory as if I were still standing out on the porch on a clear, icy night under that vaulted ceiling so populated with stars that the light from them printed my shadow on the porch boards. We had but one native tree on the acreage, a small Jeffrey pine, and so we hooked up the utility trailer to the jeep and drove to the nursery in Reno, Nevada, where we picked out three five-gallon trees—an amber flame maple, a hawthorn, and a mountain ash. When we planted them, Karen was concerned that we dig big enough holes with lots of loosened soil and that we add compost and bone meal and other nutrients for the roots to grow in. And when we sat the trees in place, she was careful to free the roots and not plant the trees too deep. "The root crown needs air," she said. We worked at it most of a day, imagining all the while the shade our new trees would someday give us and the fall colors that would brighten up the yard. Not long after, we bought five apple saplings as well, hooking them up to a drip system that we strung out from a backyard faucet, fencing each tree from the deer that were already showing an interest in our undertakings. Our "apple orchard," as we thought of it, was outside our bedroom window where we hoped one day to begin our spring and summer mornings in the sight of apple blossoms and ripening apples. That first summer there, I'd begun as well to turn under the native sod in a plot I'd marked out for a future vegetable garden.

It was in early spring after our first winter in Sierra Valley that I was hired to monitor the peregrine falcon eyrie on Beckwourth Peak. The male of the nesting pair was marked with a color-coded band, which identified it as part of the reintroduction project begun four years earlier. That the male was here with a mate was only slightly less than a miracle. With all the historical pairs of peregrines in the area extinct, the Forest Service had resorted to introducing peregrine falcon eggs gathered from coastal nesting pairs into the nest of a pair of Sierra Valley prairie falcons. So the only parents this breeding male had ever known were not peregrines but prairie falcons. It was the call of prairie falcons that he heard from the day of his birth to the day he fledged. It was prairie falcons that leaned in over the nest and stuffed bits of prey into his hungry mouth.

Not only that, but the prairie falcons were in the habit of wintering over in Sierra Valley, while the peregrine, if he were ever to find a mate, must migrate to traditional wintering sites as far south as Mexico. And should he somehow be moved to abandon the only parents he had ever known and undertake this migration without adult peregrines to guide him, would he even know that he was a peregrine and recognize a female of his own species as a mate? This young male had never seen his own kind. But in the fall of the year he was fledged, the young banded male peregrine disappeared from Sierra Valley, leaving the project directors with nothing to do but wait and see.

A peregrine is typically four years old when it first mates, at which time it will return to the place of its birth to raise its young.

Against all odds, the falcon had returned on schedule. He was a peregrine, not a prairie falcon, and he somehow understood that. Still the likelihood of the pair succeeding in raising their own young was doubtful. Peregrines feed high on the food chain, other birds being their prey. Because of this, they take in so much pesticide that the shells of their eggs are weakened and thinned to a degree that prevents their successful incubation and hatching. The use of these pesticides in the Mexican wintering areas is still prevalent, and this mating pair had been feeding there for four years.

Monitoring an eyrie is an intimate form of watching. I was required to keep a journal of all movements and interactions of the nesting pair. Noting such behaviors as prey delivery by one of the pair to the nesting site would tell me when eggs had been laid in the nest, and when brooding began, and when chicks (if any) were hatched. So day after day, hour after hour, I watched and wrote entries in my journal, not knowing until time and luck had finally run out, that I was recording the history of a failure.

The peregrines were both new at this, and the first mistake they made was to pick a bad location for their nest. In their inexperience, they passed up an almost perfect site on a ledge where the nest would be sheltered and chose instead one that would expose them to spring storms and the coming heat of summer. At first the weather favored them. Had it not, they might have relocated their nesting site. But as it was, they sailed above the Beckwourth cliffs under clear spring skies, calling and courting and mating repeatedly, the young male suddenly slanting off down the mountain toward the valley floor to find prey to offer his mate. In time, there were eggs in the nest, and at first the female did almost all the brooding, relying on the male to bring food. Later, both she and the male took turns brooding while the other hunted food for itself, finding it, I imagined, more efficient to sustain themselves that way.

There was a time when I knew that the brooding had gone on too long. The period for hatching had come and gone. The weather had turned against them with slanting rains that left the pair sitting on eggs soaking in a puddle of water. There were other days of such heat that the brooding adult could be seen standing over the eggs trying to cool them with what little shade spread wings might provide. It was painful to watch and record this day after day. Still the peregrines would not abandon their nest, and their prolonged and courageous effort was breaking my heart.

Though new to our mountain home, neither Karen nor I were children. We knew that things sometimes fail—as they did that year when sheer exhaustion and a late and particularly violent spring storm finally drove the falcons from their first-year's nest. It was bitter cold the morning I climbed to the Beckwourth cliffs and was met with silence and an empty sky. In the abandoned nest only scattered fragments were left of that thin shell dividing what goes wrong from what goes well. I knelt to gather the pieces to be sent to the laboratory for analysis, and when I straightened up to go, I saw for the first time what the falcons must have seen all those long weeks that they spent on this exact spot. I saw how the mountain descended into the valley where the wetlands spread among the grasses and reeds. And I saw as well the high peaks of the Sierra coated with snow in the far distance. Here was space enough to absorb the whole event in such a way that it would pass unnoticed and never be known by anyone at all had I not been hired to watch its occurrence. I thought of all the little failings that go unseen, swallowed up in the anonymity of those vast cities and fields of human indifference. I was glad that I'd been here to witness and record the story of the falcons.

The trees Karen and I planted struggled to survive in their mountain location where the growing season was so brief. They clung precariously to life, lashed by harsh winds and dragged to the ground by the weight of winter snows. Our first planting of garden vegetables was decimated by a hard freeze in the middle of July during weeks of otherwise-ninety-degree weather. Such a freeze we were told could come any month of the year. But long before Sierra Valley, Karen and I had seen how the best any two can make will bend and sometimes break. But we had seen as well the power of mending, healing, and repairing, finding heart and warmth, enough to spare so that the worst failing is brought to cure like any common ailing we humans must endure.

The falcons returned yet another year, drawn back on the will of some design we cannot name—surely the same that draws any of us back, whatever we lack, whatever we fear. This time the peregrines chose the better location for an eyrie and hatched four offspring when two at most is the usual limit. I spotted all four, still alive, and self-sufficient, before they left the valley for their winter grounds. That same summer, Karen and I bought row covers for the vegetable garden, put up some wind shelter for the struggling trees, laid down sod for a small lawn, and discovered that lilacs thrive in mountain conditions.

The Song Not Heard

There was no sound but that of the wind. It swept
down off the mountain, scouring the stiff autumn grasses of
the Sierra Valley basin and rattling the fields of sage. I had
come in search of Brewer's sparrows but the wind had put everything down and nothing on wing stirred.

Suddenly there it was—a Brewer's sparrow clinging to a
clump of sage not ten feet from where I stood, so near at hand
that I didn't need binoculars to make out even the subtlest of its
details. I held still, and the Brewer's sparrow either accepted me
or didn't sense my presence at all. Then I saw it stretch its head
and neck forward and its little bill opened. Its throat pulsed in
and out, and a tiny tremor ran through its whole body, the bill
itself vibrating delicately for an instant before it closed in repose.
This was repeated several times: the outward inclination, the
parting bill, the throat working, the rising shiver, then all of it
pulled back in again to perfect containment—a rhythm I
received like the expansion and contraction of my own heart.

In all of this, I heard not a note of the bird's song, only the
voice of wind that flowed around us and between us and swayed
this little creature on its perch where it seemed to throw its very
body into every rising of song. I saw the living anatomy, the phys-
iology, of the bird's call. I saw that sound and note, could I have

heard them, were only the extension, the outermost extremity of pulsing blood and feathers, breath, flesh, and hollow bone.

To see like this is much like losing the sound portion of a TV program, when the framed image suddenly lapses into a silence that communicates a reality unavailable when sound is present. The figures on the screen move about in mute animation, their faces and bodies telling you something you could not otherwise have known. At length, I moved and the sparrow flew away. I saw then that the clump of sage where the little bird had sung its song was itself singing in the wind.

Real Estate

a morning in late May. Kneeling on the ground, I work a cultivator into the soil of the vegetable garden I tend here at our Sierra Valley home. The day warms, the shadows shorten toward noon. The soil turns up moist and dark beneath my hands.

All through the night while I slept, the planet revolved eastward, bearing this little western garden of mine back toward the sun, bearing the mountain night toward another day. The garden that comes to my hands today emerges out of a yesterday that traveled the distance of two vast oceans and three continents in its daily journey to the present.

The plot I cultivate is a raised bed four feet wide and twelve feet long. It is one of sixteen such beds in the garden. Like the others, it was dug and screened for rock. Its soil is rich with compost and earthworms. My digging here this morning releases the scent of warming soil.

The garden is fenced against the deer who come out of the woods to feed in the open grassland where the garden is situated. Adjacent to the garden is a toolshed, a pump house, a well, and four compost bins. Down slope from the garden are a few apple trees and beyond these a house and garage finished in board and batten. The house opens onto a fenced yard landscaped with young trees and shrubs. A woodshed is joined to the garage. This household as I have described it sits on twenty acres of grassland sloping from a pine woods down to the county road below.

When Karen and I retired we bought this land. I know of course that it's perfectly ordinary to buy property. I can scoop up this garden earth and, though it is just a fistful of dirt like all the other dirt comprising these twenty acres of mine, even as I cup it in my hands, it is spinning in orbit round the sun. Nothing is holding still here. The whole place is in a state of rapid transit. This quickened soil that I hold in my hands owes its unlikely stability to sources as obscure as they are fantastic.

It is a dizzying proposition to think that I can own such a thing. Apparently I do, for such ownership is recognized in a joint tenancy grant deed issued by Cal-Sierra Title Company for Plumas County parcel number 025-420-10. But what can it really mean to "hold title" to so active a thing? What exactly is it that I own?

I ask these questions of myself because I know of no one else who will ask them of me. Yet they are questions that need to be asked. "Real estate" has become our most common designation for the earth upon which we live, and its fair market value has become the common measure of its worth. We think of land as property, a commodity for exchange. We ascribe to its ownership certain rights that we believe are due to us.

For four years now I have tended this garden. I broke the native sod and turned it under to rot. I screened the soil for rock and added manure hauled in from a neighbor's horse corral. I composted and watered and seeded and harvested and returned all waste to the ground. I have done these things, yet I have been helpless to effect any outcome except what the earth provides. And the earth provides not just a little, but all. The very body and mind with which I tend the earth are themselves of the earth. I am but earth tending earth. Were the earth not to roll this garden toward the sun today, were the clouds not to gather above the sea, the waters not to flow, the soil not to brim with its billions of microorganisms, were all or any part of this to fail, I would fail as well, my body numbed to a fixed stillness, my slightest thought cancelled.

This truth is so obvious that it is a wonder we can forget it so often and so easily. The fact of it defines who we are. To forget this is to forget who we are, a species suffering from amnesia that bewildered seeks its own name.

It is here in this garden that one can see how trivializing and irrelevant are the notions of property and property rights. This garden feeds me; it yields up life that I might have life. I am joined to this garden by an urgent interdependence. It is a salient, sacred, soul-sustaining fact that the best any of us can do is to harmonize our will to that of the earth. It is a teaching learned in humility and gratitude; it has no rights to press.

My body knows exactly how this stands; it taps not only into four years tending this garden but a lifetime bent to the task. Our bodies always know where we are even when we don't. Seasons rise and fall within us on blood tides of hunger. Daily need roots our mouths to the subsoil. When we lose sight of this, the fundamental wonder of it still lies fallow in our very tissues to be called forth again as joy. This wonder, this springing joy, is our only health. Our sanity is measured by the presence in us of such wonder. Lose it, and we go mad. We deal in real estate. We become incoherent with talk of "property" and "title" and "rights pertaining to thereof."

I can survive the ownership of this mountain property with my mind intact if I never forget where I am and what I am doing. We humans have been entrusted to the earth, the earth entrusted to us. When we do not tune ourselves to this trust, the discord is fatal. Our only true song perishes on the instant, though we may seem to sing on endlessly.

Zen

One of the first Zen writings I ever read was written by an ancient Soto Zen master, Torei Zenji, who called on his students to "Preserve well for you now have. This is all." It was a surprising statement for me to absorb. Is this really all? Is just this what I must preserve well? It would be some time before I would understand that Torei Zenji was saying more than just that I should take good care of what I've already got. He was also saying that there's nothing I lack, that nothing more is needed. From Torei Zenji's viewpoint, there's nothing fundamentally wrong with ourselves or our world. He isn't denying our human greed and our violence, just pointing out that none of that would be necessary if we'd wake up to the fullness of who and where we are. We could relax our ambitions and our fears: everything's fine just the way it is. I can say this now, but I couldn't always. I thought instead that there was something very wrong and lacking in me, and so of course I found a great deal lacking in the world as well.

The practice of Zen is particularly good at exposing how arbitrary are our notions of what's wrong and what constitutes a problem. The notion of problems is especially interesting to me. Most perceived problems merely become problems because we believe that they are so. This is true even of extremes such as disease, old age, and death, which are after all universal and inevitable. It's equally true of the sorrow and grief that often accompanies these events. To define the universal experiences of our species as "problems" is to define the whole human life system as a problem. And when something is seen as a problem, you feel compelled to do something about it. A problem, like a leaking faucet or a flat tire, is something that needs to be fixed. You can exhaust your life in the effort to do so.

Some years ago Jim Soren, a psychologist acquaintance of mine, designed a backpacking retreat for a group of his clients, who were mostly wealthy professionals and who had become quite glib at "doing therapy." Jim's idea was to get them into a situation that would deprive them of their usual supports and see if, for once, he could get something unexpected to happen. I'd had several years of training in Gestalt therapy and knew the high mountains well; so Jim asked me to act as trail guide and co-therapist for the outing.

By the time we were two days' walk from the trailhead, one young couple had more or less become attached to me. The two of them, as it turned out, specialized in problems having to do with their relationship. They were extraordinarily articulate in explaining the nature of these problems, which covered most categories of marital difficulty from the philosophical to the spiritual, professional, parental (in anticipation of offspring they'd not yet had), temperamental, practical, sexual, and so on to matters of household economy. Further, their grasp of the psychological complexities that underlay these problems was more impressive than anything I could manage. Of course they expected me to help them resolve their problems, though I wondered what they would have left to think about should I actually succeed in doing so.

The truth is I liked this couple a lot. They were intelligent, lively, and good humored, but I must admit to being bored with their problems after a few days. I figured they were probably bored with them as well. So one afternoon when they'd caught up with me taking a walk in a meadow near Isberg Lake and were consulting with me regarding their problems, I told them that their problems weren't interesting. "You need some new problems," I suggested. I was amazed at the flexibility of this couple—because they got it. They saw how it was, and they began enthusiastically to invent new problems for themselves. I tried to help them out, seeing if I could come up with a few good ones myself but they were way ahead of me in the original-ity and variety of problems they could imagine afflicting their lives. I got a letter from them about a year afterward, telling me that they'd decided to give up problems altogether and instead had bought themselves a sailing yacht and planned to sail around the Pacific for a while.

This was before my Zen days and so I didn't know at the time that the three of us that afternoon in the meadow were acting on the Buddha's teaching that suffering exists and that most of it is self-inflicted. When I was that couple's age, I thought my whole life was something of a problem. For one thing it seemed to me at the time that my tenure on earth was marked more by personal error and failure than anything else. So when Karen and I got together I didn't want to repeat mistakes I'd made before. There'd been too much hurt, and I'd had enough of it. I wanted a way out. I might have returned to the religious practice of my youth, the boyhood feelings of refuge that I sometimes felt on Sunday mornings sitting in a pew with the congregation of the Trinity Episcopal Church, watching the choir rise to sing in their white robes, my life for the moment as secure and orderly as a hymn. But I couldn't go back to that, because I'd be expected to share beliefs that I'd been unable to hold as a boy when I left the church for that very reason. That boy-hood lack of faith I counted now as just another of my early fail-ures. It was in this state of mind that I turned to Zen.

At the first, there was Katharine Thanas, a Soto Zen monk who taught me how to sit zazen, as the practice is called. Back straight but not stiff, she instructed, legs crossed, knees resting on the floor, left hand resting in the palm of the right hand with the tips of the thumbs touching, eyes turned downward and slightly parted but not shut. Get it exact. Hold your place. There's precision and discipline in this practice Katharine told me. And always, always, the breath. Follow the breath. When the mind wanders and you awaken to that fact, come back to the breath. Always come back. "If you persevere," Katharine said, "you will find that nothing is missing." With that first instruction, she left me to sit an hour. The next day I sat at home on my own. And the day after that, and again the next day, and somehow I just never bothered to quit.

When Karen and I retired to the mountains where there was no teacher or other Zen practitioners, I sat alone for the better part of two years before I first traveled to the monastery at Shasta Abbey to train with the monks there. On the day of my arrival, monk Kodo, who was showing me around the cloister, asked why I had come to the Abbey. I had reasons in mind—to experience a Zen community, train among others, find a teacher to work with—but that isn't what I said. What I said was that I didn't want to do any more harm. And that was when the figure of monk Kodo began to blur and I had to wipe at my eyes and I understood that that was, in fact, why I'd come to the abbey. Kodo said that if I didn't want to do harm, I must raise the heart of compassion.

She took me then to the meditation hall where the shrine of Avalokiteshvara, the bodhisattva of compassion was kept. There I found the figure of the bodhisattva etched in clear glass. The delicate tracery on the glass, representing the thousand eyes and the thousand arms and hands of the bodhisattva, was alive with the flickering light of candles that shone through from behind the glass. This was my earliest acquaintance with the Buddhist image of compassion. Monk Kodo asked, "Do you understand now what you're asking for?" I did understand, but I wasn't sure how to go about acquiring the eyes and arms of compassion. When I asked Monk Kodo about this, she set me to doing exactly what Katharine Thanas had taught me to do two years earlier. "Stay put," she told me, "and in time you will see for yourself."

My first effort was to will myself to feelings of sympathy and kindness. But you can't really generate loving qualities by simple intention. At most, you can only open yourself to the possibility of their occurrence. Compassion's not something you can simply do on purpose. The thing is I wanted to "feel compassionate." The problem was that I often didn't. Not only that, but when I did feel compassionate it came of its own accord so that it wasn't exactly attributable to me. The feelings that arose were not something I could own or lay claim to or take credit for.

I don't remember when I first came upon the exchange between the ancient Chinese Zen masters, Yunyan and Daowu, regarding Avalokiteshvara. Yunyan asked Daowu, "How does the bodhisattva of great compassion use all those hands and eyes?" Daowu answered, "It's like someone in the middle of the night reaching behind him for a pillow." You don't really plan to reach for a pillow in the night. You may not even be conscious of doing so. It happens naturally. If the eyes and hands of compassion are like that, then it is our nature to be compassionate. It's not something we have to acquire. It was these words of the old teachers that brought back the image of the little boy washing the farm dog in the washroom tub, trying with soap and water to scrub away the suffering that had happened there, and the memory of the boy who day after day washed and ironed his sick Mother's bedding so that she wouldn't lie on stale sheets. These things were done without any thought of "being compassionate." The boy simply did what his heart called him to do. As Master Daowu was later to add, it's not so much that our body has hands and eyes, it's rather that our whole body *is* hands and eyes. What I sought had been there all along.

I'll never learn to live without doing some harm, but that doesn't mean that my life's wrong somehow. In Zen I found something kinder and more nurturing than troubling myself with whether my life or anyone else's life is a mistake or not. An ancient Zen teacher, Ikkyu, was asked by a monk, "What is Zen?" and he replied, "Attention. Attention. Attention." I came in time to see that the compassion I'd imagined to be a virtue in its own right was just this quality of attention. It remains a wonder to me that if I really look at what is before me, I invariably give my heart to it. Compassion is the gift of oneself, the willingness to show up, to bear witness, to be with others. It's not about mistakes or about being right or wrong. It's better than that.

Empty Fields

*E*ven *before I parked the Jeep* I could see that the field
was empty. Still, I went through the motions, standing at
the fence line scanning the field with binoculars and then
scanning it again with a spotting scope on the chance that somewhere in the acres of grain stubble stiffened under a cold November sky, I would detect the movement of horned larks. But the
effort served only to confirm what I already knew—that there
were no horned larks in this field or in any field where they were
accustomed to flock.

The absence of horned larks in the grass and sage habitat of
eastern California—particularly in fall and winter when they
gather by the thousands—is disorienting. Horned larks are normally so abundant that their presence frequently goes unnoticed.
But the most familiar is also the most pervasive and the most
likely to assert its presence by change or disappearance. When I
realized this year that the larks had disappeared, I felt their
absence as some fundamental disorder, some distressing departure from the usual way of things.

*My father died this winter in early December. And where I sat by
him in his last moments, I saw the living presence in his eyes yield to
absence. Where there had been two of us an instant before, only one
of us remained to count the loss.*

Despite all the birds that have come to occupy their space, my mind still dwells on the absence of horned larks. When Mac McCormick called this winter to tell me he had discovered a rare mountain plover (the first ever reported in our area) in an eighty-acre field otherwise devoid of birds, anxious memory repopulated the field with a flock of four thousand horned larks he and I had come upon two winters ago. Shortly after Mac's call, when I went to see if I could confirm the sighting, the plover was gone, the field still and silent.

In late December, our local Audubon group conducted its annual winter bird count, and from daybreak to dark, teams of birders searched the fields for every individual bird of every species they could find. And when night overtook the effort and we gathered to total up the day's count, only one counter, Dave Shuford, could report even a single horned lark. I took this as confirmation of loss, a last hard fact that no hope of mine could debate. Later, when I looked through Dave's written field report, I saw alongside this entry the notation "heard only." In an area that had recorded over six thousand horned larks in a day's count, we had come down to one thin call that had reached Dave on the still air of a December afternoon.

Had Dave seen as well as heard the horned lark, he would have seen its bright little forehead and face and throat of yellow; he would have seen the black bib and stripe below the eye and one black feather on each side of the crown like miniature horns; he would have seen it fly in short bursts that hugged the ground; and when it landed, he would have seen it like some feathered insect, sprinting in rasping jerks among the stubble. I have clung to Dave's report of that single call as to a ghost crying of continuity and possible return.

My father left behind a wife of sixty-six years, three children, seven grandchildren, and seventeen great-grandchildren. We gathered at his grave this winter to mourn the subtraction of one from the count. Occasionally he calls to us across strangely altered fields of change.

It is the inmost nature of nature to change, and to change absolutely. Nothing can be held back, nothing kept, nothing saved. And however distressing this might seem to us, our survival lies in such radical regeneration, the workings of which are generous beyond the count of loss or gain. The Sierra Valley horned larks are wintering now in some far field unknown to me. But wherever that field is, perhaps someone will be there to see the larks skittering about, gleaning waste grain left from the autumn harvest. Here, some burrowing owls are setting up house in the field the larks left behind.

And Father? Father has gone as well. I don't know where or to what end. I can only witness his absence, accept its necessity, and listen for the still voice of gratitude that whispers within.

The Mind of
the Mountain

een from the north, Mount Shasta rises from the uncompromising flatness of the Klamath Basin, a great snow-crested pyramid thrust into the sky. It's a country where vertical and horizontal are vividly realized as qualities of a single geometry, where the eye, traveling from the plain to the mountain, from the mountain to the plain, sees that in every going up there is a going down, in every going down, a going up. I visited the Klamath Basin in February of the winter my father died, where I saw in the chill waters of the marsh a flock of migrating swans suspended in the inverted image of the mountain, looking as though they had stopped to rest on a mountaintop.

The morning was cold. A wind swept across the waters, insinuating itself into whatever gaps remained around my throat or the back of my neck or my sleeve ends or wherever my woolens did not quite connect. I would have retreated to the shelter of the car but, before I thought to do so, a bald eagle pushed off from its perch and soared through a melee of thousands of scrabbling pintails, the whole event played out in the silent and unassailable presence of the mountain. Ten thousand snow and Ross geese, whose whiteness stood out starkly against the brown winter grass, rose into delicate obscurity against the white flanks of the mountain, their black wing-tips disembodied, stroking white on white. A pair of mating red-tailed hawks in courtship flight soared in dark silhouette across the face of the mountain and, dropping down, led my eyes to where a stack of twigs and grass, layered round and concave to a precise purpose, clung to a cliff face high above Tule Lake. All those lives, like the wind flowing over the basin, were borne forward with the same selfless absorption with which the mountain rose in fire ages ago and with which it now drinks the winter snows.

Whatever swam the basin waters that day, or flew its skies or sunk roots in mud or layered twigs on cliff faces or huddled in heated cars, was secured within the vast scale of the basin and the long reach of the mountain that guarded it. The smallest gesture, the least consequential thought, was given its place in that greater order. The dying father uncurling within my mind brought me to wonder if it was this that his dying eyes had opened on.

In early March, I traveled north again to join fellow Buddhists in a week of meditation at Shasta Abbey, the Zen Buddhist monastery a few miles north of the town of Mount Shasta. On the evening of my arrival, we gathered in the dining hall for our evening meal. As is our custom we ate in silence, the only sounds those of utensils or dishes or the occasional chair sliding across the wooden floor. As is also our custom, we placed the palms of our hands together before our faces and bowed to receive each item of food or drink as it was passed to us along the length of the table. By chance, I was seated facing a long bank of windows that opened toward the north.

When the first dish reached me and I bowed to receive it, I raised my head to see that there, overshadowing the north windows of the dining hall and overshadowing the whole of the monastery and the little town of Shasta itself, was the great upward sweep of the mountain converging to a summit flushed crimson in the late evening sun. And each time I bowed to receive food it was as if I bowed to receive the mountain as well.

The food comes to me and is passed on. The mountain comes and is passed on. In this way we receive our lives and in this way we relinquish them, not once only, but again and again in every moment of our being. Our very mind comes to us in the exact instant of its passing on.

The mind of the mountain is our own mind. There is nothing mystical in this, nothing at odds with the ordinary. We would all see this could we but call ourselves fully into view. In the monk's enclosure beyond the dining hall hangs the temple bell. It waits to be struck that it may call forth itself. In her quarters off the enclosure, the abbess takes her meal alone, her legs paralyzed by the ravages of diabetes. "I am dying from the bottom up," she once declared to the monks. Thus, the abbess yields herself to fact.

Season after season, the mountain called Shasta is wearing down to an inevitable symmetry of its own becoming. Yet, under the thrust of the shouldering oceanic plate, the whole mass of the mountain lifts so that it forms itself by ever rising into its own going down. The abbess too is wearing away into exactly what she is. She rings true when struck. It is just such ordinary stuff that binds our human minds over to that of the mountain. It was this that rose to the minds of the dying father and his son in the time of the father's going down. We are shown this from every side at all times. It inheres in all we are and all we do.

Here in the dining hall when the meal is finished, I will gather up my table things and carry them to the wash stand where I wash each item with the same mindful care with which the nurses of Western Medical Hospital bathed my father's body, taking up one hand at a time to wash between his fingers. When all is clean, I will stack the bowl on the plate and the cup in the bowl. I will lay the knife, fork, and spoon on the plate alongside the bowl. I will drape the white napkin over the stacked items with a name tag showing. Then I will put these things in the cupboard on the dining hall porch and join the others for evening meditation.

I Speak for My Father

My father lived and died without speaking for himself. His thoughts and feelings were sometimes conveyed to me by my mother but, aside from matters of common utility, I got little from him directly. I say now for him what he did not say for himself. I have set myself to do this because I need to know what shape my father takes when put to words. Should I, from the grave of his long silence, unearth some remnant of his unspoken mind, I will surely bring to light something of my own. If I falter along the way, it is because I reconstruct my father's perspective from the most disparate of sources and because the language that describes his world is yet new to me.

Harslev, Denmark, 1916. The Percheron stallion shows dark against the horizon, its coat of blue-black darker even than the rich earth curling off the shearing edge of the plow. The plow strains against the resisting soil but the Percheron moves forward with a containment and strength that never breaks stride. There where the field slopes down to the shore, an evening light streams in across the North Sea, painting the water silver and reflecting off the rippling muscles of the great draft animal.

My father, small and slim, only a boy of seventeen years, follows the plow. He doesn't stumble along in the furrow as so many do, struggling with the plow handles and jerking the reins to bring the horse back on line. Instead he walks easily on the unturned edge of earth, one hand teasing the plow to its proper depth, the reins resting lightly on his shoulders, his free hand telegraphing its message along the reins, telling the Percheron what is required.

My father, who has hired out to work a neighbor's fields, is the youngest of the hands on Jens Pederson's farm. Yet he alone works the stallion. The morning my father came down from Eilskov, Jens Pederson led the animal from its stall and put the halter lead into my father's hands. "This is the best I've ever owned," he told him. "He needs to learn harness. Were your father able, Jochum Christian is the only one I'd trust the animal to." And so my father brings the big stallion down the day's last pass of the field toward the sea, the Percheron pressing itself against the hames, the traces drawn tight, my father guiding the bite of the plow so that nothing goes slack. Beyond the field, the surf runs with the tide up the shallow rise of the sea's edge.

At the foot of the field, my father tilts the plow out of its furrow and brings the stallion to rest. He unbuckles the traces and secures them to the hames for the return to the barn. But then he pauses, his eyes searching the sea, his hand resting on the animal's flank. He has decided what to do. He drags the harness from the stallion's back and hangs it over the handles of the resting plow. He takes up the reins and starts the Percheron down to the water.

The Percheron strides onto the slate gray stones of the beach with my father trotting after. Flocks of gulls scatter and wheel overhead, their cries riding away on the breeze. The Percheron reaches the water, hesitating, its knees lifting high. For an instant, father fears that the stallion will balk. Then a ripple of gathering strength runs through the haunches of the great animal and it plunges forward, legs pumping against the pull of the surf, the salt spray staining its coat even darker.

The long shallow slope of the beach gradually deepens, the Percheron parting the incoming waves. Father crowds in behind to escape the drag of the water. Still he goes on. He does this for the boy he once was who, at seven years, stood with his younger sister, Annette, and his younger brother, Acten, and his older brother, Johannes, and his eldest brother, Julius, the first born, in the courtyard of the Eilskov farm where the women had told them to stand. He drives now deeper into the sea for this boy who watched when the men came from the isolation hospital dressed in white coats buttoned tight at the throat and wrist, with white gloves and gauze masks concealing their faces under heads bound tightly in cloth. He does this for the boy whose mother was taken from her bed and carried past him to the waiting wagon as she lay on the stretcher, her face turned toward him where he stood with his brothers and sister, her large, soft eyes searching her children's faces. He urges the great stallion on now for the boy who saw in his mother's eyes a presence that frightened him and who started toward her but was pulled away by the women just as he heard his mother's sharp command, "Stay back!" He goes deeper now for the boy whose father hid in the house until the hospital wagon had disappeared in the mist beyond the hedge.

And my father goes on for the boy whose father lost his mind to a stroke, his eyes crazed, his high, pale forehead twisted by paralysis, all his beautiful, articulate speech turned to gurgling incoherence. He goes on for the boy whose father shivered and drooled and coughed up whatever he was fed and whose once-gifted hand which coaxed to harness the most willful horse, fidgeted uselessly now at the bed covers, but who still could not die.

And most of all, he goes on for the boy of seventeen who, night after night, hearing his father cry out in startled madness, held him to his bed so that he would not go raging about on his knees in the darkened bedroom. He does this for the boy who, fearing the loss of his own mind, pleaded with his brother, Julius, to take over the care of their father for him because he couldn't bear the horror of it anymore. He goes on for the boy who, broken and disappointed in himself, ashamed that he had abandoned his father's need, retreated to the farm of Jens Pederson where he was given the reins of the great Percheron stallion.

My father, following the Percheron into the sea, is nearly afloat now. He threads the fingers of one hand through the coarse hairs of its tail, leaving his other free to manage the reins. He can go perhaps a hundred yards more before the beach drops out from under the horse, leaving it awash in the surf. At any moment, the animal could drop into a depression and be lost. My father knows that he could not face Jens Pederson alive if this were to happen. But the Percheron churns on into ever deepening water, the surf breaking over its back now, my father taking the animal to the absolute edge of his capacity to control it.

And then it steps off the ledge and plunges beneath the water. My father is dragged under, the reins stripped from his hand. He holds on by the base of the Percheron's tail and draws himself onto its back until he can reach the mane. He feels the powerful muscles of the stallion still driving its legs, seeking some firmness underfoot that will move it forward. My father has gone beyond all rules, all rehearsal, all practiced elements of control. He needs his father's gift now as he has never needed it before. Knowing this, my father suspends all judgment and, reaching beyond anything he knows to do, he wills the Percheron to calmness, until it gradually stops thrashing and, when it does, the quantity of water its great bulk displaces brings it to the surface. The animal's legs, suspended in water, slowly revolve, inching it forward until at last the hooves make contact. Father retrieves the reins and turns the horse toward shore.

Harslev, Denmark, 1919. In summer, the young people hear the music drifting across the fields from the pavilion above the town pond. The women have already ironed their dresses and bathed themselves, and now they hurry the supper things off the table, food returned to the cooler, plates and utensils scoured and dried and stacked on cupboard shelves. The men too have bathed before eating. They have brushed down their best pants and jackets, and now they make the last rounds of the stock and go to dress themselves.

The music is lively and the dancers whirl, their motions duplicated in shadows the pavilion lights cast on the surface of the pond. My father has become very popular and he dances nearly every dance. He wears a tie and keeps his jacket neatly buttoned throughout the evening, not stripping it off to dance in a shirt and loosened tie as some others do. His hair is rich auburn and lies in waves, his forehead smooth, and broad. Some sort of dark knowledge shows in his eyes, which is at once troubling and attractive to the women. His mouth is full and sensual. The young women put themselves in his way by design, hoping he will ask them to dance. If he doesn't, they sometimes ask him. A few have seen him in the fields stripped to the waist, his body lean and muscular, the big stallion moving easily under his command. At twenty, my father is a good prospect for marriage. Some of the women view him this way. Others simply want to feel his arms around them.

My father is only vaguely aware of his attractiveness. His mother gone so early, he has learned little about women. Outside the work of the fields, he has felt mostly uncertainty and shyness. How to talk to a woman, how to walk with her or dance or ask for what you want from her—all this is beyond my father's knowing. But Jens Pederson's wife has made him shirts, and Jens Pederson himself has sent to Odense for proper dress clothes. The young women—Pederson's own domestic help and daughters from neighboring farms—have coaxed my father out of his shyness. His dancing is not polished. When he takes the women in his arms, his lead is more insistence than request. He feels a certain mastery in this. He feels wonderful.

Harslev, Denmark, 1920. Lying on the cot in the darkened stable room, my father has no clear hopes or fears. He has only pain. He has lain here, fevered and delirious, until time is only a vague uncertainty. He remembers everything that led up to that exact moment in the hay loft when something gave way in him— the shortness of breath, the dizziness, the gradual onset of weakness, the will it took to finish a day's work, his refusal to speak of these things. He remembers the bale being passed up to him. He remembers taking its weight and shifting it onto his knees, burying the hay hooks and swinging it up, the force of his body behind the lift. And then he remembers only pain, the hot shock of it beneath his shoulder blade.

Pain was all there was—the lantern hanging from the stable room rafters, my father's eyes swimming up into the dim glow of it, the women wiping sweat from his eyes, the gasps that escaped him from the sheer pain of breathing. He does not remember the fever that came as a blessing to blot out his mind. Nor does he remember the light that came and went from the stable room window in the days that followed, nor the ice that was packed around him, nor the bedclothes that were stripped and freshened daily, nor even the broth that was spooned into him as one of the women propped him up while another tilted his head back to get him to swallow.

He remembers finding himself here in the night, a gradual and dim awakening. He remembers rolling onto his stomach, his face pushed into the cot, straining to get his arm over his shoulder, reaching for the source of his pain, his fingers tracing the contour of what he discovers there, the full extent of his deformity, the awful ruin of it, his hand clamped hard over his mouth, his own father's agonies piercing his ears. Afterward, he can't tolerate the sunshine and asks that the window be covered.

In the kitchen and in the milk barn, the young women whisper of my father as of one dead; they speak of pity and loss that such a young beauty has been brought down. My father, lying in the darkened room, has made a decision. His own father, forever blighted and wasting away, will surely die soon, and Julius, the eldest son, will inherit the Eilskov farm. There is no future here. If my father heals enough to work again, he will save his earnings and emigrate to America.

Orange, California, 1927. My father is having his picture taken. He has bought himself a car. The car has a retractable cloth top and full seats, front and back. He has already met Lucy Goslee, and the car is big enough to take her and her parents or her friends wherever they want to go. He poses for the picture in a suit and tie with a dark overcoat. He stands by the car, one hand resting on the window ledge, declaring his ownership. With the other arm, elbow cocked out, he holds a dress hat to his side. He has already secured his citizenship and has steady employment caring for a local orchard. He feels prosperous and looks directly into the lens.

Laguna Beach, California, May 1, 1928. My father walks on the beach below the lighted windows of the hotel. It is his wedding night and the newlyweds have come to the little resort on the cliffs above the beach that Lucy chose. It has cost them a lot of money and their stay will be short. They are both virgins, and my father, gripped by sudden shyness and uncertainty, has excused himself and gone out "for a little air and a quick smoke." My mother has never even seen him with his shirt off and, though he has spoken briefly of its existence, he has never exposed for her the hump that projects from his back. He paces back and forth, postponing for just another moment the very thing he wants most of all. In the room with the elegant curtains, where yellow roses repeat themselves in the dressing table mirror, my mother waits for his return. She is not yet eighteen and has no experience to guide her. Yet, when my father returns, she will behave as if she believes he had only gone out for a smoke and some air, and though she aches for him to have what she offers, she will bring him to it as gently as she can.

Later, lying warmed and delighted, they touch each other everywhere and he tells her she is not Lucy Goslee anymore, but Lucy Jensen. They do not know they have wed on the eve of the century's worst depression.

Orange, California, 1934. My father is indignant that my mother and Doctor Robbins refer to his condition as a "nervous breakdown." His back hurts and he can't sleep nights. He's just tired, he tells himself. People with nervous breakdowns end up in the county mental hospital. Is that where they think he belongs? Then who will put food on the table? He hasn't time for a breakdown.

He watches Mother now as she clears away the dishes. It's Sunday noon after church. Father sits in his dress pants and white shirt at the head of the table. Mother has baked a cake and Rowland has been told he can't have any until he finishes his vegetables. He picks desultorily at some cooked carrots, his chubby fingers separating them from the onions, which he hates. I sit in an infant chair pulled up to the table. I am towheaded and my teeth are bucked, pushing my upper lip out. Mother moves back and forth from the kitchen. She wears a summer dress and an apron pulled snug at her waist. She lifts her hair from her neck to cool herself. Father's mood is softened by this. He thinks she is beautiful. He wishes he had her alone to himself. He wishes he felt better.

Later, Father will change into work clothes and go into the back yard to clean the coops and feed the small flock of turkeys he is raising there. His neighbors think this a nuisance and complain of the noise and smell. But Father thinks he can make some money this way. In time, he thinks, he can lease some acreage and expand his flock. He would like to buy Mother something nice.

Garden Grove, California, 1940. Mother has given birth to my sister, Evelyn, who, six years after my own birth, was not intended. The delivery, difficult and prolonged, has left Mother badly shaken. She suffers frequently from what she calls "sick headaches" and goes to bed claiming she is ill. She complains that she can't control Rowland and me. "They're out of hand. You have to do something," Mother insists. He does something. He orders us to the bedroom and flails away at us with a lath stick, beating once and for all some lasting order into his life.

Later from behind his newspaper, he sees Rowland come down the stairs and go into the kitchen. But I am the son who crawls up on his lap insisting on how sorry I am. And neither father nor son has any idea what the son is supposed to be sorry for. My father is fearful of his son's softness, his easy tears, his unguarded capitulation, his hunger that love be made known. It bends him in places he thinks ought to remain straight. This son of his exposes an injury in him like that of the hump on his back.

Awakening in the night, he hears my mother crying in an adjacent room. He is certain she wants him to hear her. For a moment, he pities and forgives her this weakness. But his own old night dread stiffens him and prevents him from going to her. "Come to bed, Lucy," he calls, hearing a sharpness in his voice he had not intended.

Santa Ana, California, 1964. My father sits in the farm office, a lined and columned financial ledger opened on the desk before him. To his left are a pad and sharpened pencils lined up in readiness for his use. To his right is a calculating machine with numbered keys and a handle that cranks out the tape. He wears glasses and holds a fountain pen for making finished entries in the ledger. The ledger documents three consecutive years of heavy losses. Mostly he has leased cheap land to raise his turkeys on, but by sheer chance the single forty acres he bought for its good house and hatchery buildings has become more valuable than he or any of his neighbors who have been selling off their land for retirement ever thought possible. Father knows now that he will do the same. He can't make a living raising turkeys anymore. And though the boom in Orange County has bailed him out of otherwise certain bankruptcy, my father, who has worked for years to make the turkey farm pay off, resents being rescued by accident.

Rowland, whom he has kept at home, will have no farm to inherit. It angers my father that he can do nothing to make the outcome otherwise. He is glad I have found a place elsewhere teaching at a college. He imagines me among those books he so often saw me read when I was still a child. He wonders what it is that his wife and son talk about when I come to visit. He thinks of Evelyn, married now, she and her young husband already wealthy from real estate investment. Perhaps he has been too cautious? He remembers the Percheron powering its way into the surf. He remembers the women, turning flushed and young in his arms at the pavilion above the pond. He remembers the car in which he drove Lucy Goslee to the movies. He cannot believe it all ends in a ledger page that won't balance.

He locks the door to the office and goes into the house to ask my mother something he has not asked her in years. He finds her in bed. She is not feeling well and thinks she should lie down for a while. He asks her anyway. He asks her if she'd like to drive over to Long Beach to Vivian Laird's. "We could have supper and dance." She asks if she can take a raincheck.

Orange, California, spring 1993. Gradually this house of his retirement has taken my father prisoner. He has lost the will and the strength to leave it. He relies on my mother to help him through the day. He sleeps most of the time. He is ashamed of this and tells Rowland that this is "no way for a man to live." None of us knows the extent of the cancer that eats his body away and makes his least effort heroic.

He tells Evelyn that he needs to die. He wants her help. She tells him she can't help him that way. He asks her to draw the curtains because the light hurts his eyes. But in the darkened room he sees once more the long night of his father's eyes, vacant of any mind a son might recognize. He sees his mother, carried helpless and doomed, beyond his reach, to the waiting wagon.

Tustin, California, December 8, 1993. The nurses, alerted by the monitor, converge on my father's bed to confirm what I already know—he is dead. The nurses know only his remains—that he has no pulse, that respiration has stopped, that his temperature has plunged, that his hair will continue to grow for some hours yet. They do not know that in my father's last moments the gift of his own father returned to his hands. They do not know that he took up the reins once more and, looking beyond his fear, drove himself into the sea.

This body of mine—eyes, ears, nose, lips, chin, forehead, height, weight—owes more to my father than to any other source. I look like him. Now, in these paragraphs, I discover that I think much like him as well. I acknowledge him once and for all, the last of whatever opposition stood between our two natures put aside. I am my father's son. I hear in all I say the language of his long silence. He survives in what I do and what I am. I have entered the deep waters with him.

Shaking Down

At a recent stay at Shasta Abbey, I happened to learn of a practice the monks kept while traveling by car. Whenever they saw the remains of a road kill—some squirrel or deer or raccoon, some dog or cat or magpie or hawk all scattered, torn, or crushed along the swift margins of pavement—all but the driver would raise their hands, palm to palm before bowed heads, and intone a brief memorial to the slain animal. When circumstances permitted, the monks sometimes stopped and performed a short roadside burial and service. "It's one way," they told me, "to pay homage to the source of life."

It's not possible, the monks said, to live without doing harm to others—and this is as true of driving as with anything else. But, they explained, you can do a lot less harm by slowing down and by braking or swerving to avoid collision wherever possible. No one, they told me, could drive the agricultural roads of California's Central Valley in spring or summer without killing insects, whose tiny deaths accumulate in splatters on the windshield. "But we have learned that if you drive slowly in these areas, it's possible to kill far fewer. And when we stop, we can say a brief memorial for the ones we have killed."

At the end of a week I left the monastery and drove home. I had not gone thirty miles when, along a stretch of road lined with deep woods, I came upon a smear of fur and raw flesh stamped onto the pavement by the continual passing of automobile tires. Flung against a cut bank nearby was the crumpled blackness of a raven that had been drawn to feed on whatever had been killed trying to cross the road. I was alone in the car but in my mind's eye I saw the monks from Shasta press their hands together and bow to the two lives that had ended there.

My thought goes back to a brief incident of this past winter. It was early morning, a dark half-light and quite cold. I awoke to find that Karen had already left the bed. Getting up myself, I found the living room warming from a fire Karen had started in the stove, but she herself was nowhere in the house. And then I saw her from the living room window. She was bundled up in a parka with a hood, and she wore gloves and snow boots that irregularly broke through the frozen crust of the snow as she walked, causing her to sink suddenly and struggle to keep her balance.

I saw then where she was headed in all that frozen darkness. She was making her way to the seed feeder we had set out for the winter birds. The seed on the platform and in the feeder tubes was covered over and frozen, and she was concerned that the wakening birds would be deprived of a food source they had come to depend on. It was a simple act; just a natural sympathy that had arisen in her, some sense of responsibility she felt for having raised expectations in a flock of thirty or so juncos.

At the feeder, she scraped some stiff snow off the platform. Then she took each of the two feeder tubes in hand and shook them until seed fell down to where the birds could get to it. How sensible and ordinary an act. And yet, in that shaking there, something shook down in me, settled, and was taken up again in nourishment throughout the whole of that winter day and still feeds me now.

My mother, eighty-four-years-old, called me recently on the phone. She was newly widowed this past winter and she said to me, "You know, son, I have never before lived alone." But she'd no sooner said that then she launched into the latest episodes involving Mike, an aging dog she and my father had shared their lives with for many years. She was telling me about the relationship Mike had established with Charlie, a yearling cat my sister had brought to help keep her and Mike company. Apparently, Charlie had done the trick, for here was our mother telling me not only how much Charlie cheered her up but how his kittenish antics had finally coaxed Mike off the foot of the bed where her husband had once lain and which Mike had refused to leave for hours at a time. As she went on about these things, I saw that my mother was not, in fact, living alone.

We humans are not living alone. The earth teems with countless lives other than our own. If we listen, our hearts are always telling us this. We are well advised to slow down, be prepared to brake or swerve if necessary, reduce the extent of our harm, pay homage. Everywhere I look, I see some shaking down to be done.

Window Birds

In early October I crawled down off a ladder where I was caulking some siding on the house, doubled up with a pain that emanated from my lower back and traveled down my leg. I went into the house and lay down on this very bed where I now compose this essay.

Today is November 16th and with the exception of the most necessary movement inside the house and a few outings, such as being driven to therapy or to the Reno Diagnostic Center for an MRI or for consultation with a neurosurgeon, I have lain exactly here since I descended that ladder a month and a half ago.

From the bed, I look through windows that open to the southwest. I can see a forested ridge that rises from the grassy field where the house is situated. Today the ridge is shrouded in gray and snow blows through the trees. Gusts of cold wind shoulder against the house causing the snow to whirl about the windows, and through this gauzy dimness I can see trees thrashing on the ridge above. I can see all this, lying on my back with my knees elevated to ease the pain that is perpetually with me. I can also see five little apple trees that Karen and I planted and the vegetable garden with its neat little plots all laid out and carefully fenced against the wind and the browsing deer.

It was on a day such as this a couple of weeks ago that the window birds came. Karen had gone to town for supplies, and I was alone in the house. It was about three in the afternoon, and the pain had come upon me in a hard way. I had taken a tablet of Vicodin, a narcotic prescribed for severe pain, and I was lying right here as I am now, trying to resist the futility of squirming about. I was exhausted. The best that could be said was that if hope had collapsed for the time I was still holding on.

And then great tears formed, overran the sockets of my eyes and spilled down the sides of my face. They did not feel like tears of my own making. They came as from the recesses of some common well of sorrow beyond the depths of any personal grief I might have known. They dropped silently. Through the smeared lenses of my eyes, beyond the window I could see the snow turn on the wind of a darkening sky.

Then there fluttered up into the window space, their wings brushing the very glass itself, the silhouettes of a small flock of sparrows. They seemed blown up against the window, carried like the snow on the force of the wind. They dropped out of sight beneath the level of the sill and rode up again into view. The wind swung them through the apple trees where they grabbed perches on the winter-bared limbs that pitched and shuddered beneath them. As they clung there for a second, I could make out the dark hoods of the juncos among them and the lateral crown stripes of a few white-crowned sparrows. There were perhaps a dozen of them gripping the tossing branches of the little trees, their feathers blown backward. Then as one they all let go and disappeared in the darkness up the ridge.

But even before the little flock was lost to sight, while I could still see them bobbing in the wind, I realized that an unlikely and surprising delight had overtaken me in the midst of my pain and that for the moment the whole circumstance of my life was taken up in this momentary joy.

Joy is an act of love. I loved the little birds and the wind and the trees; the tears that blurred these same eyes loved the birds and the wind and the trees; the wet skin of my face loved the birds; the breath that moved in me loved them; my whole body, where it lay injured with its useless legs propped up on pillows loved them; the very pain itself where it rolled out in waves from my injured spine loved the little birds and the wind and the trees.

The window birds are memory now. Beyond the window, I see the garden buried in snow. The wintering earth lies fallow and waits, as I lie here fallow and wait, as everywhere, in all places, at all times, and in all beings, joy lies fallow and waits.

Maintenance

These words are being written from a room in a house that has recently become for me a temporary residence. The walls and ceiling of the room are covered in rare and beautiful vertical-grained Douglas fir, all heartwood, rescued from a fire-burned ridge in the Santa Cruz Mountains of Northern California. The windows and doors are framed of clear, kiln-dried redwood. The floor is laid with Spanish-red paving bricks underlain by an inch of mortar, small-mesh wire, thirty-pound felt, and a tight sub floor. Each brick, 3460 of them, was lifted by hand and grouted in place by Karen and me. Every wall and ceiling board, every inch of trim, was milled and cut and nailed in place by the two of us. From the first spade full of rocky earth torn loose to allow for its concrete footing, to its cabinets and bookshelves that now hold all the personal possessions either of us owns, this house was built by we who were to live in it and who would come in time to know it as "home."

But now, only seven years since the Plumas County building inspector signified that our work was finished and that Karen and I could move in, a sign has been posted at the entrance to our drive declaring to all who travel Plumas County Road A-23 that the house we built is for sale. I can see the sign from our kitchen window. It is about four feet square, tacked to a post and cross arm and, though it faces away from me toward the road, I know its message by heart: LYNN WELCH REALITY, 20 ACRES, CUSTOM SOLAR HOME.

When Karen and I retired, she from a hospital pharmacy and I from teaching and carpentry, we had thought to live out the remainder of our lives on these twenty acres, in this house, within walls grown as familiar to us as our own aging images in the mirror. But now, whenever I return from some outing with a load of groceries or gas for the snow blower or anything else, Lynn Welch Realty is there to remind me that I am once more a person in transition.

When buyers come to look at our home, we point out everything good about it: the yard that Karen landscaped so beautifully, the vegetable plot with raised beds, the compost bins, the garden shed, the woodshed where cords of firewood are stacked. We fairly glow with enthusiasm, so naturally we are sometimes asked why we are leaving. When confronted with this question, I offer up the obvious and plausible response that a recent injury to my spine prevents me from continuing the heavy work of maintaining the place.

What I don't tell the questioner is how much I regret not doing the things that need doing and that Karen and I have always done together. I don't tell how the demands of our mountain life measure with distressing accuracy the exact extent of my daily inadequacies, and of the loss that this evokes in me. I tell of it now because I want to show how loss itself cancels the source of its own distress.

My knowledge of the self-healing qualities of misfortune came with a shocking injury to my spine that left me lying helplessly in bed with legs so useless I was reduced to crawling to the bathroom in order to reach the toilet. Throughout those days, I could hear Karen moving about in the other rooms, hauling in armloads of firewood, shoveling snow away from the outside doors and digging her way to the woodshed so that she might haul in wood again, and then mopping her own muddy tracks off the floor. I could hear her cooking and washing and carrying kitchen waste to the compost bin and doing these things over and over again. Beyond all this, I had no option but to watch her care for my needs as well, bringing me water and food and tablets of codeine and Vicodin, endlessly bringing me these things day after day, night after night, week after week. And still in the early morning, when she herself was hopelessly exhausted, she would try just this once more to rub the pain away.

I could do nothing to ease the burden on her. And I knew (for I had been explicitly told) that when the surgery I was awaiting had restored me to my feet, much that I had always done I would never do again: "No weights over twenty-five pounds, no repetitive movement of an extended duration, no twisting, compacting, or sudden bending of the spine." I would never again do any sustained carpentry or turn clover under in the garden or drag up a few bales of hay for mulching or split wood. I would never backpack or turn a somersault or jump to the ground from even the most modest height or run the length of half a block. I lay in bed looking up at the ceiling Karen and I had nailed in place, and I felt once again the familiar fear of losing myself, of not knowing who I was or how and where I might ever be found again. Nailing ceilings, one nails a wood tongued-and-grooved board in place while standing on planks laid across sawhorses. A partner helps secure the board while the nailer bends backward pushing the groove hard onto the tongue with one hand and driving the nail in with the other. I would never nail another ceiling. The life I had lived for all these years was impossible now and I had no option but to let it go. And in that yielding I saw more clearly than ever before what sorts of ceilings and walls I'd been building all these years.

I saw that I had tried to construct my life as I had built this house, with some fixed and lasting sense of myself nailed securely in place. I saw that no life so constructed could be held secure against the exigencies of time and circumstance, that I must inevitably exhaust myself in futile maintenance of such a structure. A lifetime of certainties fell about me in disrepair. I could no longer conceptualize who I was, and in that very loss the healing was found.

Knowing we must move on, Karen and I recently drove over the mountains to see if Chico, California, might be a place for us to live. The town has a state university, and Karen thinks she would like to go back to school for a while. Of course, there's much adventure in an excursion like this, yet at times we both felt a little forlorn. The motel room was unfamiliar, its papered walls not those of our own making. The toilet was sealed sanitary with a strip of paper, a precaution some stranger had taken on our behalf. The towels smelled of detergent we were unaccustomed to. And when we sought out the weather channel on a TV so awkwardly hung as to be viewable only while lying on the bed, the meteorologist bore a face we didn't recognize.

But we persisted in our intent and were able to join a small group of local residents on a wildflower outing to nearby Table Mountain. On the mountain we walked with the others on a windswept plateau where tiny flowers of yellow and blue hugged the rocky earth. Karen and the other women talked among themselves, and when they turned down along a little stream toward a falls, I was drawn uphill to see what species of sparrow it was that moved so low among the grasses. The birds turned out to be lark sparrows. In my trailing after them, I found myself on a prominence that lay an unobstructed horizon about me on all sides. I turned slowly, 360 degrees. In all that space there was nothing, not even a trace of the very steps that had brought me there, to suggest where one might go next. I understood that I could, at that moment, walk in any of all possible directions.

We invent ourselves that we might know who we are and what we are to be. But the consistency we seek in these inventions can't be maintained against the fabulous inconsistency of actuality. Sensing this, we clutch at cherished constants ever more urgently. The builder of the house of ego can never rest, for he is ever at work to control outcome and limit alternatives. His structure makes its appeal to our longing for the familiar and the safe, but in the end, he delivers only diminishment. I am weary of maintenance.

Noise

T *he sound of the bees* reached me even with the windows closed and the refrigerator running. I was washing the breakfast dishes, water splashing into the sink, my mind intent on the task, when I became aware of the beginnings of a sound like that of wind trapped against the eaves of the house or like the first hushed vibrations from a cello when the bow is drawn across the strings.

Karen and I have recently moved from the mountains into the town of Chico, and here where we live there are lots of competing sounds. Noise, mostly, I call it. It's hard to distinguish one sound from the other: the sizzle of tires on the nearby freeway like fat perpetually frying; the whine of power mowers and leaf blowers and chain saws; the moaning hydraulics of trash trucks and street sweepers; the thump of stereos from passing cars; the hysterical utterances of triggered alarm systems and the sirens of emergency vehicles; the clatter and grind of trains along the rails west of town, their horns marking the crossings; the whine of the helicopter lifting from the roof of Enloe Hospital; dogs barking from the confinement of backyards; the voices of humans, their shouts, laughter, fragments of conversation. Sometimes I am so drowned in the noise of others that the sound of my own life is rendered mute. I can't hear myself.

That's the way it was the morning I stood at the sink washing the breakfast dishes. So it was all the more surprising that I heard the bees at all because they had to penetrate the peculiarly distracting racket that noise makes. But the bees reached me with a sound that separated itself out from the rest. I shut the faucet off. Listened. Wondered. I went to the door and when I pulled it open the sound was suddenly and greatly amplified. On the back porch, it took me a minute to realize that the space above my head was alive with a great swarm of bees.

A catalpa tree overhangs my back yard. Its heart-shaped leaves, some as large as the spread of two hands, arch overhead like the hollow of a parachute blown open by the force of its descent. The slant of the sun that morning lit up the catalpa leaves so that their undersides showed translucent, shimmering greenly with a radiance that seemed self-originating. It was here that I discovered the bees, hundreds of them, in streaks of random intricacy, crisscrossing the hollow beneath the tree, their bodies glowing like tiny golden satellites flung against a firmament of luminous leaves. The bees had reached me with the sound of light. They were gathering me into the sun's song, into the source of my own song.

We can't fabricate our being, we can only receive it. To be alive means to receive ourselves, not once only but ever, and not from our own hand but always from the hand of something other. We exist as ourselves through the agency of what is not ourselves. "To be" means to be in relationship. Our eyes, ears, tongues, bodies are the gates of our being, the hinges upon which our minds swing. It is not so much that we take hold of life by going out through these gates as that life takes hold of us by coming in. We enter ourselves in this manner.

A sound like that of the bees has this power of confirming, of gathering us into the moment of our mutual presence. This gathering is an act of mind. It is reciprocal: mind recognizing the presence of mind, mind receiving mind. In what we call noise, the mind fails to discern the presence of itself.

We may frequently judge noise annoying, but it is not the annoyance that defines noise as such. The crows in my neighborhood are feeding their young these days. Sometimes they persist in their raucous cawing from dawn to dark. My neighbor, on his way to work the other morning, couldn't contain his annoyance any longer. He stood under the tree in his front yard and ordered the crows to "Shut up!" The sound of a crow shares with the sound of a leaf-blower the capacity to be judged annoying, but the sound of a crow arises from the common well of silence; it lives in itself and is thus capable of calling the mind into a living relationship. The sound of a leaf-blower is noise, not because such noise is an irritant, but because noise is a sound in which all the spaces are crammed allowing no entry for the living silence from which our own voice arises.

Our human voices, in speech or song, in laughter or weeping, in sigh or gasp or groan, would be incomprehensible without this attendant silence. The dawn song of a meadowlark, the rasp of a cricket under the darkening hedge, the notes of a violin concerto, the chime of a doorbell, the crunch of footsteps on a graveled path would each be only noise except that their silence is as audible to us as their sound.

This silence, which is both space and pause, is inherent in all beings. Our body manifests it as pulse, the pause between heartbeats, the point of rest between the exhalation and inhalation of breath. Such silence resides in the very tissues of which we are formed: in the spaces separating the material components of our cells, in the structured vacancy that allows for the dance of molecules, in the infinitesimal vastness of the atom where electrons orbit the charged nucleus, in the furthest descent into the microbeing of our existence where matter dissolves into space, and silence is all that is left.

The mind too is characterized by space and pause. Our perceptions arise as intervals of motion within a ground of stillness. Such stillness is integral to all thought and makes consciousness itself possible. In December 1995 I underwent spinal surgery, and for five hours I lay unconscious. Later, when consciousness returned, it came to me first as sound. I heard someone say, "How are you doing, Mister Jensen? The surgery went fine." Then through the haze the face of a woman took shape bending over me where I lay. Tufts of red hair showed at the edges of her nursing cap, freckles, the eyes coming clear and as green as the gown she wore. "Doctor Fleming will be in to see you soon. The surgery went just fine," she repeated. I could not have expressed then what I know to say now: that the anesthesia that had temporarily taken away the motion of my mind had also taken its stillness; that, with the return of sound, silence was returned to me as well. It spoke from each of us to the other, her silence and mine.

I speak of this incident because we are all exposed, chronically and fatally, to the numbing assault of noise. Everywhere we go the incessant noise of our machinery wears away at the life-sustaining stillness of our natural minds. It invades even our speech where the dulling monologue of television, allowing no response, closes all gaps, shuts tight all spaces, squeezes out all stillness, so that we are put to sleep long before bedtime. In such an environment either we awaken or we ourselves become machines.

The silence within us seeks the silence without; the silence within is the silence without. In this way I am gathered into the sound of the bees. The hum of their tiny wings holds deepest converse with the spaces between things, the silent interstices of the mind. The being that arises from this silence arises every moment and is common to all, at once singular and universal, neither one nor many, forming itself out of its own absence.

Night Talk

Karen *awakened me* in the middle of the night a few weeks ago to tell me that she loves me. I lay looking up into the darkness while Karen explained as carefully and completely as she could exactly how much and why she loved me. She had thrown an arm over me, and as she talked, she patted me in a most comforting way and tucked the bedding around my shoulders to keep out the winter chill. She told me that I was the best thing that had ever happened to her and that no one had ever listened to her or cared about her in the way that I do. She thanked me for the most ordinary things: cooking supper, cleaning up around the house, changing the bedding, helping her to word a letter to the editor that she was particularly concerned to get right. She told me that I am her "very best friend" and how sad it was to think that some people never had a friend like that. She herself, she explained, might have gone her whole life without such a friend, might have died without having known anyone who truly loved her.

Then she said, "You be careful when you work on the roof tomorrow. I don't know what I'd do if something happened to you." I heard in her voice that old, plaintive wish that what was certain to happen someday would please not happen yet. The fifteen years that separates our ages occupied the room like a third presence. It passed like a shadow across the east windows where the sycamore limbs swayed under the lash of a wind-driven rain; it sat on the foot of the bed, where it threatened to insinuate itself under the covers and wedge itself between us.

When Karen reaches my present age of seventy-three, I will be eighty-eight—should I live that long. She is almost certain to end her life alone. How often, since first we talked of this and chose nonetheless to join our lives together, has this outcome passed in detail before my eyes? I see the bag of groceries hauled home from the market, the key turned in the lock of a darkened house, lights switched on, a supper cooked and eaten alone. What does one do when the supper things are put away, a shower taken, phone calls made, reading grown stale? Sometimes when I am absorbed in some task, as I am now writing these words, Karen will call to me from another room—and I imagine that solitary call resonating, unheard and unanswered, through the vacant rooms.

Yet there's tenderness unlike any other in these night talks of ours. It radiates, like the midnight stones of some south-facing wall, a collected warmth that darkness itself seems to generate. Someday, our two lives, like all lives, will be torn apart. Knowing this gives rise to the darkest and bravest of our conversations. At such times, we place our hearts unguarded into each other's hands.

There are other times of course when the difference in our ages and what that might mean to either of our futures doesn't distress us at all. Yet it seems to me rather wonderful that loss, or the fear of loss, can redeem itself in moments of such treasured intimacy, as if mortality chooses love for its companion. Sometimes our deepest love holds conversation in the darkest places. And after all, none of us knows what will actually happen in our lives. But in the meantime it's easy to see that anyone's separation is only a breath away, and the goodness in really knowing that makes every breath your very last and your very best.

Bicycling

he fact that a bicycle is mounted on two wheels, not three, makes it possible to crash. It is also this feature that makes not crashing so indelible an accomplishment that one need never crash again. Resume bicycling in your mid-sixties, as I have recently done, and you will find, barring having had a stroke or similar problem, that you don't crash. Yet the first time through, beginning with the afternoon Dad dropped the training wheels from your new Schwinn, you were taking out hedges and rearranging primroses in your mother's favorite flowerbed and remodeling corners of the house until your elbows and knees were plastered over with the last of the Band-Aids in the medicine cabinet.

Then one day you managed the length of the driveway without mishap, and that was that. You never had to fear crashing again. Oh, you could accidentally run into things, or things could run into you, but the intrinsic certainty of crashing was put aside for good. So learning to ride a bicycle is not properly a matter of learning at all, but rather of getting the feel of the thing. It turns out that the feel of the thing requires an exquisite sense of balance maintained by delicate and intricate mechanisms of instantaneous adjustment well beyond the scope of anything one could ever do on purpose. In riding a bicycle, one becomes an intuitive instrument of self-correction, sensing the exact and only point of equilibrium available in the instant, and doing so without benefit of decision. The feel of riding a bicycle is beyond the mechanics of choice.

I myself enact this ordinary little improbability almost daily now. Chico, the town that is my home, is located in California's central valley where the land is flat and bicycling is a common means of getting about. We have bought a modest, older house in a neighborhood known as "The Avenues" where the pavement is shaded by the arching limbs of mature trees, and sidewalks are raised into little hills by the spread of their roots. We are at most ten bicycle-minutes from the campus of the California State University, about the same from Chico High School, Enloe Hospital, Bidwell Park, the farmer's market, and Cory's Restaurant in the center of town. Finding automobile parking at any of these destinations ranges from difficult to impossible—so nearly everyone in circumstances such as ours rides a bicycle.

With the car retired to the garage, my travels are more public now. Everything one does on a bicycle is done more openly than in a car. On a bicycle, no steel or glass wraps around you to divide your activities from the activities of others. No sounds or utterances of any sort are sealed in or out. No carpeted floorboard disguises the pavement that rolls beneath your feet. No windshield turns away the weather. No suspension smooths the ride. Bicycling is exposed and unavoidably social. On a bicycle, one confronts the world more nakedly, the whole sudden shifting immediacy of one's affairs opened out to the affairs of others.

Whatever you are by nature, whatever you have willed yourself to be, concentrates and distills itself on a bicycle: your timidities, your daring, your generosity or lack of it, your clumsiness or grace, whatever poise is naturally yours—all are telegraphed to others by the way you handle your bike. There's no effective rehearsal for a circumstance like this. What is needed is self-monitoring of a sort that lies outside anticipation and intent.

My favorite bicycle route takes me to the university library. Along the way, I cross a narrow wooden bridge that spans Chico Creek on the edge of the campus. Not long after I had gotten my bicycle, I was entering this bridge from the north side of the creek just as a young woman on a bike, backpack over her shoulders and a stack of books bungeed to the carrier, entered from the south side of the creek. There is just width enough on this bridge for two bicycles to pass one another, provided both riders stay alert and steady at the moment of passing. Following the custom of automobile travel, I inclined to my right. She simultaneously inclined to her left: thus we were opposed. I corrected to my left and she to her right; I again to my right, she left; whereupon we both hit the brakes and came to a standstill in the center of the bridge with our front wheels resting against each other's.

Her eyes flashed with irritation as she attempted to push her bike past me. I, concerned to clear a path for her, yanked my own bicycle aside and managed to block her way again. I was preparing phrases of apology when she turned to look at the creek where it flowed beneath our feet. And then she said to me quite matter-of-factly, "I'm so hurried these days I seldom stop to look at the water." In the midst of her vexation, she had restored balance and averted a crash. It was an instance of the most accomplished bicycling.

In December of our first year here in Chico, a heavy night storm swept through California's Central Valley. In the morning the soaking rains and high winds had toppled trees and dragged down power lines. Since Cory's Restaurant had power and we did not, Karen and I opted for breakfast out. In view of the weather, we took the car out of the garage and drove ourselves downtown where we found parking near enough to the restaurant that, with the aid of umbrellas, we got ourselves into Cory's in about as dry a condition as we could hope for.

Meanwhile, during a relative lull in the storm, Professor Stillman, who teaches music at the university, walked to the campus music department to instruct his morning class. Under the scant protection afforded by the pink umbrella he habitually carries—woefully undersized for a man as tall as he—he managed to arrive fairly dry. But he arrived only to find the university without power and his class cancelled.

Since Professor Stillman was already out and since he had no class to teach, he decided to head over to Cory's for some coffee and warmth. But on the way he was caught in a phenomenal cloudburst, which the wind drove in under that pitiful little umbrella of his, leaving him soaked to the skin from somewhere above his knees to the very undersides of his socks.

What I saw from where I sat at Cory's that morning was the sudden presence among the others waiting for a seat of a tall man in a tweed jacket folding down a miniature pastel-pink facsimile of an umbrella with the canopy ripped half off its ribbing. At the time I didn't know that the person I saw was Professor Stillman or that he was a concert pianist or that his class had been cancelled; nor did I know any of his other morning activities or thoughts. I was to learn these particulars a short time later in an extraordinary exchange of pleasantries.

Even from the distance of our table, I could see the extent of the soaking Professor Stillman had suffered during the assault of the storm. I recall feeling sympathetically distressed by his condition. The fact of him standing there inside the door with his pants plastered to his legs weighed on me just enough that it was hard to enjoy my own favorable circumstances. He, on the other hand, seemed perfectly oblivious to his situation and to the way in which others inclined away from him to avoid wetting their own garments. I tried to put his discomforts out of mind, which

I more or less managed successfully to do until the professor came sloshing after the hostess in shoes that had taken in so much water that he was wetly audible as he waded his way to a table not more than a yardstick's distance from mine and Karen's.

I witnessed then Professor Stillman's first and only concession to the discomforts of his situation. I saw him pluck at the fabric of his pants, squeezing up a bit of the soggy garment between his finger and thumb, and then I heard him comment in a remark directed only to himself, "I'm soaked." And that was that.

He then set out in a most detached and methodical manner to modify his circumstances as best he could. He removed his shoes one at a time and emptied the water from them. He took off his socks and wrung them as dry as he could. He carefully rolled up each pant leg, squeezing water from it as he went. He did these things with an exquisite precision of the sort one might well associate with the performance of a difficult piano concerto, as though the process required the utmost talent and presence of mind. In the end, these improvements left him sitting clothed in nothing but his own damp skin from his knees to the floor, his bare feet resting in a puddle of his own making.

When Professor Stillman finished eating the heated muffin with sweet butter on the side that I'd overheard him order and had settled into sipping his coffee, I engaged him in an exchange beginning with a comment on the extremity of the weather, something like, "This is some storm we're having." He acknowledged that it was and introduced himself. I asked how he'd managed to get caught in the downpour and he told me, but he quickly turned the conversation to our own recent arrival in Chico. He wondered if Karen and I found the community to our liking, and he told us of some of the town's advantages and pleasures. He did this with such absorption in the details of our conversation that it was possible to forget I was talking to a man whose wet knees projected nakedly beyond the hem of the napkin he had unfolded on his lap.

For all his composure, it was evident that the professor could not help but know that his circumstance was exactly as it was and nothing other. Whatever ease he'd achieved was not gotten by putting his situation out of mind but by including it, taking his wetness and his nakedness fully into account. As commonplace a social skill as this might be, Professor Stillman rode out the storm of his little morning miseries with instinctive poise, negotiating at each turn the exact and only point of balance that would suffice.

I had seen Holly several times before the day of our first encounter. I had seen her helped to the car by her mother. I had watched her father carry her out to the yard to see the Christmas lights when she was too weak to get there on her own. I knew that she was only eleven years old, and that her blood circulated deadly leukemia cells that threatened to take her life, and that she was driven regularly to a San Francisco medical center where she underwent the most rigorous of chemotherapy schedules. I knew that she could no longer maintain her schooling and that, in dismay at what had become of her, she had told her mother that it wouldn't be so bad if only she could be "like the other kids for a while."

I first spoke to Holly at a neighborhood potluck to which Karen and I were invited so that we could meet our neighbors. Holly was having a "good" day and had walked to the potluck with her mother's help from her house two doors away. She sat in a lawn chair in the shade of a tree. She was bald, her scalp like pale glass reflecting speckles of sunlight that sifted through the leaves. Looking down on her, I caught a hint of my own reflection mirrored on the naked surface of her head. Her eyes looked remarkably large in a face grown thin with illness. Her whole head looked as if it might topple from its insubstantial neck.

We'd been given name tags to wear and Holly had written on hers the name "Fuzzy." I said, "I thought you were Holly, but I see I'm wrong." "That's okay," she responded. "People often confuse me with Holly." The disaster of her young life had taken away nearly all her options. But she held on to one of the few that was still hers and refused to be helpless. If she couldn't be like the other kids, like the kid she once was, then she would be exactly the kid she was now and wear her baldness as though she'd chosen it.

Behind this precarious play I saw a weariness that could topple this child off into a despair from which she might never right herself. Yet she had not toppled; she had intuited the need to tilt, sensing, in that yielding, an accommodating response essential to her survival. She had taken up the hand of death as a most unlikely playmate of her childhood and had tripped along the very edge of chance where the slightest misstep would surely bring a fall.

Bicycling incorporates tilt into balance. Unless one is willing to tilt toward a fall, one cannot avoid falling. We are at all times poised for imminent fall. That we do not continually crash is the working of a grace beyond our will. Do not think that we are held upright by the force of our own intent, for balance of itself seeks itself. We discard our training wheels when we acquire trust, when we discover that what is needed for our travels is already given to us in the very nature of things.

Seeing

Twenty years ago, Mother was seated at the kitchen table. I was seated beside her, near enough to touch her if I were to reach out. It was the second day of my visit. Father, who always treated me as a guest upon first arrival, was settling once more into his customary routine and had gone outdoors to sweep leaves off the drive. Mother was taking advantage of his absence to talk to me about a book she had been reading and some ideas in which Father had little interest.

Her face was turned from me toward a window that opened on the back yard so that as she talked I watched her in profile. The sun from the window lit up her face and hair. She was absorbed in what she was saying, punctuating her words with crisp little bobbings of her head and emphatic hand gestures. I recall that she asked my opinion on something, the content of which I have long forgotten or never knew, because it was exactly then that I realized I was seeing my mother as if I had never seen her before. Her hair, gray now in her late sixties, the wrinkles radiating from the corners of her eyes and around her mouth, her lips, thinner than they once were, pressed together in the pauses between sentences, the sharp insistence of her gaze when she turned to inquire for my response—nothing about any of this was new to me. Yet for the moment these features seemed divested of all my forty-four years' experience of her. I needed to recite to myself that this woman was Lucy Beatrice Jensen, that she was my sixty-six-year-old mother whom I knew to be, in every detail, exactly the person that sat opposite me.

She was suddenly still, as though holding her breath in anticipation of what was to come. The eyes behind the lenses of her glasses were questions. I took up her hand, as though it were something I had just found. Mother said, "Yes, I'm growing old." I understood that she referred to the liver spots that had appeared on the backs of her hands. But that was not it; I had long been aware of such changes. How could I explain to her, or to myself for that matter, that in all her familiarity she was utterly new to me at that moment?

My mother, eighty-six now, still lives. I have known her for sixty-four of her years. Yet this tiny episode of two decades ago, little more than a single minute, persists. It has a reality that refuses to be ignored. It resists all my ideas of it. So for most of the twenty years since Mother and I sat down to talk, that brief moment with her at the kitchen table has stuck in my mind like a buried splinter that refuses to be dug out.

There is a seeing that occurs before thought, which means, of course, before recognition. And though as yet momentarily nameless, the object seen is not featureless. It is in fact more nakedly and vividly present in all its detail than it can ever be after the intervention of thought. All of us naturally see in this elemental way; to do so is unavoidable. It's just that we fail to notice its occurrence, and the reason for this failure is that our natural sense of seeing is overridden by our ideas regarding the objects of our sight. A sudden splash of yellow and orange, singular and unprecedented is so readily and habitually converted to the categorical generalization of a rose that all we end up seeing is our idea of a rose rather than the living rose itself. Anything that looks familiar to you, even if it is the face of your own child, is not truly being seen. If you were really seeing your child, the features of her face would appear as if for the first time. Our perception of the familiar is an idea about something, a generalization intending to fit many occasions and thus never really fitting a single occasion at all. Still there's always that fresh instant of seeing before even the simplest thought intervenes. If you notice this, it's possible to cultivate eyes that see beyond thought regardless of how busy your mind might seem to be.

Adjacent to "The Avenues" neighborhood of Chico is a cemetery with wide lawns, ancient valley oaks, and a few maples whose fallen leaves paint the ground in the shortening days of late October and November. It's a stretch of ground as intimate to me now as any I've ever known, and yet more and more often these days it appears to my eyes as to those of a stranger. At such moments, the landscape seems to reach for me before I can reach for it. The blossoming myrtle tree, the scrub jay pecking at the lawn, the sprinkler splashing water on the gravestones, the oak with its limb broken away, a squirrel motionless on an elm trunk, leaves scattering on the wind, children running on the far lawn of Chico Junior High, a vapor trail spread high above the Sacramento Valley—all this coming upon me fresh and nameless, without the familiar qualities I attribute to things. I have entered a visual universe where even the most marginal objects come to me with same living insistence I felt at my mother's kitchen table all those years ago.

The present moment is swifter than thought. My body, in its intrinsic and native power of sight, has always understood this. It reads life directly and is teaching me now to do so as well. It has loosened my hold on things that they might move, as they must, along the sequence of the moment. It has shown me that this sycamore rooted to the banks of Chico Creek on this blustery afternoon in mid-October cannot be held in place beyond the instant of my seeing it here any more than its yellowing leaves can be held from their fall to earth. I know now that the only sycamore I can hold on to has its roots sunk nowhere but in my thoughts of it.

I have not risked seeing the world as it actually is. My eyes have snatched at things, picked and sorted them, until there was little left to see but an arbitrary arrangement of my own thoughts. Between classes at Chico State University, students by the hundreds crisscross the quad on their way to various destinations. Watching them I have discovered that most of them look down, their eyes controlling the short patch of ground into which they forever walk. Others stare ahead with such singleness of purpose that I marvel they do not collide with each other. Only a few have eyes that risk the present moment. These few know one another on sight.

I soften the edges of intent that I not reside within the fixed and narrowed center of my will. The eye that sees forever opens on the fullness of itself where edges join the center and sight receives things as they are.

Five hundred miles south of Chico, my mother lives alone now that Father has died. I will visit her soon and I will give her a hug. In the meantime, I must settle for the mother I hold here in my mind. But there is no such mother, and when I make my visit I will see that this is so. The mother I hug will only be herself, a fact my own mirror now teaches me daily where, search as long and hard as I will, I cannot find the person I thought I was.

Swallowing

other couldn't swallow. She sat propped up in bed on the fourth floor of Saint Joseph's Hospital with a spoonful of pudding in her mouth that wouldn't go down. And when she tried to wash it down with water, her hands shook so badly she could barely get the cup to her lips. She tilted her head back and dumped in a little water and all she succeeded in doing was to add to the volume of diluted pudding she was already holding in her mouth. She pinched her lips together to keep it in but most of it dribbled back out onto the towel I'd tucked under her chin.

I tried to persuade her to give up but she wouldn't. It was like asking her to stop breathing. She was eighty-eight years old and she had always swallowed and now she couldn't, a bewildering circumstance like that of a bird with a broken wing that suddenly discovers it can't fly. It flaps its wings up and down as it has always done and is astonished to find itself still on the ground.

The medical staff was threatening to insert a tube into her stomach. "Don't let them do it, Linley," she implored me. "I want to feed myself." I sat on a chair at the foot of her bed. The second-hand ticked interminably round the face of the wall clock. The towel under Mother's chin was soaked through to her nightgown. Every few minutes she'd put another spoonful of pudding in her mouth.

At length she quit. Defeated. Her mouth fell slack. The last of the pudding drained in a smear down her chin and throat. Her hair was askew, matted down by the pressure of the pillow. Her scalp showed through patches of gray that had once been a cascade of auburn reaching to the small of her back. Her face was gaunt. Skin hung from her in leathery folds. She cried when I brushed her hair. At the nurses' station, they were preparing a stomach tube.

Sometimes things fail us that shouldn't. And when they do, it can seem as if the sun had suddenly reversed its course. You can never know when this might happen or what form it might take. But its arrival can bring you to doubt your most unassailable certainties, things you never before thought to question.

One hot August day at about three in the afternoon, I was standing at my workbench in the garage of the Sierra Valley house Karen and I were building. I was holding a window frame in my hands that wouldn't fit the window I'd made it for. Two others just like it lay on the bench before me. What with all the set-ups that had to be made, the cutting, gluing, clamping, and sanding that had to be done, the three frames represented the better part of two days' labor. Add on the expensive materials that had gone into their making and they represented a considerable cost as well. Yet they were useless, a complete waste.

I had twenty-two such frames yet to make, and thinking I ought to try out at least one prototype before committing myself to cutting all twenty-two of them, I'd put one together for a laundry room window. It didn't fit. This threw me a little because it was something that had rarely occurred in all the years I had been building. But it didn't throw me nearly as much as did not being able to discover where I'd gone wrong. I went over the plans again—which I'd drawn up myself and of whose accuracy I was convinced—and found no error. I carefully checked the math on the length of the rails and stiles. I subtracted once more the depth of shoulder cuts on the tenon joints. Everything was just as it should be, except that the resultant window frame was nearly an inch narrower than the space it was meant to occupy.

If the specifications were right, I must have made a mistake on the saw. I built a second prototype, which turned out as much too large for the space as the first had been too small. I recalculated everything. As before, I found no error. I built a third prototype, and by this time I was so unraveled that I didn't expect it to fit either—and it didn't. I had no idea where I'd gone wrong. I felt as if I had lost my mind, or had somehow lost the world in which a mind such as mine could properly function.

Besides the twenty-two window frames I still had to make, I had all the cabinets ahead of me. Weeks of labor, thousands of dollars of expensive hardwoods, forty-eight drawers and thirty-nine cabinet doors yet to build—and I couldn't put together a single window frame!

The thermometer on the garage wall read a hundred degrees. Through the open door, I could see where heat waves distorted the fields, putting the whole landscape out of focus. I muddled about in the heat of the garage, aimlessly rearranging tools, straightening up the workbench, sweeping shavings into a little pile on the floor and then leaving them there to be tracked around the garage again. A stack of clear, kiln-dried boards rested on a pair of sawhorses near the workbench. I lifted a board from the stack, set it down again. I couldn't bring myself to cut a single piece of it.

Then Ron McCaffrey was there. He'd come up the half mile of graveled driveway from the county road and was parked in front of the garage before I awakened to the fact that anyone was around. Regardless of the heat, Ron was wearing the same old

Montgomery Ward's coveralls he always wore. He came into the garage carrying Dolly on his arm, a ratty little chihuahua that was as inevitable to his visits as were his coveralls. Though our talk had never gone much beyond comments on the weather and such, I poured out the whole story to Ron. I told him everything, all the perplexity, the panic, the fear, everything. By the time I got it all out, I had somehow ended up holding Dolly, petting her and consoling her as if she were the one who couldn't build a window frame.

We were quiet for a while. Then Ron said, "You don't have to work alone." He means God, I thought. I should have known. But the truth was I liked hearing him say it. I recited it inwardly: "I don't have to work alone." "Take the rest of the day off," Ron suggested.

I did. After Ron left I shut the garage doors and went up the wooded ridge west of the house and sat under some Jeffrey pines. In a clearing beyond the pines stood a single western juniper tree. It had grown in the thinnest of gravelly soils and yet its trunk was of a girth you'd find hard to get your arms around. It was an ancient specimen, rooted in soil that was eroding on all sides. A huge boulder broken off from the cliffs above had come to rest within a few yards of its trunk. It was a most unlikely survivor and looked as if its long uncertain life had been lived in hazard.

The evening wind came up, the sound of it pushing its way through the surrounding woods. I saw the stiff grasses rattling against themselves at the base of the juniper, saw the dust rise from the bare patches of earth. I saw the nighthawks wheel overhead, and everywhere I heard the restless whistling of the wind among the rocks and brush. It was dark when I came back down the ridge. In the garage I switched on the light and looked once more at the failed window frames. It was not a world in which one could take result for granted. In the morning, though my hands trembled to do it, and without ever knowing what the previous days' error had been, I successfully cut the materials for the window frames.

We brought Mother home with a tube inserted in her stomach, a case of liquid nutrient, a stand to set up by her bed with a machine mounted on it that delivered the nutrient to her in measured doses throughout the long days and nights. She submitted to this without showing interest or resistance. We were certain she was dying. For a few days it was all she could manage to respond to the call of her own name. Then by degrees, at a pace heartbreakingly slow, she began to strengthen. And one day, after weeks of being fed by tube, she asked for her supper. She wanted it served at the table. And so we got her into her wheelchair and wheeled her to the table and set a small plate of creamed peas and potatoes in front of her. But she had to spit out the few spoonfuls she managed to get into her mouth, because she still couldn't swallow.

Nonetheless, she now insisted on being brought to the table for every meal. She pushed little bits of food around on her plate with a fork and every once in a while stuck some of it in her mouth. She would hold food in her mouth for what seemed to an observer like interminable periods of time, trying to will herself to swallow. And then one morning at breakfast, she swallowed. She didn't repeat this feat again for nearly a week, but in increments you'd have to measure by weeks rather than hours or even days she swallowed more and more.

Mother eats three times a day now. She lives by her own volition once more. But she knows her world too well to count on any outcome. I see it in her eyes; I see that whenever she takes a spoonful of food into her mouth, she's never quite sure it will go down.

Harmony Creek

In early July of the eighty-ninth year of her life, my mother, Lucy Beatrice Jensen, took her last walk. She pushed her walker from the bathroom to her bedside, where she lay down and shut her eyes on the world. She's not risen since and rarely looks at anything except to squint in the direction of the few voices that manage to penetrate her isolation. Meanwhile, we have moved her from the bedroom to a bed near a living room window so she can look out if she wants to.

Outside the window, a simulated waterfall circulates a trickle of stale, chlorinated water over stones. A tiny footbridge, hardly wide enough to accommodate a child's feet, spans a rock-lined pool dwarfed by a flowering bird of paradise. Just to look at the setting makes the mind squeeze down to the scale of a doll's house.

Secreted among the shrubbery are a dozen ceramic squirrels in various postures of feigned animation. They constitute the only wildlife other than a few adaptable species of birds that have managed to survive the monthly pest control poisonings. Along with a pathetic little patch of grass and a few miniaturized palms this constitutes the entirety of my mother's cramped backyard.

Beyond the chain-link fence that separates the backyard from the Santiago Drainage Canal, sprawls the municipal wasteland of

Orange County, a gray grid of pavement, sidewalk, subdivision, shopping mall, industrial park, and freeway interchange, its name the only and last remnant of the fragrant groves that once stretched across Orange County from the foothills to the sea. In the twelve weeks she has lain by the living room window, Mother has not once bothered to look outside.

My sister, Evelyn, calls. "Mother is weakening," she tells me. "Perhaps you should come." I begin the familiar drive southward from Chico, down California's Central Valley. Two hours bring me to Sacramento, another forty-five minutes to Stockton, both cities sweltering in mid-morning heat beneath a seemingly interminable smoky haze. Trucks churn past me. The odor of diesel exhaust lingers. The shoulder of the road lies littered with the peeled carcasses of overheated truck tires. Everywhere trash blows: strips of paper and tissue, bags of all sorts, cigarette butts, discarded six-pack cartons and rings, bottles, cans, cups with straws stuck through the lids, Styrofoam and plastic containers—all strewn along the roadside, lodged against freeway fences, scattered among fields of corn and lettuce and ripening grain.

The stench of the cattle-fattening yard reaches me long before I see the first corral. It drifts northward on the hot wind. I know what I will see when I get there. The highway soon climbs a little grade along the shoulder of a grass hill. At the crest of the hill, the fattening yard comes into view: thousands of cows crammed into an intolerable proximity to each other. A few mill aimlessly about, most stand motionless in a kind of stunned and fixed stupidity with flies crawling into their dripping nostrils and into their eyes, while the steaming waste of their own bodies piles up under their hooves. Not one tree shelters them from the heat. Not a blade of grass, not one weed, survives their unspeakable confinement where they sicken on salted feed so alien to their appetites that only a constant dosing of antibiotic prevents their dying before the time of scheduled execution.

I wonder that the sight of this place doesn't stop traffic. I wonder that we do not—all of us, truckers, travelers, commuters—abandon our cars in the lanes of California's Interstate 5 and converge upon this horror, pleading relief for these suffering creatures. Instead we pass by with our windows rolled up so as not to gag. At length, I climb the long grade to Gorman and descend into the Los Angeles Basin where smog turns the sun a sickly yellow.

My sister was right. I find Mother even more feeble and unresponsive than before. She breathes. Her heart beats. Her body manages to digest the nutrient liquid we pour into her each day through the tube that has been reinserted in her stomach. It is this act alone that keeps my mother from sliding into death. She has no capacity to sustain herself at all.

Bonny, a caregiver my sister has retained from a local agency, is torn between watching a gameshow called "Who Wants to Be a Millionaire?" and taking advantage of someone she can talk with. Her attention bobs back and forth between the TV screen and a conversation she has launched into with me involving just about everything that's on her mind. She's apparently upset about some public assistance she has recently been refused and she's concerned to convince me that it's the result of "illegal Mexicans taking all the money." "I've got nothing against legal Mexicans," she is at pains to have me know, "but it's not fair that the illegals take what's mine." Though I haven't volunteered a single objection, it seems urgent to her that I concede her viewpoint. But urgent as it may be, she's also terribly distracted by the game show where apparently a contestant is on the verge of winning $250,000. "You should see what they do in Anaheim where I live," Bonny complains. "They throw dirty diapers right out on the back lot."

The contestant wins, and Bonny looks as if she'd like to climb right into the image on the TV screen and congratulate the winner in person. When she turns back to me, her eyes are swimming in tears. She plans a trip to Las Vegas over the weekend to try her own luck. I go for a walk.

An asphalt bike path borders the Santiago Drainage Canal behind my mother's house. I strike out along it, walking as hard as I can. I was raised here in Orange County. This was my childhood home. I once walked through fields and orchards on my way to school. This engineered atrocity that I walk along now, this barren ditch, was once Santiago Creek. It flowed year-round from out of the hills through pasture and croplands to the sea. It resounded with crickets on warm summer nights. Frogs and snakes lived among its damp grasses. Warblers hunted insects in the willows that overhung its waters.

I come to a bridge spanning the canal and I cross over attracted by the promise of trees and shrubbery among the houses on the far side. I find my way blocked. I have come upon a closed community. The road and sidewalk are barricaded with metal gates locked tight against intrusion. A man in a white Jeep Cherokee pulls up from inside. The gates part momentarily and he drives through and disappears over the bridge. The smell of his exhaust lingers.

On the site of what was once a eucalyptus grove, this gated complex now stands declaring itself to be "HARMONY CREEK APARTMENTS." But the so-called creek is nothing but a cement underpass littered with trash. It is this final absurdity that moves me to grief. I sit on the curb in the shadow of these ridiculous apartments and I know the sorrow of all those Harmony Creek Apartments and Sun Village Acres and Blossom Hill Estates and Oakwood Manors and Sea View Terraces across this nation whose names belie the tragedy of what we have done to our earth.

Back at the house, I prepare Mother's night feeding. I shake the can of liquid nutrient and pull the bedcovers back to expose the feeding tube. Lucy Beatrice Jensen, born in Missoula, Montana, brought to Orange County at age seven, wed to my father at seventeen amid fields fragrant with orange blossoms, lies now inert and unseeing in one of the same frilly nightgowns she has worn to bed the whole of her adult life. Her face and throat are ashen and wrinkled. Her mouth, without dentures, is sunken and shapeless, her lips hardly existent. "What a pretty nightgown, Mother," I say to her.

Though she has lived eighty-two years of her life within ten miles of the bed where she now lies dying, my mother has nonetheless journeyed into the furthest reaches of an alien world. My mother is trapped now in this place, imprisoned by consequences of her own doing, the farm she and her husband traded for their retirement converted now to a shopping mall. If my mother has shut her eyes on this, so have we. We retain the organ of sight yet refuse to see the awful waste we lay about us. In our blindness we prepare a deathbed for our own demise.

I uncap the feeding tube and position the funnel. I have urged my sister and brother to suspend this intervention and let Mother die. They say they can't condemn her to death. I pop the top off the can of nutrient and dump the contents into Mother's stomach—condemning her to life.

Lifeguard

Every time I surface, Mother is still there. If she thinks I'm looking at her, she waves to me. I wave back. I clear the faceplate, blow the snorkel clear, and kick my way down through columns of kelp with an abalone iron in hand. Ten, fifteen, twenty feet under, I still feel her eyes on me.

Nearly an hour has passed since I entered the water and she hasn't moved at all. The wind has come up, raising dust and blowing her hair about, which from time to time she tries to pat back in place. I wish she'd get back in the car. After all, I'm old enough to have a driver's license. I'm not a kid anymore.

My mother isn't very large, a slight woman, almost frail. She looks no bigger than a child waving to me from the high cliff above the beach. She's not daring at all. Under any ordinary circumstances, she would never consider risking the climb down that cliff face. Besides, she can't swim. Yet my mother is doing all she can to guard my life.

What does she do when I'm under? Does she hold her breath? Does she know when I need to surface for air? What if I failed to reappear? Or came floating to the surface, my body washed lifelessly back and forth on the swells? Would she scratch her way down the cliff and come into the water in her skirt and sweater and hose trying to reach me?

Mother is afraid for me. She doesn't think I should come diving here alone. I could drown she tells me and no one would know where I went down. So she comes along to keep watch. Again and again I disappear into the deep water and she is never certain I will come back up. When I do, she waves to let me know she is still here.

Sixteen years old and hot with self-intent, I don't want my mother watching over me. Her presence on the cliff puts me in doubt, troubles me with a lesson I'm not yet willing to learn.

Yet within a year that lesson will be learned and my mother watching from the bleachers of the Anaheim High School football stadium will have her worst fears realized. The son who was needed at home for after school chores and who'd repeatedly nagged to please be allowed just once to go out for football lay unconscious, his flesh split open, his skull fractured, his helmet awash in a pool of blood. The son to this day retains scattered fragments of that event. He recalls the blurred outline of his mother's face, her voice reaching him through a haze of searing pain. He remembers what she said, her words following him the whole of his life. "I'm here, Linley. I won't leave you." He recalls as he was wheeled into surgery her plea to the doctor to please do all that he could, that cost was "no consideration," that she could pay whatever it took. It was a guarantee without basis in fact, just so much hopeful waving from a cliff top.

There are certain lonely offices of the heart undertaken in the absence of either hope or means. These are the lowliest of our duties, the tasks from which we wrest our humanity. For Mother it meant attending to my survival when the Anaheim surgeon told her I probably would not survive. It meant not despairing when it was explained to her that, should I live, I would never be normal again. It meant watching her son waste away through weeks of semi-consciousness until his robust young body, once so manly and firm, weighed less than her own. It meant bringing him home, too weak to walk on his own, his head hanging perpetually to one side as if shielding itself from some anticipated blow, his world repeated in duplicate from the severe double vision with which he suffered. It meant coaxing him, spoonful by spoonful, to eat again. It meant awakening in the night to his screams and holding him down in his bed until the doctor arrived to sedate him. It meant putting aside her own affairs for nearly a year that she might devote herself to drawing her son back into life, hauling him to doctor's appointments, providing for his special dietary needs, tutoring him in his schoolwork, slowly, day by day, returning him to the natural world.

Mother looks so tiny in her coffin, something like a life-size doll, her cheeks lightly rouged, her lips reddened, her body clothed in a gray suit I don't recall her ever wearing, her hands folded beneath her breasts. Rowland has yet to arrive from his home in Santa Maria, and my sister, Evelyn, and I have come to say goodbye. Mother's hands and face are cold to the touch, as unyielding as plaster, not at all like living flesh. Her eyes, that once searched the sea for my reappearance, are sightless now.

I start to go, but turn back again to the coffin. Evelyn is seated on a wooden pew in the front row of the chapel. The others have left. I look at Mother and then at Evelyn. I say, "I'm sixty-seven years old and something in me hasn't grown up until now. There's no one to look out for us anymore. We're it. There's no one else to do it."

"Yes, we're it," Evelyn replies.

At the coffin I taste the true sorrow of guarding another's life. "I'm here, Mother," I tell her. "I won't leave you." Then I turn and go.

Swimming Lessons

The chubby little boy had a puffy face that made his eyes look unusually small. He had a short thick neck and hair sheared close to the scalp. His fat little hands clutched the concrete wall of One-Mile Pool on Chico Creek.

"Just let go, for Christ's sake!" his father ordered.

The father stood at the pool's edge directly above the boy so that when the boy looked up, he would be seeing his father from an angle virtually under the parent's feet. The father too was stout and thick necked. He wore shorts and a T-shirt and a baseball cap. He stood in clogs of some sort with his thick legs spread apart and his feet turned outward. His arms were crossed over his chest.

"Just let go!" his father bellowed again. "God, the water's barely over your head!"

The boy's mother stood in the water where a set of steps descended from the wall into the pool. "You can let loose now," she instructed the boy in a tone of contained sternness. "Let loose and swim to me."

Twenty feet separated the mother from the boy where he still clung to the wall. She inched toward him a foot or two. "Look, I'm closer now. You've swum this far before."

"Why don't you just hold his hand while he does it?" the father said in disgust. "He can hang there all day for all I care," he added. He turned his back and walked away.

"Just let go!" the mother insisted, an anxious fear rising into her voice.

The boy's knuckles were white where they gripped the wall, and he had begun to shiver from cold or fear. I had taken to swimming at One-Mile Pool since moving to Chico and I happened to be close at hand when all of this took place, and intervened in a way in which I probably had no right to do. All I seemed to see was the boy's predicament, and setting aside his parent's prerogative to treat him as they chose, I pushed my way through the water to where the boy held on.

"It's okay," I told him. "You don't have to if you don't want to. I won't let you sink,"

He looked at me, gauged the distance between himself and my outstretched hands, and then let go, thrashing his way through the water toward me. His fat little hands closed on mine and held on fiercely. I floated him to where his mother waited on the steps. She met my eyes without disclosure of any sort.

Later, as I waded in the river shallows, the boy was suddenly there. I saw his mother and what was apparently his sister nearby. When we came to a spot where the river moss made the footing slippery, he took my hand for help. I saw then how it was, how the slightest tenderness, the merest sliver of acknowledgment, had won from him an affection and trust that his parents daily forfeited. Neither of them understood that their child was on the verge of drowning.

From the distance his mother called to him to come away. Her voice reached us hard and sharp, provoked perhaps by his attachment to me, distrustful perhaps of my motives. The boy showed no sign of having heard her. She called again.

"Your mother's calling," I said to him. "You'd better go back."

His eyes, suddenly wary, looked at me out of his puffy face as if I had sent him into deep water. He turned away and walked disconsolately back toward his mother where she waited in sourness with her hands on her hips.

"You come when I call you," she scolded.

Perhaps she would not have scolded him had she known that the boy was struggling to reach the surface and that he was giving all he had to the effort. But she did not know this, as most assuredly her husband had not known earlier when he stood spread-legged at the pool's edge and ordered the boy to swim.

I watched them go, the mother, still scolding, heading back toward the pool with her daughter in tow, the boy trailing after them. My heart hurt for this little boy who must learn to swim in waters so dangerous he might sink from our sight at any moment.

The Bidwell Park Goats

The goats are telling us something. I'm possibly the only one in town who has noticed this. Most don't know they're being told anything at all. The goats themselves aren't conscious of doing any telling. But the telling is real, and those who are exposed to it are getting the message whether they realize it or not. I only recently realized it myself. But its discovery serves to explain why the goats are such a compelling attraction to the townspeople.

Of course one element of their attraction is the sheer novelty of keeping a herd of goats in the middle of town. We got the goats to keep down the blackberry vines that invaded Bidwell Park, choking out the native plants, cutting off access to the creek, threatening the canopy of sycamores and valley oaks that line the riparian corridor. The goats were an alternative to herbicides which none of us wanted to use if it could be avoided. So a contract was drawn up and in the spring of 1999, just as the blackberries were sprouting new growth, Danny Mitchell pulled his trailer into Bidwell Park, set out some electric fencing around a patch of blackberry vines, and released a herd of eighty goats into the enclosure. You couldn't miss them. The enclosure was within hearing distance of the Community Recreation Center, and within sight of the parking lot at One-Mile pool with its five lifeguard stands and its picnic tables. The herd was visible to traffic on Vallombroso Avenue and from the front yards of houses adjacent to the park. You could smell the goats from the doorway of Chico's main post office. Everyone who came to pick up their mail knew where the herd was.

The goats were universally popular from the start. They weren't satisfied to let you do all the looking but would study you in turn, their dark eyes curious under soft lashes peering at you from the other side of the fence. They telegraphed responses with their ears, which were soft and floppy or stiff and pointed depending on the breed. Their whole caprine posture was extraordinarily expressive, the slightest tilt of a head conveying an emphasis as readable as are the facial expressions and hand gestures accompanying human speech. They seemed able to express the equivalent of smiles or frowns or to even make inquiries through attitudes of body.

A few of the nannies had suckling kids. Baby goats are irresistible. To see one is to have cuteness defined. So Chico's children came in droves. They arrived by bicycle and on foot. They came with parents or grandparents or older brothers and sisters. They were carried on backs, pushed in strollers, or towed along by hand. Busloads of them arrived from area grammar schools.

When the novelty wore off, I noticed something. I noticed that long after most children lost interest the adults usually hadn't. They stayed on. They lingered by the enclosure, reluctant to leave, their children fidgeting at their sides, tugging at them, asking to go. It was then I began to understand what the goats were telling us. I think I wasn't alone in this. It's just that the others were, and remain to this day, innocent of having received any understanding at all. I can best explain this by describing how the goats eat blackberry leaves.

They eat them with a single and sustained concentration. By "single" I mean that their eating is all of one piece. Goats have long nimble tongues. Their mouths are flexible and mobile. They use these instruments with an intelligent precision. They project their faces with their dark eyes into the most daunting confusion of blackberry thorns and capture leaf after leaf, extracting them without the least hesitancy or uncertainty. To watch them is like watching the violin section of a symphony orchestra. Every musician is exactly on the point; no one strays from the task even the slightest. The goats eat with this kind of undistracted absorption. They show us what it really means to pay attention. It all seems so natural. We wonder if we could learn to mow our lawns or answer the phone or fry eggs with any comparable presence of mind.

The way the goats eat pretty well describes the way the goats live. We can see exactly how they live because, being contained as they are, they don't go anywhere else or do anything other than what they are doing. They browse among the blackberry vines and shrubs. They eat a little grass that comes up in the clearings. They rest in the shade of the sycamores and oaks. They breed and give birth and suckle their young. They drink from the creek and bed down together at night. There's not a whole lot to see. It's a wonder anybody hangs around to watch.

But that's the point. The goats are telling us that at the irreducible core of our lives we are single and whole. The goats live with a directness that calls our complications into doubt. Watching them, we begin to discover the inadequacy that underlies our need to acquire, the fear that drives us to so relentlessly consume. The goats expose the anxious source of our greed.

In the alleys behind our houses, trash barrels distributed by North Valley Disposal await collection, bearing within them the remains of the great harvest we have required. Among the discarded containers of paper and foil and plastic, among the emptied bottles and cans, lies the waste of our own depleted lives. To peer into this mess is to know the expense of spirit squandered.

We can clamp the lid back down but we already smell the odor of regret in our nostrils. We yearn at such times for the harsh hand of need, the exposed spine of ourselves beneath the flabby excess. We long to nibble blackberry leaves on the banks of Chico Creek.

Things

A *January night.* I wrap up in a scarf and push my hands into my pockets for the walk home from an evening lecture at the university. Cold moonlight silhouettes the winter-bared limbs that arch overhead: silver maples, twenty-one of them in all. Here, where I turn off Laburnum onto Sacramento Avenue, I can see most of these maples at a single glance. Just saplings when the city first set them out a half century ago, they line the avenue with trunks grown massive, their roots lifting the sidewalks, their limbs crossing each other from opposite curbs. I can count them: thirteen on the south side of the avenue, eight on the north. I can count as well the ones that will soon be missing—eleven of the largest maples condemned by the city as unsafe. They are slated to be cut down, three now, the others within the next two years. Tonight, for all their present beauty, the stark and shifting geometry of their shadowed limbs in patterns against the lighter sky, I count the impending loss.

In the middle of the block, a short strip of plastic ribbon tacked to a trunk marks the first of the trees to go. In the dark, I can't make out the color of the plastic but I know it to be orange. The ribbon flutters limply in the night breeze. Overhead, clouds drift southward. From the windows of the houses, patches of light fall onto the lawns. The ribbon-marked tree is a giant. Two people could not join hands around its trunk. I try anyway. I push myself against the trunk and stretch my arms around the curve of its circumference, the side of my face flattened against the rough bark. I strain to bring the tips of my fingers together. Of course it's useless. I'm not even close. I need help to do this.

Those of us who live on the two blocks of Sacramento Avenue between Laburnum and Palm have grown accustomed to the presence of these trees. Many of us have known them only in their maturity but a few were here to see them planted, so that season by season with quiet stealth the trees came to overshadow the whole of their lives. Hardly any of them noticed this. There were other matters to attend to—the growth of their own children and, after that, grandchildren. The trees grew out of mind, as it were. Yet, all the while, the trees, in increments of hours, minutes, seconds, stretched their limbs in ever widening arcs that tower now above the streets and rooftops shading lawns where great-grandchildren take their first steps.

But out of mind or not, the trees have filtered into the lives of all of us who reside on the avenue. We wear the trees in our consciousness in the same unacknowledged way we wear our own skin or hear the sounds of our own voices. It's an intimacy that is likely to go unremarked. But when recent notice came from the city of the trees impending removal, all of us on Sacramento Avenue realized at once the extent of their presence in our lives. "Why?" we asked. "Because they're old and ready to fall," we were told. Of course! We should have known: after all, there were three widows on this block and another soon to be, her husband confined to a wheelchair, unable to breathe on his own. Still, it had not occurred to us that this selfsame mortality that overtakes our lives had overtaken the lives of the trees as well. We weren't ready for it. We looked in dismay at those that were condemned, eleven of them, marked with splashes of paint, orange ribbons tacked to their trunks. We didn't see how we could give them up.

We made calls to city officers, spoke out in opposition at council hearings, demanded a tree-by-tree assessment led by the city forester while we tagged along to be shown the deterioration that required each condemned tree to be cut. We took up the offer of the city to get a second opinion by an independent arborist, a last hope which ended with all of us gathered round the city forester's pickup on a late afternoon, the doomed trees with their orange ribbons visible up and down the block, the forester telling us that the second opinion concurred with the first.

We're waiting now. Sometimes it's a little like holding one's breath. Something inheres in a thing like a tree or a park bench or a familiar lamp by the bedside or the feel of one's own hand in a pocket or a stone found by the creek, something that so compels us, that so draws us within its sphere of influence that we feel shaped by its presence. It is this shaping presence that we stand to lose in the death of the Sacramento Avenue trees. It is a loss that reaches us beyond the mere loss of their familiarity, beyond the loss of whatever comfort of shade or enclosure they might provide, beyond even the loss of their beauty or the sheer length of their proximity to our lives. Beyond anything we know to name, there moves a force arising from the pure juxtaposition of things, a force that draws us into being, that allows us to dwell fully in our lives.

All pure juxtaposition is a gathering. It gathers the Sacramento Avenue trees and those of us who live here into mutual dwelling, and through the agency of this dwelling, it gathers us into dwelling with all things. It roots us to the subsoil, raises our eyes to the sky, lifts us to the moon on night branches, speaks to us in veined leaf the language of the sun. It teaches us the dropping away that sheds itself, the moldering silence of deepest shade, the coming again in proper time. The naked power of juxtaposition to gather us into dwelling functions beyond any sentiment or thought of relationship. It is as direct and out of mind as is our mutual exchange of carbon dioxide and oxygen, the trees breathing us and we them.

So it is that we dwell in things with a surety beyond conscious perception. However set apart we might feel, there exists a concreteness in things that impinges directly and immediately upon our bodies, sometimes sustaining connections otherwise forfeited to circumstance. If you spend your childhood in a backyard under a great weeping willow tree with a swing hung from it, you carry the sweep and descent of those shading limbs with you the rest of your life. You bend without breaking, and when you least expect it, you find yourself swinging back and forth in some cool recess of your mind. Had the willow been a pine, you'd be a different person. If you live long enough in a two-story house, you always carry an upper story on your mind. Your viewpoint bears the imprint of a staircase and little that you do seems entirely horizontal.

Count them. Eleven silver maples soon to be cut down. Their loss will leave gaps in the arrangement of our lives. We have dwelt with these trees in ways deeper than thought can fathom. We have been gathered into being with them by force of simple presence. It is certain that when they are gone we will be other than we are now. We will bear the shape of their absence, and dwell where we have not dwelt before.

The Questioner

"**What is it that Buddhists want to learn,**" he questioned, though no one had asked him to question anything. We were supposed to be listening to to the dharma talk Susan was giving, her explanation of some aspect of Buddhist teaching. Besides his question had nothing to do with Susan's talk. It was all very strange.

It was Thursday night at the weekly session of the Chico Zen Sangha, our group that comes together to meditate weekly. We had settled into a circle to hear Susan's talk, when Karen noticed this young man outside who seemed to want to come in. So she asked him, and he came in. He was tall, graceful and poised, and he carried himself with an air of quiet purpose. He found a place in the circle and sat down on the floor cross-legged with the rest of us. He looked as if he'd been sitting meditation his whole life.

Susan got out her notes and put on her reading glasses. Her topic, she informed us, was gossip. I believe she intended to make reference to the Buddha's teachings concerning "right speech"— but I never found out because no sooner had she got started than our visitor spoke up. He interrupted Susan in mid-sentence and he announced to us that he was in possession of a "Toastmaster's International Certificate of Completion." He had the document in hand so we could all verify it. I was trying to make out the wording from across the circle when, with a sort of measured solemnity, he said, "I have been sent to ask this question with eloquence and dignity: What is it that Buddhists want to learn?"

None of us thought to ask who sent him, but I've since come to accept the fact that he was, in some sense "sent." At any rate, being a resilient group we set out to tackle his question. I suppose we thought that we could give him a few answers and then Susan could get back to her planned talk.

Susan tried first. She offered him something somewhat pat like, "We Buddhists want to learn the four noble truths and the steps of the noble eightfold path." She added something to the effect that these teachings were central to the Buddhist Way, and then she resumed her talk—but she'd barely gotten her notes back in order when the questioner interrupted her again. "What is it that Buddhists want to learn?" he repeated. Apparently he hadn't bought the noble truth and eightfold thing; he was looking for answers.

I tried: "We Buddhists are seeking the true nature of self." I thought that was pretty good, but when he responded again with "What is it that Buddhists want to learn?" I could see for myself that I'd merely uttered words. Whatever it is that Buddhists "want to learn," it can't be passed off as "seeking the true nature of self."

We tried other things. We fed him assertions about impermanence, compassion, the dissolution of ego. We kept this up until it became increasingly clear that this question of his, invariably repeated, was the only element of honest discourse going on at the Chico Zen Sangha that night.

He'd stumped us. With an innocent insistence like that of a curious child who really wants to know, this graduate toastmaster had quickly brought us to our limits. "What is it that Buddhists want to learn?" Though we'd previously thought we did, we didn't actually know what it is that Buddhists want to learn. We were beginners after all.

I made one last effort to restore familiar circumstances. "Would you be willing to just listen to the talk that Susan has prepared for us?" I urged in as conciliatory a tone as I could muster. "Perhaps you'll get some answers from that." His response: "What is it that Buddhists want to learn?"

Karen, who'd gotten us into this in the first place, came to our rescue and got us out. "Meditation," she announced. With that, we all retreated to the comfort of something we figured we knew how to do right. Sitting there in proper cross-legged posture, I felt the chagrin of not knowing how to explain even the simplest, most basic thing about Buddhism. It was a lesson that the questioner, with eloquence and dignity, had come to teach.

I'm glad to have gotten that lesson. The questioner brought me to doubt whatever certainties I was holding that night, his unanswered question demonstrating once again the inadequacy of even the most unassailable "truth" to explain the great mystery of existence. His visit to the Chico Zen Sangha released me once more into the freedom that resides in knowing that I don't know.

Eclipse

"**I'm Gerald,**" he said, as if it were suddenly important to him that I know who he was. "I'm Lin," I told him. We shook hands. Of the brief mutual history Gerald and I shared, it is that moment that stands out most in my mind.

The Chico Zen Sangha holds its meditations at a local church and in the winter the town's homeless gather in a room adjacent to the meditation hall. We can hear them talking among themselves as they bed down for the night.

One evening I arrived early. On the altar table, I set out a small statue of the Buddha, an incense burner, a few candles, and some flowers. Knowing there would be a lunar eclipse that night, I added a large framed photograph of the earth as seen from the moon.

When I got things set up I went to unlock the restroom but found it already open with the lights on and the door standing ajar so that anyone passing by could look into the room. The door to the toilet stall was open as well, and someone was in there. It took a moment to register what I was seeing. There was an empty wheelchair drawn up to the toilet and a man sitting on the toilet seat trying to wipe himself. I saw as well that the man had one leg amputated just below the groin and an arm that was scabby and raw and swollen and patched up with dirty bandages.

For a moment I thought that perhaps I should just leave. The man on the toilet didn't appear to have seen me. I could save him the embarrassment. But suddenly he knew I was there. Our eyes met for just the briefest instant and then he looked away. The bathroom door had failed to catch and had swung open, leaving him helpless and exposed. "I'll shut the door," I told him. He didn't respond. I shut the door and locked it and went into the stall next to his to urinate and to give him some privacy. I could hear him shuffling about and grunting and exhaling little bursts of breath as though he were straining to do something. He smelled of old sweat, and shit.

When I came out of the stall, I saw that he had drawn himself up to a standing position. His pants had fallen to the floor beyond his reach, exposing the stump of his leg. His buttocks were smeared with shit, gobs of it still trapped between the cheeks. He gripped the metal handicap bar, struggling to keep balance. He looked as if he could fall at any moment. "I'll help you," I said.

I wiped him with toilet paper, spreading his buttocks apart to do so, trying to clean him where the feces had gotten into the hair on his testicles. He held his face turned away from me and he didn't speak, but he submitted because he had no other choice. I got paper towels from the dispenser and wet them at the sink and washed him as best I could. There was no hot water and the bathroom was cold. His wet flesh where I scrubbed it looked pink and chilled. His whole body shivered from the cold or from the exhaustion of holding himself upright, or both. He leaned his weight on me whenever he could.

When at last he was dry and relatively clean I pulled his pants up, puzzled at first to find where his underwear was until I realized he had none. He sort of angled himself toward the wheelchair then and more or less collapsed backward into it. But he struck his injured arm in doing so and I saw the pain of it shudder through him. He looked up and for the second time that evening our eyes met.

Then he looked away again and everything about him went suddenly limp. He sat in his wheelchair in pants wet with urine. His single leg terminated in a shoe scuffed and colorless as cardboard. He wore no sock. He had a faded leather jacket jammed into the seat beside him, its surface worn and cracked with age. On the empty footrest of his wheelchair, lay a cigarette butt and a partial cup of lukewarm coffee that the two of us had somehow managed not to spill throughout the whole of our ordeal. These were items of value to him. I washed his hands with cold water and soap and turned to wash my own when I heard him say, "I'm staying in the shelter." "It's a cold night," I said, "good to be indoors."

We were silent again, embarrassed by what had passed between us. And for all the painful intimacy we had shared, we were nonetheless separated by the awful disparity between our circumstances: he with nothing of his own, I with suddenly far too much. We found it hard to look at each other. "I'll get the door for you," I told him.

He had passed through the door and a little beyond, when he touched the controls on his wheelchair and came to a stop. I watched him turn the chair around, and I heard him say, "I'm Gerald." He held his hand out to me and we shook hands. "I'm Lin," I told him.

When he was gone, I went to join the meditation group. From beyond the wall, the sounds of the homeless reached me. The flickering candlelight imparted just the suggestion of movement to the photo of the earth so that the planet seemed to turn in black space above the altar. I sat with the others, cross-legged and silent. The shelter room grew still. And at that very hour in the skies above the meditation hall the long shadow of a lunar eclipse was sliding onto the face of the moon.

Later, we went outside to watch. The moon hung in the limbs of the winter-bared trees. It dulled to a glowing rose-colored ball and gradually fell into darkness. Beyond the darkened moon the heavens streamed with stars. For an instant, everything that had ever happened to Gerald and me happened then. All that we have become, all that we are, was right there. Gerald humiliated and helpless, the two of us held in the pity and love of it, our brief meeting played out under the vast night sky. Gerald, you should see this. Did you drink your coffee? Are you asleep now? I don't want to lose you.

The earth released the moon from darkness. Chill moonlight flooded my eyes and spilled into the windows of the darkened shelter room.

"I'm Gerald," I hear him say again.

"I'm Lin," I reply.

Not-My-Cat

My neighbor's cat is named Not-My-Cat. Well, I say it's my neighbor's cat, but my neighbor, Robin, denies this. She professes no knowledge of the cat's origins or residence. Not-My-Cat eats and sleeps at Robin's house; in fact, it sleeps on Robin's bed right between her and her husband, Dylan. But Robin remains completely ignorant of these circumstances, and she does so because her landlady, Mrs. Jennings, has strictly forbidden pets of any sort. Therefore, Robin has no cat, and Not-My-Cat is not her cat.

Robin maintains this pretense at all times so as to have it ready should Mrs. Jennings suddenly show up one day. There's more than just a little strain in this for Robin. She's not very good at lying and so she has to sort of practice it. When any of us refers to Not-My-Cat, our conversation assumes lack of any ownership whatsoever. But Robin is so transparently honest that I'm not sure she's capable of lying to Mrs. Jennings if the need ever arises to do so. "Oh, you mean that cat? Gee, I don't know. It's always hanging around here. I wonder whose cat it is?" Nothing like that seems very likely, knowing Robin as I do.

When Robin and Dylan moved in next door, Robin came over to introduce herself. Karen and I were out in the front yard at the time and, while the three of us were talking, this cat that I had never seen before kept rubbing itself against Robin's legs with its back arched up the way cats do. It was purring loudly and walking back and forth over her shoes. Robin acted exactly as a person would who did not have a cat walking on her shoes. Finally I was driven to ask what the cat's name was. Robin sort of glanced down at the cat then as if she'd just noticed its presence. "I don't know. We were moving in and it just showed up," she explained. "I don't know whose cat it is."

I can't say that I knew at the time that Robin was lying. But I knew something was amiss. For one thing, it took Robin more than one swallow just to get her disclaimer out. And her eyes, which are so naturally engaging, were suddenly anywhere except in contact with my own. I can tell you that she was not even remotely convincing.

The explanation for all this came the next day. It was evening and I had just gotten back from a walk. It was starting to rain and I was congratulating myself on making it home dry when Robin intercepted me on the way to the front door.

"It's my cat," she said.

The cat's name was Kelley, she told me. She'd rescued her from the roof of the apartments where she used to live. No one seemed to know whose cat it was so Robin fed her, got her some shots and a flea collar, named her Kelley, and brushed her every day. While she was telling me this, the rain was coming down harder and both of us were getting soaked. "I know I'm not supposed to have pets, but I couldn't leave Kelley behind. Who would take care of her?" And then she looked at me with rainwater running down her face and she said, "I had to tell you. I didn't want to start our relationship with a lie."

At the time I was thinking that I'd seldom started a relationship with anybody in a way that I liked better. I'd chanced upon a treasure. "As far as I'm concerned" I told her, "it's not my cat and I have no idea whose cat it is." She brightened a little at this prospect and she said, "All right, then it's not my cat either." That's when Kelley became Not-My-Cat.

And that's also when the rain let up and the sun came out and the whole world was brighter than before.

The Jury Room

Nancy is the first to break out a deck of cards. We are to discover that a good deal of our time during the course of the trial will be spent waiting in the jury room. Nancy seems to have anticipated this. On the first day of the trial, when the rest of us are watching the clock on the jury room wall tick away the long minutes and hours, wondering when—if ever!—we'll be called back to the court, Nancy is absorbed in a game of solitaire.

The doors to the jury room and courtroom face each other across a narrow hallway. At best a mere dozen steps separate the table where the twelve of us sit from the courtroom where *The Case of the People versus Trevor Bird* is underway.

We jurors are under the strictest admonition to avoid all media of any kind and to avoid any conversation regarding the trial, not only with acquaintances and family but with each other as well. For the twelve of us, the trial is everything. It is, for the moment, our whole life. Even though we are silenced on the matter, our common concern regarding the trial is disclosed in every word we utter regardless of what we say. Its unspoken presence can be heard in the least comment on the weather or on what one is having for lunch or what one does for a living.

Not only that, but we are also instructed to form no opinions regarding the trial until the time of deliberation. Thus we're enjoined not only not to talk but not to even think about the one thing that's on all of our minds.

So we do everything else instead. Nancy, one of four alternate jurors, shows up with a book titled *Card Games One Can Play Alone* and settles down to solitaire. Marilyn, a third-grade teacher, brings her iBook, intending to work on lesson plans but succumbs instead to a computer game. Dennis, who recently retired and whose wife is critically ill with Lyme disease, donates a jigsaw puzzle. Jake, once a racehorse trainer and groom, reads from a book called *New Trails*. Rose, a grandmother of six grandchildren going on seven, hangs a dartboard on the jury room wall but complains that darts is not a game she can play sober. Terry is tearing her hair out for want of a cigarette. And so it goes: a cribbage board appears, several books, some knitting, and two more laptop computers. All of us busily engaged in doing anything other that what we are here to do.

Lance, the bailiff, tells us when it is time to go back to the courtroom. He unlocks the doors that separate the jury room from the courtroom and we file into the jury box. I am Juror Number Eight. Barbara, an elementary school teacher who takes notes on all the testimony, is Number Seven. She sits on my right. Jake, wearing jeans and a silver belt buckle in the shape of a horseshoe, sits on my left. He is Number Nine. In the abrupt traverse of a few yards, we have come from our card games and puzzles and innocuous conversation to sit as jurors on this elevated platform with the whole courtroom spread out before us.

We are here to judge the guilt or innocence of the defendant Trevor Bird, charged with murder in the first degree. We hear Judge Roberts declare that "The Case of the People versus Trevor Bird is in session" and that "the jury is present and ready."

Gradually, the evidence in the case takes shape. We listen, along with Trevor Bird and his mother and father and grandparents and the nameless others who have come out of curiosity or concern, as witnesses describe the beating death of Lloyd Brown in an alley on a cold November night in Chico, California. Brown, we are told, was a homeless man of undetermined age. An alcoholic and long acquaintance of the Chico Police, he was known in all the local AA groups. We learn how the twenty-year old college football lineman, Trevor Bird, overtook Lloyd Brown who was fleeing from him down the alley. We are told how Bird slammed the flat of his palm into the back of Brown's head, tumbling him face forward onto the pavement and splitting his chin open to the bone. We learn that Trevor Bird and another lineman, Derek Phillips, proceeded to kick the helpless and unresisting Lloyd Brown where he lay on the ground until blood ran from his ears.

We are told how Trevor Bird pulled a fence board from an alley fence and began to beat the victim with it, repeatedly swinging the board overhead and shouting, "Who's a punk-ass now!" We're shown the board itself, which, although heavy and solid, was fractured into pieces from the force of the beating, Trevor Bird whaling away at Brown until there was so little left of the board that he was more or less flinging his bloodied fists against Brown's body. We learn how he and Derek Phillips turned Lloyd Brown face up and, finding a filled five-gallon glass water jug in the bed of a pickup truck, dropped the bottle repeatedly into Brown's unprotected face. We are shown a forty-pound tire and wheel, its projecting hubcap stained with blood, which the two of them took from the truck bed for the same purpose. We hear a 9-1-1 tape of a caller who stood at an apartment window overlooking the alley and who witnessed all of this. "They're beating the crap out of him," she says, and then, "Oh my god! Oh god! Oh my god!"

The county forensic pathologist diagrams the extent of Lloyd Brown's wounds: the base of his skull fractured in five places, his whole face caved in, his brain flooded with blood, his ribs broken, his liver lacerated, twenty-eight distinguishable wounds in all, thirteen of them deemed fatal. A picture of Lloyd Brown after the beating that is circulated among us reveals no recognizable human face at all. We all silently echo the 9-1-1 caller's anguish, "Oh my god! Oh god! Oh my god!"

The jury is released for lunch and I drive to a nearby lake to eat alone. I park where the grass slopes down to the water and a few willows line the bank. There are some mallards resting on the grass and a covey of coots going in and out of the water. Further out on the lake, bufflehead and grebes are diving for food. I watch as they disappear below the surface and then bob up again, their bills dripping with tufts of brown waterweed. A flock of Canadian geese drops down from the sky in long gliding descents. I watch as their wings flair and their feet touch water and they slide to a stop. I want to go down among the grasses and the water. I want to pull weeds from the lake bottom with my teeth. I want wings to carry me into the sky.

After lunch when we reassemble in the jury room Gail complains that court security has confiscated her nail file and Terry says, "Come on ladies, let's not be brandishing weapons." We all laugh much harder and longer than the humor itself requires.

The days of our isolation continue, each of us carrying the life of the trial in the confinement of our own minds. We long to speak of it to each other. And then suddenly, one day, the testimony's complete and the case is ours.

Now we're not sure we're ready for it. We're given final instructions on the law and the twelve of us are locked into the jury room, charged with the task of arriving at a verdict. The four alternates—Nancy, David, Marilyn, and Rose—are sent away.

We miss them. When the door shuts behind their departure, we feel all the more alone.

Released at last to speak of the trial, we don't know what to say. We select Phil as our jury foreman because he has done it before, but that takes only a few seconds to accomplish and we're still stuck with what has to be done. For the first time since the trial began, the jury room is silent. Maybe Phil can get us going.

The eventual verdict is unavoidable. Still, it takes us four hours to arrive at it. Phil says that's because we're "shooting for the stars." He means that we want to be absolutely sure that the verdict we reach is the right one. But we already know what the verdict must be; it's just that we aren't able to say so yet. We go over and over the evidence trying to wring from it any mitigating circumstance that might justify reducing the charge. We have watched Trevor Bird through these long days of testimony, where he sat beside his attorney, wearing his tie and slacks, looking as if he's not used to dressing up that much. We have seen how he wears his hair neatly parted on one side, and how he blinks sometimes as if to clear his eyes of some obstruction. None of us wants to send Trevor Bird off to prison for life.

An hour into deliberation, we take our first straw vote. Terry unfolds the slips of paper bearing our votes, stacking eight of them into the guilty pile and four in the not-guilty.

"Couldn't it possibly be a case of second degree murder? Wasn't alcohol a factor in the crime?" Gail asks. "He's just a boy," she continues. "He got to drinking and made one bad choice after another. Isn't that how it happened?" Yes, Trevor was drinking, but he wasn't too drunk to recognize a police siren and race the length of the alley and up the street, and duck in among some houses, and climb onto a rooftop and leap from roof to roof in his effort to avoid capture. We've all tried Gail's argument but it simply won't work.

"I'm just not ready to vote on it," Leslie explains. "I can't bring myself to write down guilty." She wants to hear the law again governing first-degree murder by torture. Phil offers to read it aloud but Leslie wants to read it for herself.

Four hours after we began deliberations, we watch as Terry stacks twelve slips of paper into the guilty pile. We've convicted Trevor Bird of first-degree murder.

Phil wants to hear each of us say it. So in turns around the table we all say "Guilty" and Phil hears himself says it last. He fills out the verdict form, reading it aloud as he goes. "We the jury find the defendant, Trevor Bird, guilty of the crime of murder in the first degree." He dates the document and signs it. And then one of us starts weeping, silently, with streaks running down her face. And then, quite remarkably, we are all weeping, looking across the table at each other and no one saying a word. And then Terry gets up from the table and pushes the signal that will bring Lance, the bailiff, to the jury room. "Who wants soft drinks?" she asks.

We all want soft drinks, even I who haven't drunk one in years. Lance authorizes Terry to go after the drinks and we all divvy up coins and put in our orders. We ask how long it will take for the court to reassemble and Lance says we have about a half-hour. It's a half-hour that we need because we know that when we file into the jury box for this last time Trevor Bird will be waiting there and his family will be waiting. Each will be hoping, as we jurors have hoped, that there be some way to avoid the inevitable.

Too soon, the doors separating the jury room from the courtroom swing open. For the last time these long days, *The Case of the People versus Trevor Bird* is in session. The jury is present and ready. "Have you reached a verdict?" "We have, your honor."

The clerk reads the verdict to the court. "We the jury find the defendant, Trevor Bird…" I watch Trevor as the door to his future slams shut. He stares fixedly forward, as the merest tremor of a movement passes through his body. Trevor Bird, twenty years old, will be forty-six before he is even considered for parole. He will never graduate from college. He won't again ski or fish or take hikes in the woods or swim in a mountain lake or walk to the corner store for a magazine. He won't marry or have children of his own. In all likelihood, he'll never be released from prison.

I hear the stifled outcry of Trevor's mother. Her husband sits stiffly beside her, his body rigid with the effort to control himself. And surrounding these two are the stricken forms of grandparents, brothers, sisters, friends. In passing judgment on Trevor Bird this day we have sentenced all these others as well. We have sentenced ourselves. In violation of our own hearts, we have voted to discard this boy. Nothing we can tell ourselves will ever alter the consequence of having done so.

I watch as Trevor is led away. I understand then that whatever innocence the twelve of us may have brought to the jury room, none of us will know such innocence again.

The Cry of a Fawn

I'll begin with a simple recitation of the facts. Perhaps that's all that's needed. The facts may be the best anyone can do. Karen and I were driving south on Highway 395 in eastern Oregon. It had been raining heavily, but the storm had broken up and a late afternoon sun slanted in from the west. The highway had just descended from a conifer woods and was gradually flattening out into the sagebrush and grass country of the Great Basin. Karen and I both saw the sign indicating a deer crossing and had noted to each other that we should stay alert. The highway climbed a little rise and then descended into a shallow pocket where a small fenced enclosure set off a few acres of seeded grass from the surrounding sagebrush.

We both saw the fawn as soon as we came over the rise. We saw that it had been struck and that it was struggling to get up. Highway 395 is a mere ribbon of road at that point, two narrow lanes separated by a faded line of yellow paint. The stricken fawn was exactly in the center of the road, its thin legs splayed out on both sides of the lane divider. We found space to park the car and ran back to get the fawn.

The fawn, terrified, tried to escape us, stabbing at the pavement with its front legs, its little sticks of bones flailing about, its cloven hooves clattering on the asphalt, its whole rear section, rump, thighs, calves, dragging behind it. I could hardly bear to look at it. It was brought down like this, its little body ruined beyond recovery. I picked it up and carried it off the road and laid it on the grass. In the near distance, a doe paced back and forth along a fence line. The fawn would never again rise. It would exhaust all the life left to it trying to do so, bewildered that legs that had propelled it into a sustained run on the very day of its birth would not now carry it across a hundred yards of sage and grass to its mother.

"What are we going to do?" Karen asked. She knew, of course, but neither of us wanted to say it. "It might take days for it to die," I said, my eyes searching the roadside for a stone heavy enough to smash a deer's skull.

Then I heard the sound of an engine and the whine of mud tires on pavement. I looked up to see a pickup truck coming over the rise where it caught the late sun, revealing the unmistakable silhouette of gun racks in the rear window. A hunter! I hailed the truck down. The driver, his eyes screwed to the road, seemed to take notice of me only at the last moment. As he slammed past us, I thought he was gone, but then the tail lights of his truck flashed and he skidded to a stop.

When he reached us his eyes went first to the fawn, where it was struggling once more to rise. He watched it for a moment. He was chewing on the stub of an unlit cigar, and he took it from his mouth and shoved it into his shirt pocket. "You hit it?" he asked. "No, we found it like this," I told him. "Do you have a gun?" "I don't," he said. "You wouldn't often hear me say that. We could sure use one now." "I've got a pocket knife in the truck," he said. "We can cut the jugular vein."

When he got back with the knife, he opened the blade and ran his finger over it to test its sharpness. He looked at me and shrugged, pulled his cigar stub out of his pocket and stuck it back in his mouth. The hunter got down on his knees by the fawn. I got down beside him and turned the fawn's head to the side to expose its throat. From that angle, its eye stared up at us in terror and confusion. The hunter punched the blade into its throat.

It was then that the fawn cried out. I'd never before heard a deer make any call at all. I suppose I thought the species was mute. The hunter was clearly as startled by the sound as I was. He said, "Sorry, old buddy." I needed words myself, but I hadn't any of my own at the moment, so I too said, "Sorry, old buddy." The hunter sawed his way through the flesh of the fawn's throat, and said again, "Sorry, old buddy." And I said, "Sorry, old buddy." Blood gushed from the torn throat as the hunter and I pressed it against the earth. Neither of us could bear to see it try to rise again. The hunter said, "It helps to say something," and he repeated, "Sorry, old buddy." And I echoed him a third time, saying, "Sorry, old buddy." A second later, the fawn's eye went blank and its brief encounter with humans was over. The hunter wiped the blade of his pocket knife on the grass and a minute later I heard the pickup start, and he was gone.

But the cry of the fawn was not gone. Its gaping throat and blank eye still reverberated with the sound of it and gave expression to all the suffering I've ever caused or witnessed. The fawn was dead by my own hand; its bewilderment, its terror, its innocence were facts as hard as the stones that littered the shoulder of the road. There was nothing I could look to that would soften or mitigate these realities. I couldn't imagine retracing the fifty yards that separated me from the car, turning the key in the ignition, and driving myself back into that banal and false normality where the death of a fawn is merely an unfortunate incident to be kept in perspective.

How can I make anyone understand this? How can I show that the death of the fawn was not a matter merely pitiable, not a matter simply of regret or guilt or remorse? How can I explain that none of the deaths of my lifetime will ever again be merely regrettable? How can I touch the tenderness in all this, convey the degree to which the cry of the fawn exposed my heart?

It was a cry like that of Karen who, twenty days earlier, working her way down a Nevada trail so steep and eroded that it was little more than a ditch of teetering rocks, caught the toe of her boot and fell. With the leading foot wedged and the following foot trapped behind the first, her body tilted and, arching outward and down, slammed full length into the rocks with nothing but the ineffectual failure of one thin arm to break the fall. She lay for a long instant, blood running from her mouth and from a hand split upon some sharp edge. Her eyes swam up from their sudden bed of stones like the eyes of one drowning beneath the waters of her own life's current. She saw from that sunken and solitary depth how the canyon walls rose into the blue summer sky, and she said, through bubbles of blood forming at her lips, "I've done it now." She sat in the trail trying to comprehend what had happened to her while I bound her split hand in moistened clothing I had stripped from myself. She probed her bloody mouth, trying to see if her teeth were still there, and she said again, "I've really done it now, haven't I?" She spoke a language of wonderment that what she had always feared might happen had, in fact, happened. Weeks later, she would remember how the canyon walls carried her to the wonder of blue sky from the very place of her fall.

It was a cry like that of the man who, paunchy and middle-aged, rushed up to a urinal alongside me at a rest stop on Interstate 5 and confided to me that he'd wet his pants. We stood there side by side, just inches between our elbows, utter strangers to each other. He didn't look at me or preface his disclosure in any way. He simply said to no one else but me because no one else was in the restroom, "I thought I was gonna make it, and I almost did, but not quite. I dribbled a little." I looked at him then, his face so near that without my reading glasses it appeared blurred. He stared straight ahead, his neck and cheeks red with embarrassment, his throat working up and down as though there was more he wanted to say or wanted to prevent himself from saying. "Can you believe they recommend diapers for my condition?" He couldn't grasp what had happened to him. He needed someone, anyone, to hear the voice of his humiliation, the anguish he felt over the betrayal wrought upon him by his body.

It was a cry like that of children anywhere when war or poverty or disaster has left them stunned and wise before their time. A cry like that of their parents who could not save them, and of all of us who have seen the young taken down while we ourselves survived. A cry like the hunter's own "Sorry old buddy," recited like a prayer of contrition for the hard work of his hands.

We cry out from the place of our ambush, where the certainty of accident, disease, infirmity and death lies in wait for us. Our innocence is assaulted on all sides. Were we not capable of being surprised by this, we would long ago have succumbed to despair. Were we not capable of sorrow, we would be brutes.

If you look at a map of Oregon, you can pretty well pinpoint the exact stretch of road where the fawn was struck. You can see it in relationship to the rest of Oregon, and with a more general map, you can see its relationship to all of North America. It was, as I told you, on Highway 395, forty-one miles south of John Day and twenty-nine miles north of Burns. I tell you this because I want you to understand how Oregon spreads out from the place where the fawn died, out into Washington and Idaho and California and the Pacific Ocean. And I want you to see how none of these neighboring territories limits the extension of space, so that being, of its own nature, spreads itself across the face of the earth and beyond.

Any astronomical chart will show you that the whole universe is contiguous to the exact spot where the fawn cried out, so that absolutely everything was gathered into that cry. The cry was voiced everywhere, heard everywhere, and not just at that time, not just at 5:30 pm on August 25th, 1997, but at all times. You can hear it now. It is the voice of our dismay, the cry of our innocent bewilderment. It is the injury received of our ears, the wound from which our saving sympathy bleeds forth. Listen! Listen! It calls us to the site of our deepest redemption.

Gathering

The gravestone is inscribed RITCHIE W. EVANS, 1936–1994. It is only one of the dozens of grave markers that I pass on my morning walk through the old cemetery at the end of Washington Avenue. Beyond this scant information, I know nothing whatsoever about Ritchie Evans. What with all of the more elaborate grave markers in the cemetery, some with beautifully artistic sculptures, I might never have noticed Ritchie's modest grave had it not been for the fresh flowers that I invariably found there. Even in the darkest weeks of winter, even when one of the severest wind storms of the decade toppled trees all over town, Ritchie's grave received new flowers.

And then one morning in early February, I saw who it was that tended Ritchie's grave. She was wearing a pale yellow dress with a shawl pulled over her shoulders and a scarf over her hair, and she was arranging some flowers in the little plastic cone that is standard on all the newer graves in the cemetery. It had rained heavily during the night, and a light mist fell on her where she kneeled by Ritchie's grave. When I got near to her and our eyes met, I said, "Looks nice." "It seems the least I can do," she responded. That was all that passed between us. She turned back to her flowers, and I went on with my walk.

I haven't seen her since, but I awaken sometimes in the early bedroom light to find that my mind has settled on her like dew dropping on the cemetery lawn. What is it that draws me to so common an act as that of the woman who tends the grave of Ritchie Evans? What is it that draws me to any of those faceless souls whose silence accompanies my morning walks?

Not long after I had chanced upon the woman, I met up with two young workers seeding lawn at the cemetery. I remember telling them that in a few months the heat would be coming back and that they'd be glad to have the oaks and maples to shade them and the sprinklers going all summer. One of the two was smoothing the ground adjacent to a family burial site, pulling a rake through the freshly dug soil. "You see this guy's name he said," pointing to one of the gravestones with the head of his rake. "I read these names every day. It makes me watch what I do. I mean there are things I don't waste myself on." He kept on raking, and his eyes followed his own movements as he talked. "When I go home and my wife is cooking or something, she's only twenty-six years old, and I know she'll be nothing but a name like this some day. This job is good for knowing stuff like that."

Along with his gloves and his lunch pail, this young husband took what he now knew home with him each day from work. He carried it into the house where it fell like an ancient, tender longing on the limbs and eyes of his wife as she set out their supper. Even in the sanctuary of his home, perhaps especially there, he read in the lettering inscribed on every gravestone in the cemetery the spelling of his own name as well. Working the graves at the cemetery, he'd discovered some newly dug warmth of heart. He was learning how our mortality runs deeply into our affections, how our capacity to love resides within our capacity to die.

A few months after these encounters at the cemetery, the Olympic flame made a stopover in Chico on its way to the summer games. Lots of events were planned for the occasion, including some evening music at the Children's Park. So after supper Karen and I walked uptown to join in the celebration. Karen had heard that a replica of the Vietnam Veteran's Memorial was to be displayed on the south lawn of Chico State University's Kendall Hall. She thought she would like to see this memorial, and we went there on our way to the Children's Park.

The memorial consisted of 128 sectioned panels made of some hard material resembling the dark granite of the Washington original. The panels were four feet high and joined end to end so that they formed two long walls that converged at an angle in the exact center of the display. The angle of the panels was such that, when Karen and I stood at the center of the wall, the far ends of it curved around us on both sides. From there, we could see all the names: 58,494 of them, etched in silver and stretching for 250 feet across the south lawn of Kendall Hall. I put a hand to the wall, feeling the lettering there, touching the last remnants of lives just like my own. And others did the same: a young student, who had come seeking a name, touched each letter as tenderly as though it were her own eyelids; an older couple lifted a child who petted a name like a puppy; a bearded man with a knapsack over his shoulder pressed his forehead to the wall and silently recited something that needed to be said.

In the hollow beyond the display, I could see the university rose garden illuminated in the evening light. Close by, the waters of Chico Creek ran through deepening shadows toward the sea. From the Children's Park, I could hear the sound of instruments and singing and the excited voices of children playing. It seemed to me for the moment that my townspeople and I were gathering at the absolute junction where the circle closes, where all our going travels in one direction, where a soldier's last cry can be heard in a child's laughter and love blooms in every occasion.

In the Children's Park, the gospel choir was singing. I stood on the lawn in front of the bandstand and the voices of the singers resonated through me. Children ran about the grounds, their calls shrill with excitement. The crowd clapped hands in rhythm to the singing, and the choir clapped, and a young woman in a wheelchair next to me clapped. The woman in the wheelchair—impaired by some condition—flailed her arms wildly in spasmodic jerks, her hands frequently failing to strike each other, crossing crazily in midair. Yet she clapped in pure abandonment, her face twisting up in distorted smiles of joy. A short distance away, Karen sat on a bench under a tree. In the cemetery beyond the avenues, Ritchie Evans lay in his grave.

I am not the woman in the wheelchair whose joy shakes through me like some spasm of my own. I am not the singers on the bandstand whose song forms itself in my own throat. I am not Karen watching from a bench under the limbs of a tree in whose shelter I rest as well. I am not the children playing nor am I any one of the 58,494 lives whose end is recorded on the south lawn of Kendall Hall. I am not Ritchie Evans nor the woman who tends his grave nor the chastened husband whose work in the Chico Cemetery teaches him daily that his young wife must someday die.

I am not the one who has known and now tells of these things, for I am ever and inseparably receiving myself from within the lives of all these others. I draw my life from this common existence, as wholly and finally and inextricably and repeatedly as breath itself is drawn from undivided air.

What I owe Ritchie Evans is what I owe myself. What any of us owes him is exactly that. Ritchie lies within the gravesite of our collective being. He persists within the common journey of our species from 1936 to 1994. I don't have to know anything particular about Ritchie Evans to know that I bear his life within my own and that I would do so had he lived his fifty-eight years somewhere on the far side of the planet in some ancient culture lost to memory.

The woman in the yellow dress tends Ritchie's grave for us all. Week after week her remembering hands lay flowers at the very feet of our passing here. The flowers are fragrant and newly cut. We bend with her now to lay them, stem and leaf and blossom, at the exact site of all our going on.

Redemption

AN EPILOGUE

One of the great Zen scriptures, "Taking Part in the Gathering," was written in the eighth century by the Chinese Zen Master, Shitou Xiqian. Within Xiqian's scripture are these lines (as translated by Zen masters John Tarrant and Joan Sutherland):

> The darkness is inside the bright,
> but don't look only with the eyes of the dark.
> The brightness is inside the dark,
> but don't look only through the eyes of the bright.
> Bright and dark are a pair
> like front foot and back foot walking.

Shitou Xiqian's verse is about awakening to the realities of human existence, and awakening Xiqian insists is not a matter of looking to the bright side of life, but rather a matter of seeing life through the eyes of darkness as well. "Bright and dark," this ancient master tells us, "are a pair." We cannot be whole, which is to say we cannot be human, if we try to live by light alone and refuse to enter the darkness. To shun the darkness is like trying to walk with only one foot. Darkness often represents states of suffering—pain, anger, fear, sorrow, and so forth. Light, on the other hand, represents various states of happiness—security, comfort, joy, love. In this context, we hope for as much light as we can get and consider the darkness of our lives to be a misfortune. Anyone in his right mind wants to be happy and avoid suffering if he can. What this viewpoint misses is the redemption darkness offers. And what the darkness redeems is the very quality of happiness one seeks.

Happiness of a certain popular sort is simply unsustainable, and it is so precisely because it mistakenly attempts to isolate itself from misfortune. So it is not this categorical happiness that redeems human life. What redeems human life is kindness, the simple offering of a loving consideration for others. And kindness is learned most intimately in times of suffering. In the chivalric tradition of the Middle Ages, such loving consideration was characterized as "disinterested," a love that did not depend on the loved one's being deserving, a love that sought nothing for itself. The ancient Greeks as well recognized such love, which they termed *agape*. Agape is a spontaneous self-giving love expressed freely without calculation of cost or gain to the giver or merit on the part of the receiver. That such an unqualified sympathy for others might result from traveling in life's dark places is easy to understand. Once you've known for yourself the sufferings and sorrows of the Bad Dog, you will be the first to come to its rescue. You will do so because you can't do otherwise. Darkness has taught you a kindness that can't be set aside. It lights your way wherever you go.

My brother, Rowland, died this winter at age seventy-four from myasthenia gravis. From the time of the disease's onset, it took but a year for him to waste away in the most deplorable manner I've personally ever witnessed. In the end, his skin hung from him in blackened folds draped over the exposed bones of his arms and legs. His face was swollen almost beyond recognition from the prednisone he was being given. It took the utmost effort for him to sit or walk and then only at the cost of great pain. By degrees he was losing his mind, sometimes mistaking me for his son or for some stranger he didn't know.

Little more than a week before Rowland died, I sat by his bed one afternoon, and he told me in the most lucid terms how it was for him. He told me how he'd managed to get to the toilet on his own the day before and that when he'd finished and was working his way back toward the bed, he saw himself in the full length mirrors that cover the closest doors. "I'm gross!" he told me. "I'm like a holocaust victim. I'm just a bag of black skin. I don't recognize my own face. I'm gross, Linley." And then he said to me again, having hit upon a word that summed it up for him, "I'm gross."

"You're not gross to me, Rowland," I said.

"Then look!" was his answer, jerking himself up in bed and holding out toward me an emaciated arm hung with scabby skin. His eyes, staring into mine from out of the puffy bloat that was once his face, were daring me to deny the truth of his condition.

"You're right," I conceded. "You are gross." With that admittance, he seemed satisfied and his head sunk back on the pillow and his eyes closed. He and I had gone about as far into the darkness that afternoon as one can go, and the journey was requiring of us a fierce and uncompromising love of the sort that only such darkness brings. Had I refused to acknowledge the obvious truth of his condition it would have been as if I'd said, "No Rowland, that's too hard a place and I don't want to go there with you." In that refusal I would have failed the great love that the moment was offering us. And then I said again, because it was of course, in its own way, the absolute truth, "You're not gross to me, Rowland."

Neither Rowland nor my father ever spoke of love as such in my experience with them. I never heard either of them say "I love you" to anybody. But my sister tells me that Father in his last years once made the observation to her that "Linley was never afraid to say, 'I love you.'" He's right. I was the one who carried the banner of love in the family. And the worse things got, the higher I hoisted it into the air, waving "I love you" in everyone's face, seeking some assurance I suppose that love would somehow survive even the most unlikely circumstances. This love crusade of mine may have obscured for me at times the love that was already being expressed in less overt ways. And if so, that's a loss worth considering.

But still, here's this kid who simply refuses to leave love out of the equation, no matter what the mathematical odds are of its occurrence. He can't imagine a situation so bad as to not expect some kindness to arise from it. He takes for granted that redemption can be found in hell itself if that's where you happen to be. In his innocence he has hit upon a truth that time would reveal to him in its fullness.

Lin Jensen
Chico, California
March 31, 2004

about the author

Lin Jensen is the founding teacher of the Chico Zen Sangha, in Chico, California, where he lives with his wife, Karen Laslo.

Nixon Under the Bodhi Tree and Other Works of Buddhist Fiction

Edited by Kate Wheeler
Foreword by Charles Johnson
288 pages, ISBN 0-86171-354-0, $16.95

Pico Iyer, Victor Pelevin, Doris Dörrie, and other renowned contributors join young award-winners in what National Book Award-winner Charles Johnson calls "an embarrassment of literary riches," sure to please fiction lovers of every stripe.

"(starred review) [You'll] relish the beauty of these well-told tales. Wheeler has assembled a stellar collection, one that fans of fiction and Buddhism hope for—full of play, insight, revelation, and diversity, and never compromising in delight."—*Publishers Weekly*

"This volume is surely a milestone in Western Buddhist literature—and a book that fiction lovers, Buddhist or otherwise, will very much enjoy."
—*Tricycle: The Buddhist Review*

Available Spring 2006:
You Are Not Here & Other Works of Buddhist Fiction
Edited by Keith Kachtick • Foreword by Lama Surya Das

Landscapes of Wonder

Discovering Buddhist Dharma in the World Around Us
Bhikkhu Nyanasobhano
192 pages, ISBN 0-86171-142-4, $14.95

"Contemplative, sensitive, and lyrically written. *Landscapes of Wonder* offers the richness of Buddhist teachings reinterpreted along with keen observations about what nature can teach us concerning life, change, and death."—*Tricycle: The Buddhist Review*

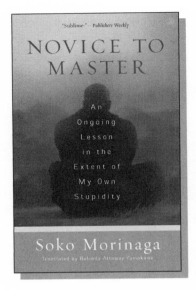

Novice to Master
An Ongoing Lesson in the Extent of My Own Stupidity
Soko Morinaga
Translated by Belenda Attaway Yamakawa
144 pages, ISBN 0-86171-393-1, $11.95

"Sometimes a book comes along with a title that dares you not to pick it up. In this case, it was the subtitle—*An Ongoing Lesson in the Extent of My Own Stupidity*. Morinaga's telling of his life from youth in Japan's army during World War II to becoming a Zen master is direct, blessedly free of jargon, and sprinkled with universal spiritual observations. There are passages that had me laughing out loud; others inspired serious reflection. Remarkable: pithy, profound, inspiring, and joyous."—*Arkansas Democrat Gazette*

The Wisdom Anthology of North American Buddhist Poetry
Edited by Andrew Schelling
416 pages, ISBN 0-86171-392-3, $22.00

This landmark anthology vividly displays Buddhism's presence and influence in modern poetry. Includes works by Diane di Prima, Lawrence Ferlinghetti, Norman Fischer, Sam Hamill, Jane Hirshfield, Gary Snyder, Eliot Weinberger, Philip Whalen, Michael McClure, Leslie Scalapino, and many more.

about wisdom

Wisdom Publications, a nonprofit publisher, is dedicated to preserving and transmitting important works from all the major Buddhist traditions as well as exploring related East-West themes.

To learn more about Wisdom, or browse our books on-line, visit our website at wisdompubs.org. You may request a copy of our mail-order catalog on-line or by writing to this address:

WISDOM PUBLICATIONS
199 Elm Street
Somerville, Massachusetts 02144 USA
Telephone: (617) 776-7416
Fax: (617) 776-7841
Email: info@wisdompubs.org
www.wisdompubs.org

the wisdom trust

As a nonprofit publisher, Wisdom is dedicated to the publication of fine Dharma books for the benefit of all sentient beings and dependent upon the kindness and generosity of sponsors in order to do so. If you would like to make a donation to Wisdom, please do so through our Somerville office. If you would like to sponsor the publication of a book, please write or email us at the address above.

Thank you.

Wisdom is a nonprofit, charitable 501(c)(3) organization affiliated with the Foundation for the Preservation of the Mahayana Tradition (FPMT).